the mystical backpacker

the mystical backpacker

How to Discover Your Destiny in the Modern World

Hannah Papp

ATRIA PAPERBACK
New York London Toronto Sydney New Delhi

Hillsboro, Oregon

ATRIA PAPERBACK
An Imprint of Simon & Schuster, Inc.
1230 Avenue of the Americas
New York, NY 10020

BEYOND WORDS
20827 N.W. Cornell Road, Suite 500
Hillsboro, Oregon 97124-9808
503-531-8700 / 503-531-8773 fax
www.beyondword.com

Managing editor: Lindsay S. Brown
Editors: Sylvia Spratt, Anna Noak
Copyeditor: Kristin Thiel
Proofreader: Michelle Blair
Design: Devon Smith
Composition: William H. Brunson Typography Services

First Atria Paperback/Beyond Words trade paperback edition May 2015

Manufactured in the United States of America

10 9 8 7 6 5 4 3 2 1

Library of Congress Cataloging-in-Publication Data

Papp, Hannah.
The mystical backpacker : how to discover your destiny in the modern world / Hannah Papp.
pages cm
1. Backpacking. 2. Papp, Hannah--Travel. 3. Voyages and travels. 4. Self-actualization (Psychology)
I. Title.
GV199.6.P38 2015
796.51--dc23

2014045113

ISBN 978-1-58270-486-9
ISBN 978-1-4767-7146-5 (eBook)

The corporate mission of Beyond Words Publishing, Inc.: *Inspire to Integrity*

For my father, Martin,
who supported every dream and cheered me on while I traveled.

And for my mother, Eva,
who envisioned a golden bubble around me every time she worried.

Mystical

1. Of or having a spiritual reality or import not obvious to the intelligence or apparent to the senses.
2. Of, relating to, or stemming from direct communion with ultimate reality or God: *a mystical religion.*
3. Enigmatic; obscure: *mystical theories about the securities market.*
    - of hidden or esoteric meaning : *a geometric figure of mystical significance.*
4. Inspiring a sense of spiritual mystery, awe, and fascination: *the mystical forces of nature.*
    - concerned with the soul or the spirit, rather than with material things : *the beliefs of a more mystical age.*[1]

Contents

Foreword

Through the bars of the stark Dubrovnik jail cell, I could see my well-worn backpack leaning against the wall. It looked as forlorn and out of place as I felt. I sunk down on the hard bed thinking that surely the floor was softer. Still, I must have fallen asleep because the next thing I realized, I was startled by the sound of a man clearing his throat. Looming over me, the Yugoslavian police chief was trying to talk to me again. To make up for the fact that I didn't understand his language, this time he spoke slower and much louder. It was as if the louder he spoke, the more understandable his words would be to me.

As he banged out of the cell in frustration over my lack of comprehension, I thought about the journey that had brought me to this point. I had been backpacking and hitchhiking alone for three months through Europe. Already I'd explored the meandering canals of Venice, feasted on freshly caught fish in quaint seaside villages on the Mediterranean, hiked high into the Croatian mountains, and even been strafed by the guns of a military plane when camping alone on an isolated island in the Adriatic Sea that evidently was used for aerial target practice. I'd arrived in Dubrovnik late the night before and hadn't been able to find lodging. Since I was exhausted, I decided it would be easier to find somewhere to stay during daylight hours, so I curled up on a park bench for the night and fell asleep, which is where I was found by the two policemen who hauled me off to their station.

Sitting in the cold cell, the gravity of the situation began to sink in and my heartbeat quickened. Although the political situation was stable in what was then called Yugoslavia, it was not uncommon for people to mysteriously disappear. As a budding journalist, when I met people, I asked questions about their lives. I asked about the politics of their country and what they felt about the current Communist regime. My mind began to spin. Maybe I had asked the wrong people questions. When you are traveling beyond normal parameters, sometimes it's difficult to reconcile what is a real threat and what is fear based.

Eventually the policemen found someone who spoke English. They explained, through the translator, that they frown upon people sleeping in their parks, but they were also concerned to find a young woman on her own at nighttime and they wanted to help, so they decided to "put me up" in their jail. I apologized profusely for sleeping on the bench, and by the time I was released, everyone in the police station was smiling and we were all shaking hands.

When you embark on an adventure, there are no guarantees, but that is precisely why the journey can be so expansive. In Hannah Papp's inspiring book, she talks about the adventures (and misadventures) that can occur while traveling and the profound insights that can ensue from these sojourns. Even though it was daunting to be hauled off to jail in a foreign country, it took me out of my normal, limited view of the world into a more expanded awareness. For example, even though I was only confined for a very short time, I now have a much deeper compassion for those who find themselves suddenly deprived of their freedom. And if I see someone sleeping on a park bench, I don't make the automatic assumptions about that person that I might have made without this experience.

One of the greatest gifts of travel is that it allows us to step out of our comfort zones to see the world through the eyes of others. This has the added benefit of opening our eyes to the vast vistas that dwell within us, that might have been hidden otherwise. *The Mystical Backpacker* carefully introduces this idea that when we expand our views of the world, this expands the views we have of our own lives, which in turn, adds depth and richness to all of our experiences . . . even when we're not traveling.

Stepping out of your comfort zone doesn't mean you need to jump out of a plane with a parachute or spend a night in a Yugoslavian jail. Sometimes it's the less dramatic experiences that can have the deepest impact. Many years ago while backpacking across Tuscany, an elderly farmer and his wife invited me to spend the night in their spare room. Their invitation was so sincere that I gratefully accepted it. The room was simple—stone floor, stone walls, and a hand-hewn wooden bed—but I slept deeply and fully beneath the feather comforter. Awakened the next morning by a chorus of birdsong and the crow of a rooster, I was invited to eat breakfast with the farmer and his wife on the terrace overlooking their vineyard. They served me fresh-squeezed orange juice from oranges on their tree, homemade bread, and robust scrambled eggs, which came from the chickens that scurried around the terrace.

Looking into the twinkling eyes and sun-wrinkled faces of the aging farmer and his white-haired wife, I felt like I had traveled back in time to a simpler era. I could feel the depth of their connection to the land. They raised their own food, made their own wine, grew their own olives, gathered salt from the sea and dried it on their roof, ate eggs from their chickens and tilled the soil in their garden. I could feel a gentle alignment with the cycles of nature in their approach to the land.

As I spent time with them, I realized that was something I was missing in my life. Growing up in United States, my family had moved about once a year, so I didn't have a personal sense of place. The food I ate came from grocery stores, convenience stores, and fast food restaurants. It seemed normal because everyone I knew lived life at the same pace that I did. I didn't have a connection with the food I ate and the land it was grown on. I didn't know what I was missing until I experienced life through the eyes of the farmer and his wife. As the couple showed me around their homestead on a hillside in Italy, a seed was planted in my heart that bore fruit decades later on another hillside, halfway around the world, in the wine country of California.

Thirty years later, my husband and I bought land on the Central Coast of California. Our roots sunk deep into the land as we planted vines to make our own wine, grew olive trees to cure our own olives, planted a large organic garden, and built a chicken pen to house our chickens. As I look over all we have created, echoes of my time with the elderly couple in Italy fill my heart. It is as if their spirit has been overseeing our lives. As Hannah so eloquently explains in her book, embarking on my backpacking adventure so many years before had opened inner doors of perception that continue to reverberate in my life.

Every journey can allow you to connect more deeply to what's important in life and open you to new ways of thinking about the world around you. Of course, there are risks on any sojourn, but I don't believe that we're incarnated to play it safe and live by the expectations and needs of others. I believe that we're here to experience life in its fullness and to love deeply and fully, as well as receive love deeply and fully. And to do this means being willing to take risks.

There are risks in embarking on a Mystical Backpacking journey, as there are risks in any kind of spiritual sojourn. But the benefits far outweigh those risks.

I'm so grateful for Hannah's gem of a book. It harkened me back to my earlier journeys. As I read her words, my fire ignited and reminded me that at the end of life it's better to fling your arms to the heavens with exuberant joy because of the adventures you've had—even if there were a few bumps along the way—than to have lived safely according to the dictates and the needs of others, without having allowed the sail of your soul to unfurl to the winds of fate.

In this book you are given step-by-step instructions to embark on a journey of the soul. Whether it's taking an adventure in the next county or the next country, this book will show you how to live large and live fully. I hope to meet you on the road!

—Denise Linn

Hannah's Mystial Travels

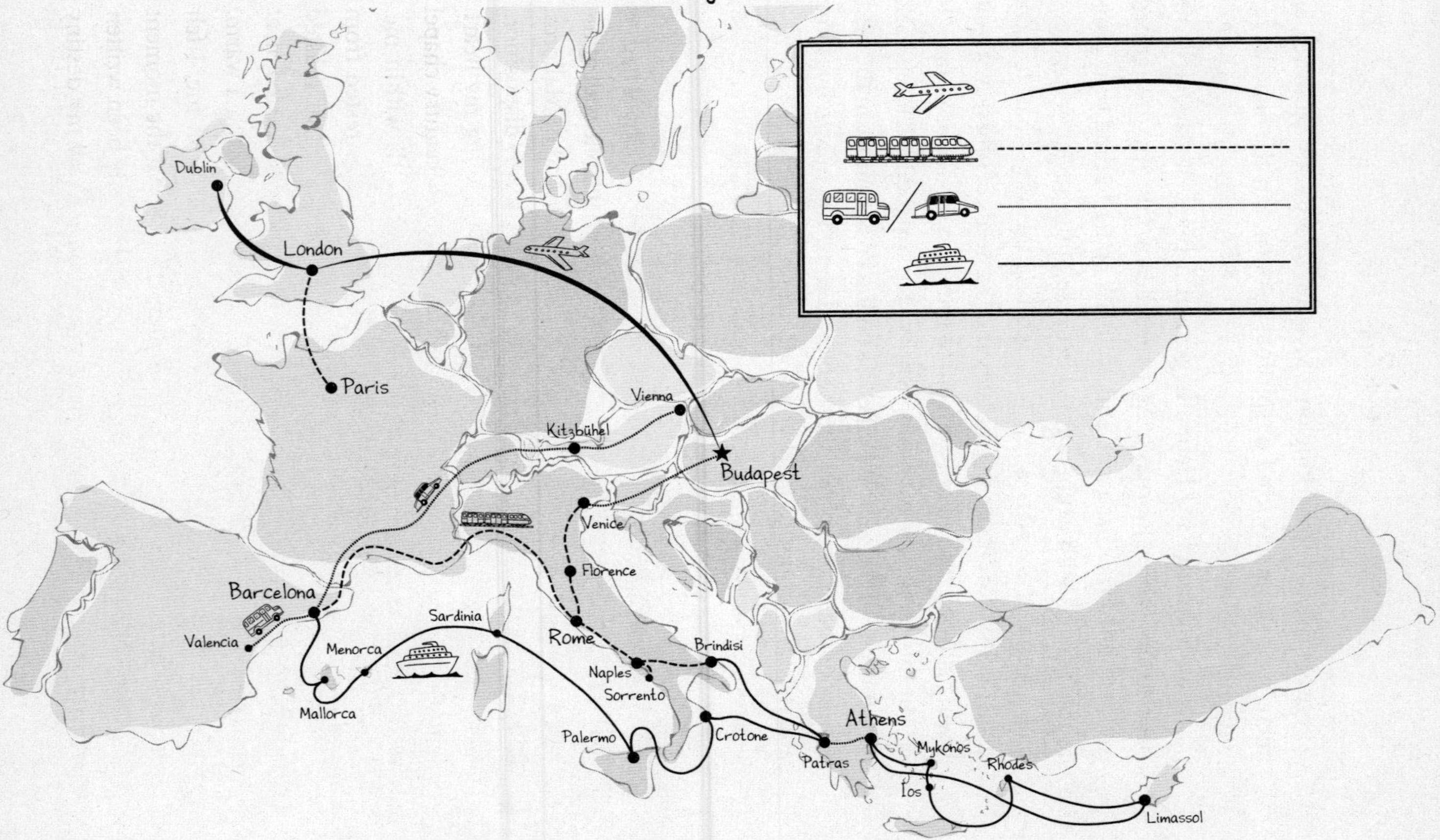

Dublin
London
Paris
Vienna
Kitzbühel
Budapest
Venice
Florence
Barcelona
Valencia
Menorca
Mallorca
Sardinia
Rome
Naples
Sorrento
Brindisi
Palermo
Crotone
Patras
Athens
Mykonos
Ios
Rhodes
Limassol

Preface

There is a distinct moment in my life when I first felt that I had, as they say, arrived. I was twenty-six, sitting on a stone wall at the top of a mountain, looking out over the Spanish island of Mallorca, and in every direction the lapis sea embraced her sunny disposition, tickling her sides. The sun shone on my face, warming my heart. Behind me, the silent, calm energy of the fourteenth-century chapel washed over me, causing a deep peacefulness to settle within me. Friends laughed and chatted around me. My muscles rested from the climb up the mountain, and my stomach was full of roasted meat and potatoes and the homemade red wine we had feasted on at the restaurant halfway up the mountain. I felt saturated in a warm, calm happiness. Then, as though a revelation was upon me, I felt profoundly that I had *arrived* to this moment and that the moment had been waiting for me for some time. It had already been written into the story of my life, and I had managed to follow my destiny simply by breaking with tradition and listening to my heart, to the very place I was meant to be. From a small town in northern Ontario where I had started to feel that the answers would be found further afield to this point, many years and thousands of miles later, where I was now on top of the world, literally and figuratively.

This was a turning point. Silent and uneventful though it may have seemed to the onlooker, my world was being devastated and rebuilt simultaneously at its core, in the very place where it mattered most. My old life was falling away behind me and new possibilities were impregnated with a breath of life that made them actually possible. I could sing! I could sigh. I could live my life differently than I had been. My very thoughts had changed. This moment had, quietly, in the sweet breeze of a sunny blue day, rewritten my very beliefs in a way that no amount of reading or listening or secondhand experience could. *I* had climbed a mountain. *I* had torn asunder a belief. And now the sky was the limit. *I* could fly.

This moment exists for each of us.

Written into the story of your life, there is a moment when your plans can swing alarmingly into another direction like a sailboat jibing with the wind. All that is calm and peaceful, but heading in the wrong direction, is suddenly shifted with great excitement into a new direction, purposefully, by choice. From the shores of your life where friends and family observe your boat's merry progress, this event appears benign; as mine might have to someone observing me sitting in the quiet afternoon at the top of a mountain trail. But from inside the boat, the experience is exhilarating, action-packed, and adventurous. All that has come before is now just the foundation for what will come after, rather than the sum total of your accomplishments.

After is new and shiny, ripe and crisp, seeded, budded, and growing your bright, bright future.

So, how do you find this moment?

Travel was an adventure I lived, but really, it was a vehicle for self-transformation. And that self-transformation has brought me here, to a much happier place. I've learned so much about the world around me, and I now know that even in the most foreign of places, our souls are mirrored back to us in a gesture, an expression, a line translated from a note scrawled on a napkin. Discovering the unknown—whether through journeying to a far-off country or an unexplored place closer to home—has the magical effect of forcing us to stand more in our truth than our stomping grounds can ever demand.

It's hard to believe that I sat on that mountaintop fifteen years ago. So much has happened since then, but I know—*I know*—that it's all very different from what would have happened otherwise. In sharing my adventure with you, I hope to inspire you to chart your own course to this very moment in your life: the turning point that puts you on your way to fulfilling the yet-undiscovered dreams of your soul.

Deep down, I think each of us knows what it is we want out of life, and we know how it is we will shine. It often doesn't feel that way because our environments try their darnedest to bury that truth under the rubble and offal and weeds of experience. And to me, it's fitting that Mystical Backpacking is about helping others to excavate their truth by way of climbing the mountain. It's up to each of us to choose to live our purpose, or not, for buried within each of us, the truth of our purpose pulses magically, waiting to be brought to light.

I feel that I have always had this book within me. I may not have known the title or the cadence, but I've known the truth of it for as long as I can remember. The journey is yours, but together (via the exercises throughout) we will excavate layers of experience like spiritual archaeologists, seeking the knowledge buried over time. It's taken me a long time to journey to this place, where now *The Mystical Backpacker* breathes its first breath and goes out into the world to live its own life. Just because we glimpse our purpose doesn't mean we can take a shortcut to realizing it. We stumble and fumble and fail and succeed and step forward and retreat as we make our way into the future. Trying isn't always pretty. Which is why so many people don't.

If you would like to sink your arms into the mud and muck of seeking out your soul's purpose and to climb your own mountains (literally and figuratively), then pull up a whoopee cushion and join me here at the kiddie pool. A veritable petri dish of life's toughest moments and greatest highs await you. I will show you how to embark on a most delicious odyssey. You will be the hero of your life! You will save yourself. You will have so much fun! And you will cry. You will wail and moan and raise your eyes to the sky while calling out, "Why? Why? Why?" You will unearth the secrets of your soul and stretch them out to dry in the glare of the hot sun. You will heal. And in the end, your own mountaintop moment will occur, and the next phase of your life will begin to blossom as, step-by-step, you create a life in keeping with *your* destiny.

Every word that takes you there is my gift to you.
Embarking is the gift you give yourself.

Introduction

> Any life, no matter how long and complex it may be,
> is made up of a single moment, the moment in which a man
> finds out, once and for all, who he is.
>
> —Jorge Luis Borges

At the start of my journey, I had no money, no ideas, and no sense of direction. I was burned out. I had degrees, diplomas, and work experience. I had the stick-to-it-iveness to succeed at what I set my mind to, but so far what I had thought I wanted wasn't turning out to be what I really wanted after all. It was rather disturbing to thus discover, by way of settling into the stagnant discomfort of what I had built and achieved, to realize it would not do. Intrinsically, I felt glad to be alive, but that feeling was diminished as I made my way through my days. My work didn't thrill me. My social life didn't thrill me. My home didn't thrill me. My city no longer thrilled me. Each day was a task. Each day had to be gotten through. What was the point?

Let me be clear: I didn't feel low. My situation felt low. While I could find reasons to laugh, enjoy life, and appreciate small things each day, I was dissatisfied with the overall state of affairs. And I didn't have ideas for what would be better. Waiting for something else, coupled with dogged forward motion through my days, was the current strategy. What was I supposed to be doing with my life? Who was going to tell me? Who could show me the way?

I didn't know then that adventure was just around the corner. I didn't know that I would experience something so profound that I would describe it as mystical. I didn't think I could afford a EuroRail ticket, let alone an odyssey.

June 1999

The kite drifts to the ground
two feet touch down
on the sidewalk
on green grass
on a beach
on a homeland
or a foreign soil.
Where do the feet touch down?

Only the kite is visible
and beyond it, the sky.
Two hands cling
effortlessly
waiting for the pain to claim them.
Windy
cool
quiet.
Just the wind
and dangling feet.

As the daughter of a lapsed-Catholic mother and atheist father and a fresh graduate with a master's degree in history, I don't think

I was trained to go through the world with thoughts of mysticism on my mind. The Catholics I knew and loved experienced miracles as facts and repented daily for the sins embodied by the lives they actually lived. The atheists I knew and loved taught me to be good for the sake of being good if only because it was easier to live with oneself that way. And the historians I knew (some of whom I loved) seemed most pleased when they were disproving truths, for the truth is a mutable opinion rarely rooted in fact. In this repenting, Godless, untruthful world, ideas were hard to cling to and beliefs something to understand rather than ascribe to. The mystical aspect of my journey was more comforting to me than Catholicism, atheism, or academia had been. It was as though a cool and gentle mist of love, compassion, and understanding washed over me. Within this experience, I was comforted and led, never alone, never left dangling.

When I use the word *mystical*, I suppose it's hard not to picture the sensational. Imagine a swami sitting cross-legged in his white toga while meditating on his third eye or a gap-toothed Carol Burnett dressed as a gypsy and hunched over a crystal ball, her bright scarves highlighting her hard-living appearance. The Greek mystics you might have learned about in school were members of mysterious religions, which in today's terms (let's be honest) definitely sound like cults. Let's not go near the mystics! And of course, who could forget the hippies of the sixties who made love, not war, while ingesting all manner of psychedelic drugs (I'm picturing Jim Morrison in the desert, arms outstretched to the peyote-induced god in the sky) and referring to these trips as mystical. *Mystical* can seem inaccessible, most especially to us mere mortals sifting through real-world days.

Spiritual seems safer. We often read spiritual people as noble and generous and participating in advancing the human race. Spiritual people are Catholic (like Mother Teresa) or Hindu (like Gandhi) or Jewish (like Rabbi Isaac Luria) or Buddhist (like Bodhidharma). None of them are flying their flag solo, they all have a tried, tested, and true group of people who live the religion and make all that mystical stuff they did okay. But all those people I just mentioned are also famous mystics. Did you know that? Even Jesus was a mystic.

Mysticism is really about creating a personal connection with a higher power. It's about using your intuition and personal experience to create a relationship with God, Spirit, Source, Universal Consciousness, Nirvana (whatever name resonates with you the most) and thereby gain a better understanding of your place in the world. It's a stripping away of the ego at the same time as attaining a better understanding of one's *self*. What's perhaps most significant about mystical knowledge is that it is gained through experience. You can read about it in a book, but you can't be taught it. While it isn't separate from or in contradiction to one's religion, it is an adjunct process that happens without the community. Your community may perhaps facilitate opportunities for you to become a mystic, but they can't make it happen for you.

It's been many years now since my mystical odyssey. At the cusp of the last century, I spent three years living abroad, and it was during this time that it happened. Altogether, I spent nearly three months backpacking, and for much of it I traveled alone, through Italy, Spain, Greece, France, Switzerland, and Austria, and crossed the Mediterranean by boat. On this adventure, I discovered my destiny. I came to know my soul and understand the yearnings of my heart. I explored the essence of my own being. I discovered new parts of the world, and I discovered a different version of myself than I had previously known: the stripped-down version that exists at the core of me. Most important, I experienced strange synchronicities and signs, feelings of ecstasy and enlightenment, things I can only describe as mystical experiences. They served to validate my thoughts and experiences, guide me in decision making, and comfort me as I questioned, pondered, discovered. Since then, I've returned to the everyday, and I've worked and moved and learned and traveled and had other adventures, but I've not forgotten the lessons learned on this pivotal adventure. They have shaped my actions in such a way that I have steadily embraced my dreams and have turned them into realities. Mystical Backpacking has never left me. It changed the very course of my life.

Of course, my mother wasn't thrilled that I had chosen to traipse about by myself like a hobo with my meager belongings on my back. I don't know that my grandparents would have approved either, had they been alive to offer their opinions. This was *not* something young women should do. But thankfully, this odyssey took place at the start of this century and the many doors that would have been closed to me in times past were now open, at least in theory. Let's face it, for many men of the recent past, this type of odyssey would have been impossible as well. With no Great Depression to warrant riding the rails, riding them anyways usually meant you had gone off them.

Being alone and traveling alone isn't typically celebrated in our culture. The family unit, the stable job with benefits, the groups, leagues, and clubs creating caste systems of belonging are still venerated and used to describe one's accomplishments and thereby ascribe value to one's worth. This is not to deride this system, for it certainly holds value to individuals and to society; without these groups, we wouldn't have fundraisers and teams and awards and all manner of fun and community. But it is difficult to grow personally within these constraints. There is no I in T-E-A-M. Yet, does membership truly yield a sense of belonging or, more importantly, a sense of purpose? We are more connected to one another than ever before in human history. We are able to instantly tweet our location to our followers, to Facebook or Instagram our photos only moments after we've taken them, to send a note and have it received within seconds via email. In a world such as this, the concept of being apart from others is counterintuitive to the lives we actually lead. We are living rapidly, continuously defined by our latest post, our latest text. Yet, this instant connectivity can be absurdly alienating. Who has not felt the sting of having every call you place to a specific person go to voicemail, yet your text to them is responded to instantly? We are somehow farther apart in our closeness, which can be emotionally confusing.

Removing yourself from the group for a time is the most generous gift you can give your soul. It provides the opportunity for you to breathe without restriction, act without judgment, create without criticism. It provides the space, mentally, emotionally, and physically, for you to journey within, to the heart of the matter. The gift of solitary travel is that it affords you the time and space to sit with your true nature and come to know who you are. When your work or home environment do not define you, when your friends and family do not define you, when you are without these anchors that hold you to the life you live each day, then you are able to take your natural shape and see where you truly fit. You end up in unfamiliar places that challenge you to use your own self as a reference point and find stability anywhere you are.

You may be thinking that Mystical Backpacking sounds familiar. The process and desired outcome are truly about experiencing a modern-day interpretation of the traditional vision quest, which many peoples of the world have engaged in for centuries. To complete a vision quest, a person leaves his or her community to explore the world and to experience the divine. This act is believed to reveal one's purpose in life. The person then returns to the community to begin to pursue that purpose.

Unlike vision quests, Mystical Backpacking is coupled with guided reflection exercises and journaling. Similar to them, Mystical Backpacking reveals inner truth and a clear way forward. You create space for your destiny to unfold before you, and you return to your community better equipped to contribute to it.

In some ways, this is the more difficult path. Mystical Backpacking is active rather than passive, assumes risk over security, and requires a dedication that can be exhaustive, especially toward the end of a long journey. But the joys, the experiences, and the adventure of it all are incomparable to any other kind of living. As I have embraced the challenges of this more difficult path and the joys afforded me as a result, I've become aware of something that saddens me. Many people experience grand adventures vicariously rather than firsthand. Many people haven't actively engaged in the time and effort required to scale their inner mountains. Many people are too busy making a living to actually live.

There is an inner voice buried within each of us. It is the voice of our authentic self and speaks to us of our dreams and the directions we would like to pursue. As young children, it was the only voice we heard. That voice was then tempered and forged by the people raising us and the experiences we encountered along the way. As a result, it has become unrecognizable to us. Those of us who do still hear it often dismiss it, intellectualizing its primal urges as unnecessarily indulgent. We dispel the authentic voice's power over us by finding its urges irrational and foreign, although these urges are in fact the most rational and self-knowing, self-revealing insights into the true direction of the life and challenges we are meant to face. By turning away from these dreams and directions because the pursuit of them frightens us, we are really turning away from personal growth, self-fulfillment, and opportunities for experiencing the divine.

Taking the first fearful step toward greater self-knowledge engages us in a process of learning and growth. We do not grow by doing what we know. We grow by doing that which is new. Engaging in the new by doing something, anything, for the first time, is frightening. Being frightened is humbling. Humility helps us to be vulnerable, kind, and open toward others. Kindness and openness help us better communicate with others and better equip us to recognize and receive the beauty of the world. Communicating with people and recognizing the beauty in the world help us to love the world and the people in it. Love helps us have greater self-awareness and, if we believe in a higher power, helps us communicate with this higher power and to *feel* the presence of that power in our lives. This entire process helps us find our paths in our lives. In pursuing our paths and fulfilling the dreams of our authentic voice, we find happiness. The answers are there. We need only to have the courage to experience finding them.

We all have a Mystical Backpacker inside of us, and I hope you access yours within the pages of this book. As an experienced Mystical Backpacker, I stand here like a roadside local, arm raised and finger pointed toward the place I think you may be looking for.

Part memoir, part guidebook, this book tells you about the places I've been on my journey, physically and metaphysically, that impacted me and provided opportunities for deeper self-knowledge. At the same time, you will engage in your own journey, your own odyssey, to embrace adventure and new experiences. The personal experiences I share along the way will resonate with the experiences you are having on your journey, and activities at the end of each chapter will guide you to places within yourself where you will unearth the layers of your thoughts and beliefs, thereby uncovering your own direction in life.

The book follows the chronological order of a trip (planning, preparing, embarking, returning, etc.), and is divided into two parts: first, the journey into the heart of the labyrinth of discovery, adventure, and self-discovery that is a Mystical Backpacking expedition; and second, the journey back into the "real" world, where you will learn to apply in your everyday life the many lessons and riches you've gained from your voyage. This book is meant to be experienced chapter by chapter, rather than jumping around. This way, the book journeys with you and you with the book. And whether you're super freaked out about traveling alone or just want to share your experiences with others from time to time, the Mystical Backpacker website can be a resource for you as well: themysticalbackpacker.com. I balk to suggest any kind of social media resource on a sacred solitary trek but also can't deny that information is a valuable commodity, most especially when you're traveling alone! The website provides videos, meditations, suggested reading lists, music playlists, recommended activities and even a forum for leaving and reading messages left by other Mystical Backpackers—me included. Using the wealth of resources available at your fingertips is a way of staying connected to other soul travelers while having necessary information readily available and without losing entire days to planning. After all, you want to be free to experience! Once you return from your Mystical Backpacking journey, the site can also help you to find a community of Mystical Backpackers. It can be a wonderful experience to share stories and insights with kindred spirits as you create a life more in keeping with your soul's purpose. Check out the Mystical Extras section at the end of the book for more.

While I can show you where to begin your journey toward feeding your spirit and embracing your destiny, I can't take the journey for you. I will point out the road, but you have to travel it. In traveling, you reconnect with your spirit, and when you find your spirit, you find your place in the world. There is only one way to find your destiny, and that is to pursue it by participating in the life you want to lead.

There is never a perfect time to do this. You will never have the money you think you need. You will never feel brave enough to do it. You will always feel like embarking on your journey is something to be planned for, carefully and incrementally—something that someday might be possible far off in the future, but not now. Believe me, you've never been so wrong. Now *is* the time, the only time, and it's as good a time as any. You will soon find that the responsibilities and burdens you were carrying weren't as constricting as you had thought them to be.

As the Taoists say, a thousand-mile journey begins with a single step. You take this first step alone but know that many have walked this path before you, and many walk beside you now.

PART I

Into the Wild Unknown

1

What Exactly Is a Mystical Backpacker, and Do I Need to Become One?

We can't solve problems by using the same kind of thinking we used when we created them.

—Attributed to Albert Einstein

Before becoming a Mystical Backpacker, I would never have articulated that I needed to experience a vision quest or anything like it in order to find my way in life. Thoughts of such matters were furthest from my mind. Art, history, architecture, and poetry: these were the subjects that delighted my soul and occupied my mind. I had no romantic notions of living in the wild or communing with a higher power or experiencing anything transcendental—at least, not beyond da Vinci or Botticelli, Gaudi or Monet. The wild of the natural world was something I had left behind once I had my own apartment and no longer needed to go on camping trips to escape parental control. Not that I didn't enjoy camping—I did. But cable and hot water were so much more enjoyable. And I wasn't looking for spirituality either. I was far more drawn to the temples of art and history (the Louvre or Uffizi) than to the temple of a god. For me, churches were places for marveling at architectural accomplishments: flying buttresses and vaulted ceilings and great expanses of incensed air within which silent prayers ascended. Nor would I have chosen an experience that, at least in my home continent of North America, might be construed as an appropriation of a Native American tradition.

A wide range of cultures around the world engage in sacred journeys of self-discovery. Many First Nations peoples of North America call these vision quests, when a young man fasts and goes into the wild for several days and nights and experiences visions enlightening him of his life's purpose.[1] Amish teens are afforded the opportunity to break from the community before choosing whether or not to commit themselves to the Amish way of life, a period of time referred to as Rumspringa, which, literally translated, means "running around."[2] Aborigine boys engage in a Walkabout, and Buddhist boys in the Theravada tradition enter a monastery for a time (typically three months) to retreat spiritually and live as monks before rejoining their communities as adults. The African Babongo, Mitsogo, and Fang peoples of Gabon drink Iboga as part of their Bwiti religion.[3] Modern users of Ayahuasca tea, found in the Amazon, seek their own enlightenment in performing the ritual (although this is not the historical reason for its use).[4] In each case, the purpose is the same: to go on an individual journey, either into the wilderness of the wider world or by sacred ritual and to encounter the intangible experiences that reveal one's purpose in life, one's true calling. Also, the physical journey is always accompanied by a spiritual journey. When you are removed from your community, you are removed from your ego. No longer worried about what they might think, you are free to explore what you think. When your environment does not mirror, reflect, or define you, then you have no one to be but your true self.

In this modern age, the desire to know the "authentic self" impels us all to explore our thoughts and analyze our actions, perhaps more so than at any other time or place in history. Religion remains a barometer of moral worth, a compass, for many. Therapy, counseling, and support groups are all available to many of us in the modern Western world, and time on the couch is no longer stigmatized but rather is seen as a way of maintaining balanced mental health and tackling stressful situations in life.

What are missing from these modern processes are the actual *physical journeys*, the *solitude* acquired while separate from one's community, and *recognition* of the mystical experiences afforded by such means. Would the journey away from our communities and the new experiences gained from this break benefit us mentally, emotionally, perhaps even spiritually?

According to some psychologists, the answer—at least in part—is yes. Dr. Julia Zimmermann and Professor Dr. Franz Neyer have conducted the most comprehensive study to date of students who have studied abroad. In their 2013 paper, "Do We Become a Different Person When Hitting the Road? Personality Development of Sojourners," they found that students who had studied abroad—even for only a semester, about three or four months—were more open, more agreeable, and more emotionally stable than those who had not. Additionally, they scored higher in conscientiousness and extraversion than those who had not. In short, their emotional development was boosted by the experience.[5] A similar study, conducted in 2010, found that people who lived abroad and had either adapted to or come to understand the cultural norms of another culture had a greater capability for creative thinking and problem solving than those who had not. These people, as a result of their experiences, are better at thinking outside the box. While these studies focused on students, it is interesting to find such significant personal growth result from relatively short experiences.[6]

Travel does not need to be lengthy and expansive in order for benefits to be gained. We also do not need to go far to realize our destiny or experience personal transformation. For so many people, even a "small" trip changes their lives forever. Take, for example, the story of a young woman studying to become a secretary at a Christian college in North Carolina who visited her sister in New York City during her school break. Her brother-in-law, a photographer, took her photo and placed it in his shop window. A young man, smitten with her image, saw it and suggested it be submitted to a movie studio. Within the year, the woman was called back to New York for a screen test and put under contract by MGM. Ava Gardner hadn't even been trying to be a star![7] In fact, upon seeing her test, Louis B. Mayer sent a telegram stating, "She can't sing, she can't act, she can't talk . . . she's terrific!"[8] And she was. The camera loved her. She had traveled only a few hundred miles away from home to meet her destiny on Fifth Avenue. This trip affected her life profoundly: whom she married, where she lived and worked, the very story of her life changed course. Which is not to say we're all going to be discovered as movie stars when we visit our sisters, but to say that even the smallest of trips can afford the opportunity for a complete transformation to occur.

Now Ava wasn't on a vision quest, per se. A vision quest is an exploration of the outer *and* inner planes. But her small trip was an adventure for her. It was beyond her comfort zone and outside her normal circle of existence. The small step she took unearthed tremendous shifts in her life. We celebrate such stories because the spirit of exploration and adventure is an inherent part of the human story. The possibility of striking it rich and changing our lives overnight is a wish that resonates with the human soul. Whether a Bedouin desert child who fantasizes about finding a genie in a bottle or a suburbanite who imagines winning a television singing program, we share the overnight success story as the ultimate adventure. And this is why we celebrate those who travel well beyond the small circles of experience and live life large: Annie Oakley, Sacagawea, Amelia Earhart, Ernest Hemingway, Gertrude Stein, Elizabeth Bishop, Neil Armstrong, Christopher Columbus, Nellie Bly, Marco Polo, Captain

James Cook, Xuanzang, and Kira Salak, to name a painfully meager smattering of examples; the list is too exhaustive to cover, the age and geography of the world too expansive to represent adequately. Television shows celebrate the traveler (think *Anthony Bourdain: No Reservations, Survivorman, An Idiot Abroad*, etc.), while whole television networks, magazines, and entire sections of bookstores devote themselves to the subject. We like to hear about people living adventurous lives not just because we enjoy the stories that result or the voyeuristic aspect of secondhand experience but because they speak to places within us that also yearn for adventure.

Travelers and adventurers seem to exist outside of the box. They aren't living in the same world as us mortals but seem to swoop in and out of our world as if gods from Mount Olympus. There is something daring and exciting about their transitory natures. In fact, the traveler is exempt from certain rules and obligations because of this: Amelia didn't have to wear skirts, Sacagawea traveled while pregnant and continued to travel with her son after he was born, and Nellie wasn't expected to marry someone before circumnavigating the globe. Allowances are made because the soul of the traveler is somehow different, perhaps even heroic. And we like heroes, because they inspire us to be the best possible versions of ourselves.

We perceive our heroes as having superior abilities, increased courage and discipline, yielding higher aptitudes for success. But I doubt you'll ever find a real-live hero who describes himself or herself this way. Most heroes chalk their successes up to hard work and dogmatic persistence. They simply choose not to quit or give up. One of my favorite quotes is by Michael Jordan, a man known as the greatest basketball player of all time: "I've missed more than nine thousand shots in my career. I've lost almost three hundred games. Twenty-six times, I've been trusted to take the game-winning shot and missed. I've failed over and over and over again in my life. And that is why I succeed."[9]

The truth is, we don't need to look to adventurers and heroes as people separate from or better than us. We can choose to make our lives an adventure and to be the heroes of our own stories. Within each of us there is an adventurer waiting to be brought to light, a hero waiting for the opportunity to save ourselves from ourselves. So, how do we unearth these magical qualities?

Self-reflection and self-analysis benefit us. Travel benefits us. But the combination is powerful. In uniting the two, it is possible to create the right conditions for self-transformation. Mystical Backpacking occurs when you have the opportunity to marvel at, to learn about, and to experience the new one-on-one. It is in part an intimate dance, a long date, a love affair with the world itself and in part an intimate dance, a long date, a love affair with your truest self, the person you are at the core. Mystical Backpacking is a process by which you establish a relationship with the macrocosm of the world at large while experiencing a renewed sense of faith, connectivity, and personal relationship with the spiritual; a coming to clear terms with yourself is gained in the process. It's not about athletic ability, physical strength, or mental aptitude. It's about whether or not you have the insight to discover your purpose and the chutzpah to manifest it.

So, what does that mean for you now? How do you know whether or not you are a candidate for becoming a Mystical Backpacker? Is this text speaking to you, or is the person beside you the one who really needs to read this book?

The Challenge

I want you to picture the planet in your mind's eye. Imagine being up there in a small, austere, utilitarian spaceship and peering out a small window. The Earth is a golden and blue jewel of miraculous life, suspended by violent, life-taking forces in a seemingly meaningless void. You'll see that there, down there, just past that vast horizon of twinkling lights and rising sun, there is a dot. On that beautiful dot, there are ten thousand buildings. And in one of those buildings, there are a few thousand people working at a few thousand tasks. And one of those people is you.

You go through your day tending, doing, moving through the actions. You're tense. Even your eyebrows are tense. Your jaw is tense. Your thighs are tense. You are one tense cookie! Your day began too early. You're tired from too many nights not long enough to accommodate the rest your body tells you it needs. You have things to do when you get off work: chores, errands, and responsibilities to uphold. You won't have any time for fun things today. Today will be a day without pleasure. Come to think of it, tomorrow will be the same. You move through days like this on autopilot. Your rest will be the hour or two spent in front of the TV or lost on a website or in a book before going to bed.

It can be difficult to look at your life this way. You've probably done what it takes to be a success. You impress your friends and relatives with how "together" you are. Your life is a carefully constructed harbor where no boat sinks. As the American author and professor John Augustus Shedd said, "A ship in harbor is safe, but that's not what ships are built for."[10] What if your life, while built with the best tools and opportunities available to you at the time, is not the life you dream of? You're successful, so why aren't you happy? Until now, you've thought maybe it's because you need a partner, a raise, a vacation, a hobby, to lose some weight . . . for most of us, this list goes on and on. But the pursuit of these so-called solutions does not make you happy. This can get confusing. You begin to suspect there is something wrong with you. It could be medical. It could be chemical. It might be your thyroid. You set up appointments and surf the web, looking for possible explanations. You become more confused. You join a gym, you get fit, you meet someone; you're happy! After a few dates, the romance fizzles, and you don't feel like going to the gym anymore. Forgetting you were unhappy before, you think you're unhappy because dating is such a chore. After years of such casting about, your confusion only deepens.

You start over. But where do you even begin? What are you searching for? Why can't you be happy with what you have? The cycle repeats, and maybe you start to feel guilty. After all, you are blessed with many things others don't have. You should be grateful for what you have. Clearly, something must be wrong with you! Maybe you've convinced yourself of this. Maybe someone else has. One thing's for certain: If you are not living the life you dream of, you are living the life you create in response to others' expectations. If you believe your existence has some meaning, even if to no one other than yourself, then the way to manifest that meaning is on the high seas of life, not in safe harbor. But you can't head boldly out to sea if you're stuck in a rut on land.

Let's talk about ruts.

At this point, your rut may be more of a suspicion than a confirmed fact. The reality is, most of us don't even realize when we're in a rut. And here's why: our ruts are really, really big.

Imagine an enormous crater. You're standing inside it, but you don't see the edges because the things you pay the most attention to are also inside it. Your home is inside it. Your car is inside it. Your place of work is inside it. Even your gym is inside it! This rut is huge. You're like an ant in a sandbox. The ant doesn't know he's in a sandbox—he thinks he's just out in the world. But his world was created using three-dollar bags of processed sand from the local hardware store. It is boxed in by chemically treated wood, and it makes up a very small area in a very large yard. The ant's world is a construct of someone's imagination (or lack thereof), but the ant probably thinks he's in the Sahara. When we ask ourselves what our souls truly need, the answers are rarely found inside our sandboxes.

If you've ever asked yourself, "Am I in a rut?" then you probably are. It's that simple. All ruts like this are serious business, because they remove you from your purpose in life. You are not fulfilling your destiny.

Whoa! Did someone say *destiny*? That's a little over the top, isn't it? The word destiny can seem overwhelming. It suggests that we must live life at heights akin to the gods. It suggests a life of greatness, perhaps fame, wealth, adventure, material success, spiritual success. Those who have been destined to exist are those who have impacted the world on a large scale. They are the Gandhis, the Mother Teresas, the Joan of Arcs, the Shakespeares of the world. But destiny can apply to you too. When I speak of fulfilling destiny, I'm talking about living happily and making a difference. Perhaps that means you are to sail the seas your entire life, never having a fixed address. Or it may mean that you are a stay-at-home parent who cooks, shops, cleans, and raises children. Maybe you work in a shop and help customers. No destiny is considered little if it is *your* destiny. Once you find it, you'll be able to see your sandbox for what it really is and to transform it into a new stomping ground that supports the deep happiness of fulfilling your soul's purpose.

The bottom line is this: life is not supposed to feel like a chore. Life is supposed to feel full and whole. As you move through your days, your surroundings and the people you interact with should stimulate you, evoking happiness and a sense of satisfaction within you. That's not to say some days won't be challenging or involve doing things you don't want to do. But overall, your precious time should always be channeled in ways that lead you to the greater picture you're striving towards, rather than have you standing still on a boarding platform where your train never arrives.

The challenge is to get yourself out of your rut. Let's begin.

The first thing to know about ruts is that you were born at a perfect time in history for overcoming your rut. Modern life (especially in Western and other developed nations) affords the opportunity, like never before in history, for us to step out of our sandboxes. We have more agency to define our own lives than most people who've come before us. You're not a sixteenth-century goat herder or a twentieth-century suffragette. You aren't trapped by a caste system, feudal system, socioeconomic system, by gender, race, or creed in anywhere near the ways in which people once were. You don't have to travel by stagecoach or Viking ship! You can board a bus, train, ferry, plane . . . or just get in your car and go. One of the benefits of the modern age is that a waitress from a small town can save up enough money to go abroad and change the course of her life—I know this because I've done it. In my teens I worked as a waitress in a small town, and now, decades later, I've lived and worked abroad, earned degrees, owned a business, and become a seminar leader and published author. I didn't have the money, privileges, or gender to mean this would all be a snap of the fingers.

The second thing to understand about ruts is that they are more in your mind than they are in time and place. The personalized rut you have created—however inadvertently—is really a reflection of the larger rut that exists in your belief system. And those beliefs took some time to create. Let me show you what I mean.

My first car was a gray Plymouth Reliant with burgundy interior. Its previous owner was an elderly woman who drove it a mere two thousand miles in as many years. When I first laid eyes on it, my teenage eagerness to own and drive my first car was rapidly displaced by the horror and humiliation of driving this *particular* car. But it was already paid for (thanks, Dad!). I drove it for many years, until there was a hole in the floor and it just wouldn't start anymore.

My second car was a red Fiero given to me by my mom's boyfriend. Somewhat cooler, although it made no sense to be driving such a small, low-to-the-ground car in our harsh Ontario winters. It was a ridiculous sight to see: my sixty-pound dog, my six-foot-two boyfriend, and five-foot-nine me crammed into the two-seater, the groceries loaded under the hood (the engine was in the trunk), and the mounds of snow towering above us. I remember it felt more like sitting on a sled than in a car, which is how it drove, too, fishtailing and sliding through Ontario's small towns. Accelerating on a highway, it sounded like a small plane taking off.

My third car was a poison-green VW Golf with tartan black-red-and-green interior. The moment I set eyes on it, my heart sank because I knew it would be my car. I just knew it. That car looked like it should be cruising in a St. Patrick's Day parade. At every red light, people would stare at my car; I imagine they were waiting to see if fifty clowns would pile out in a game of Fire Drill. If my car were to have its own soundtrack, it would definitely have been a circus theme.

Don't worry—I am making my point.

My fourth car was a silver VW Passat with black leather interior, a purring Audi engine, surround-sound speakers and Bluetooth. When I bought it, I didn't feel that I deserved it. I felt like I was putting on a false persona. The person I had grown accustomed to being drove old and crappy cars. Who did I think I was in this fancy car? Who was I *pretending* to be?

Living your life in a rut can feel the same way. At first, you are horrified by the choices made for you, as I was when my dad bought me that Reliant. Then, once you've worn them a while, they start to fit, so you're not as horrified with the next choice. And after a while, you think those choices somehow define you: I was a woman who was artsy, confident, and drove old clunkers. Your identity is tied to these choices—choices of necessity, choices of practicality, choices made by others. When you finally presume to make a choice for yourself because you have the ability to, like when I bought my silver

Passat, that first choice feels like the wrong one. The authentic self has become displaced and feels foreign. And so it is with stepping out of the sandbox and into the rest of the world.

When you first mount the wall of your rut to make your break for the world beyond, you may not feel deserving of your venture. You may not feel that it is the "real you," that by venturing out of the world you've inhabited for so long, you are pretending to be someone you're not. You may feel shallow because in your pursuit of a "better" life, you're rejecting the life you've been living. You may question your faith. You may wonder if you think you're special, and if so, who do you think you are? Your friends and family live in the rut you've been talking about leaving behind; do you think you're better than everyone else? Are you rejecting the people you love?

Orison Marden said that "The Creator has not put desires in our hearts without giving us the ability and the opportunity for realizing them."[11] If you believe in a higher power, then you most likely believe that that higher power wants you to appreciate your most precious blessing: the gift of life, and to live it fully. As for your friends and family, you may *want* to have their permission so you can escape these unsettling feelings you've been having. Perhaps if *they* think you should get out of your rut, if they give you their permission to pursue this course, then it's okay that you want to. As such, the first hurdle to overcome when you've realized that you want to get out of your rut is in giving yourself permission to do so. *No one else's permission will suffice.* You may not feel that you have the confidence needed right now to give yourself permission. You may not feel that you have the authority. Of course, if you felt those things already, you wouldn't be in a rut. Isn't that called a Catch-22?

So, where does Mystical Backpacking factor into all of this talk of playing in the sands of destiny? If you suspect that you're in a rut, the best way to climb out is by embarking on an adventure. When you adventure, you are catapulted right out of your rut into the world beyond, where you will meet new people, experience new places, reawaken your soul to the very gift of your life, and embrace a newfound enthusiasm for the possibilities that abound in your future. But because you need to return to the reality of your life and shape it in accordance with the vision you create for it en route, the adventure should be paired with inner work: a coming to terms with your own belief system, a thorough excavation of your inner world—for this inner world is largely responsible for what is created in the outer world. To overhaul your rut once you return, you not only need the inspiration and the courage to believe you can (which you will gain from the trip itself), but you also need to know—to the very core of your being—that it is possible (which you will gain from doing the worksheets and exercises that you'll be encountering shortly). Mystical Backpacking is an adventure that takes place without and within concurrently. It is a vehicle for connecting with your truest self in a powerful way. It is an experience that is physical, mental, emotional, spiritual, and ultimately transformative. This particular solution to what ails you is an outside-the-(sand)box solution. Immense progress can be made from this new, uncharted plane.

Strap in and hang on: your first step toward embracing your outside-the-box solution has arrived. Drumroll, please: it's time for your first set of Mystical Exercises.

The Mystical Exercises throughout this book will support and assist you in traversing the inner planes as you journey inward to discover your soul's purpose and unearth your destiny through the vehicle of Mystical Backpacking. The exercises that follow serve to help you find some clarity of thought and purpose on this particular leg of your mystical journey. These exercises are for you alone. You may keep them entirely private and don't ever need to share your truths with another soul. However, welcoming them into your conscious self is the only way to benefit from this process, so try to be as truthful as possible.

Mystical Exercises: Chapter 1

Acquire a Journal

It is absolutely essential you keep a record of your journey, both outward and inward. You may either keep two separate and distinct journals, one for documenting your travels and one for documenting your Mystical Exercises, or you can keep one journal and work your way through both journeys in one place. It's entirely up to you. I strongly encourage you to include your full name and mailing address with a request to ship the journal to your address if found. This way, if you lose your journal, you may not end up losing it forever.

I encourage you to keep your records in your own handwriting and not as a digital document. A lost tablet, notebook, or smartphone is less likely to be returned to you. Also, there's something sacred about looking at your thoughts in writing, running your fingers over the labels, ticket stubs, stickers, and café napkins you place within its pages, and seeing the pinched letters of distress next to the soaring cursive of a breakthrough. There are pages in my notebook where teardrops have dried, marking the location in time and place my own personal healing began. These journals have become valuable possessions marking not just my travel adventures and experiences but also the inner journey of my soul's healing.

The Practical: Buy a paperback journal or notebook to use as a journal because that kind is relatively easy to transport (it doesn't weigh a lot), both as you carry it and if you mail it home, and to write in (it bends and folds easily). It's also the least expensive to buy and the most readily available wherever you travel, so if you fill one up, you can easily purchase a second volume.

The Mystical: Make your journal special or sacred to you. Embellish the cover, inscribe the first page with your favorite quote, add your name and address to the back pages, etc. Find a way to mark this as a special place for you to go. Create a space you want to spend time in. You can see pictures of some of the journals I've kept on my travels in the Mystical Moments Photo Album beginning on page 155.

Top 5 Dreads

Make a list of the top five things you routinely dread in your daily life (feel free to record this exercise in your newly acquired journal!).

Top 5 Pleasures

Make a list of the top five simple pleasures you routinely enjoy in your daily life (regardless of whether or not they're healthy for you).

Finality Exercise

There are many fun movies and stories about people who are given the opportunity for a do-over, thereby escaping death, improving their lives, or mending their relationships. Perhaps the most famous of these is *A Christmas Carol*, in which Scrooge experiences a life review and opts to change his ways. But it's a popular theme explored in other stories as well. Off the top of my head, I can think of *Defending Your Life* with Meryl Streep and Albert Brooks, *Chances Are* with Robert Downey Jr. and Cybil Shepherd, *Ghost Town* with Ricky Gervais and Téa Leoni, and *It's a Wonderful Life* with James Stewart. In this exercise, I want you to imagine yourself as the main character in just such a story and you have just learned that you are going to kick the bucket tomorrow. Immerse yourself in that feeling of finality. From this place, knowing that all your chances are over and your life has been fully lived, answer the following questions. If you find it difficult to center yourself and go within to the truth of this moment, you are welcome to try using a free guided meditation at the Mystical Backpacker website, themysticalbackpacker.com, under the freebies section. The meditation for this exercise is "Mystical Meditation 1: Finality."

Once you've successfully connected with that feeling of finality, please write these questions and answers out on a few blank pieces of paper. You can opt to include them in your journal, too, if you wish.

1. The most important life experiences I've had to date are:
2. The relationships I cherish the most are [please explain why as well]:
3. My top five regrets are:
4. If there was one thing I could have experienced and didn't, it would be:
5. If I could go back to a turning point in my life and give myself advice, it would be:

Nicely done. Answering these questions has already moved you to a more powerful place. Even if some of the answers make you sad or uncomfortable, remember that this isn't the end of your story. You are still writing it. It's time to get into that silver Passat and drive it like you own it (because you do) out onto the open road, knowing that you'll never drive a crappy old junker again.

2

I Never Win Anything: Life Before Travel

All know the way. Few actually walk it.

—**Bodhidharma**

"If Miss Honeychurch ever takes to live as she plays, it will be very exciting both for us and for her."[1]

This quote from E. M. Forster's *A Room with a View* is spoken to young Miss Honeychurch by her pastor, Mr. Beebe. They are both vacationing in Italy, and Miss Honeychurch has been playing the piano in the common room. Mr. Beebe has been listening and pondering her choices. He appreciates her decisions to make the notes of the pieces she plays triumph and is surprised to witness such a common girl play in such an enlightened manner. In fact, her connection to something glorious and godly is so obvious to him, he cannot understand why she would ever bother to listen to his sermons. But Miss Honeychurch *is* a regular person. It is only in playing music that she is able to transcend her own limitations and feel that she is neither "deferential or patronizing; no longer either a rebel or a slave."[2]

Each of us, when moved by spirit, becomes something grand and glorious that rises above the mundane, if only even for a moment. It's entirely possible that our fascination with athletes, musicians, travelers, adventurers, and other heroes is our awareness, if even by sixth sense, of this interplay and exchange of mortal and spiritual energy. The hero becomes the conduit for divine effervescence to surprise us in our flat world, like a champagne cork flying from its bottled casements and issuing forth its precious, sparkling cheer. When we witness a person's interaction with the supernatural, we are awed less by the person's humanity and more by their superhumanity. Our perception is that it takes some kind of mighty and formidable effort of will and energy to be the strongest or the bravest or the one to defy records or conventions. But it's actually a divine spark being witnessed in a very practical way within our real world. We are impressed and moved and triumphant ourselves because we have come so close to that experience that we actually feel the magnificence of the divine and are awed by it.

The goal of Mystical Backpacking is to find and feel that connection, that divine spark. The trick is to believe it is possible, perhaps even when it's never happened to you before.

But how does one start believing?

There was a time in my life when I, like many others, was that person who said, "I never win anything!" I worked hard at school and at my jobs; I was ambitious and graduated multiple levels of postsecondary school. I had a vague idea of the future I was working toward realizing: I wanted to have a good job, earn a good living, get married, buy a house, and have kids. Everything I had, I worked hard for, and I had always known I would have to work hard. I didn't feel entitled. I also didn't feel particularly lucky. My mantra in those days, which I even inscribed in one of my journals, was a variation of a quote attributed to the writer and publisher Garth Henrichs: "The person who is waiting for something to turn up might start with their shirt sleeve."[3] The life I imagined was one that would elude me for a long time. The opportunities presented me were always taking me away from these goals. And *damn* it, weren't they the very opportunities my authentic self craved? I just couldn't see the forest for the trees.

I wish I could say I actively created the life I wanted to live, but I know I lived reactively, partially of necessity. That is, others in my life made decisions, and I adjusted my plans accordingly. It seemed as though each time I tried to make a decision for myself, it didn't work out. In my third year of university, I wanted very much to go to Belize and be the artist for an archaeological dig run by the anthropology department. The cost, after applying a student loan and small scholarship, was still several thousand dollars, and I shouldn't have been allowed to go on the trip because I was not an anthropology student. I met with the department head and won him over, my place on the dig assured. I began to save money, knowing I had several months to do so, but soon realized I wouldn't have enough. I spent months actively fundraising in the community, but nearly everything I gained was gifts-in-kind and not money toward the trip. I asked my hometown newspaper to run a story. A man and his daughter mailed me $90 and asked that I send postcards so she could learn about Belize and archaeology. I was touched and thrilled! Then I received a phone call from a woman in my hometown who screamed into the phone, "Who the #@$!! do you think you are? You think you're so special? You have no right to ask people for money to go on this trip! You're disgusting!" I cried for days. I was short over $500 to go on the trip. I returned the $90 to the little girl and her father, and I canceled my plans. But as Maria said in *The Sound of Music*, "When the Lord closes a door, somewhere he opens a window."[4]

While I didn't have enough money to go to Belize, I did have enough to go to Romania, land of my paternal family. I contacted the history department and arranged to write a thesis paper on the Hungarian women of Transylvania, beginning with my own grandmother, had my interview questionnaires approved by the Human Ethics Board and borrowed a tape recorder from the A/V department. Within a few short weeks, months of planning for Belize were displaced and I was on a plane headed to Eastern Europe. I spent a month interviewing over twenty elderly women, their stories connecting me to my family history and winning me a place in my new and unplanned future.

I returned from Europe for my final year of school and worked these oral narratives into a thesis. My advisor suggested I attend graduate school in Budapest, Hungary. So I applied to the school, even though I didn't really want to go to school in Hungary. I wanted to stay at home and marry my boyfriend, but I was too intimidated to tell my professor that. Then my boyfriend dumped me. Crap. Now I was going to Budapest.

Two weeks before my flight to Budapest (after a summer spent weeping, doing data entry, and learning to ride horses, in that order), my boyfriend wanted me back. I did get back together with him (dumb), but I didn't cancel my flight. I remember his sister telling me that if I really loved him, I wouldn't go. In the end, I left my sofa in her basement (which she later sold for fifty dollars) and rented a furnished flat in Budapest. (The reason my boyfriend left me in the first place was because he had slept with another woman, *on that sofa*.)

Try as I might, I couldn't plan my own life to save it. Destiny pushed me toward Hungary, and I went kicking and screaming. As a result, I had the best adventure of my life. And sometimes, that's how the good things in our life come to fruition: we're forced by circumstance to head in a direction we hadn't planned, and we do so with great resistance.

A Journey Begins with a Single Step: Budapest, 1997

I had never lived abroad or even gone anywhere alone. To say I was scared is an understatement. I spent my first four days in Hungary cooped up in a dorm room, missing every opportunity to meet my peers and find a community. I couldn't sleep at night. I did nothing during the day except read and wander around the empty building. Even though I spoke Hungarian with relative fluency, I was afraid that if I left my dorm unchaperoned, I wouldn't be able to find my way back to it. It was nerve-racking, and by day five I wanted to go home. The only reason I didn't quit was because what scared me more than the idea of exploring a foreign land and pursuing a master's degree was going home a fool and a quitter with no direction.

I packed my knapsack and, map in hand, took public transportation into the city, into a new world and into my new life. That year I met the most wonderful people, some of whom are still friends of mine today, and I had one of the best years of my life. I lived in Europe! I felt so continental, so brave, so exciting! I ate the most divine food, saw beautiful sites, and met with diverse people. At every turn, I learned about the world and my place in it. I dumped my boyfriend, finished graduate school, and stayed in Budapest to work for an English-language publication. I learned many new skills that I would employ several years later when I started my own business. I lived in beautiful, high-ceilinged apartments, exhausted every museum and art gallery, enjoyed every restaurant, every dance club, every twisting cobblestone laneway, every overstuffed antique shop and every marketplace. I knew the hills, the bus routes, and every metro stop by name. I knew the radio stations and all the local hits. I became fluent in the language and confident in my speaking, even though my accent always gave me away as a foreigner. I couldn't believe my life and that it was mine and not some character's in a movie or a novel! I traveled to Austria, to Slovakia, to the Czech Republic, to Poland

and Romania. I saw heaps of mistletoe cut from treetops in the town square in Krakow, bathed in oily black thermal waters during August in Romania, ate pastries in coffeehouses like the poets from the last century in Bratislava, and sipped champagne beer from crystal glasses in Prague.

So many experiences lived up to my dreams that the seam between my fantasies and my day-to-day life was nearly imperceptible at times. I felt more alive than I had ever before. I felt more interested in the world and more interesting as a person.

Once I was settled in, though, even before the second year had fully passed, I began to feel that I had taken only half a step toward my dreams. Although I had been living an interesting life, once I acclimated to my new surroundings, I realized I had essentially moved from one comfort zone to another. As the daughter of Hungarian parents, I had moved to a country I had known from previous visits with family. I spoke the language quite well when I moved there. I already knew the foods and the flavors, the music and the national identity. For me, the acclimation was quick and relatively easy, and though I enjoyed my time there immensely, I always knew that my classmates and expatriate friends had challenged themselves far more than I had. I had fallen into both the Hungarian and the university society with such ease and grace that I felt comfortable almost in the same way I did at home. I could see myself living there for the rest of my life, going to work each day, watching television each night, and dreaming of unfulfilled dreams. While the decision to go to Hungary had felt adventurous, I realized that I went to Hungary because it was the best possible option at the time.

In retrospect, *it was*, if only because it had brought me to this particular crossroad. The amazing thing about stretching your comfort zone and doing what you fear doing is that once the hurdle of deciding to take action has been conquered, the succeeding steps to face new challenges and cross into ever-widening comfort zones become easier and easier to take. During this time I saw a quote somewhere that read, *Brave people are always scared.* This became a new motto for my life. I don't think I felt less frightened as I moved toward realizing my dreams; I simply felt more comfortable with feeling that fear.

After two years in Budapest, I very much wanted to see Western Europe. I wanted to be in the places I had read about, the landscapes of literature and history—to see the Forum in Rome, to roll through the countryside in which Renoir and Monet painted, to visit the land where Shakespeare wrote, and to see flamenco dancers in their native environment. I felt that I needed to put myself in a truly foreign place and to experience places that were unlike anything I had previously known. Strange yearnings simmered beneath the surface and tugged at me during my coffee breaks. I moved through days wearing a suit, scheduling meetings, making and meeting fiscal goals for the magazine, but the emptiness and loneliness I felt repeatedly reared themselves into my reality. I had such a desire to be elsewhere.

Christmas came and went. My favorite holiday was steeped in the melancholy of missing my parents. The magazine's editor had returned to San Diego to visit his family, and I worked through the holiday in the empty office while everyone else shopped, baked, and spent time with family. I had sold a lot of advertising space and promised our advertisers the guides would be available for purchase throughout the holidays, but distribution didn't come through. The guides sat in our closet. Nothing happened for several weeks. I couldn't get meetings. We weren't making money. When our boss returned and the realization of all that had not been achieved sunk in, he berated me in front of all the staff at the office. I was shocked. I was upset. I couldn't believe that I, the least deserving of accusation, was the one being held accountable. I couldn't believe that I had continued to work while everyone else was off for the holidays and that I was the one being yelled at. I stood up, and while he continued to yell, I gathered up my things. The pastries I had purchased with my own money for our office meeting sagged on my desk. The coffee I had come in early to brew for the team turned the air bitter and acrid. My hands shaking, I pushed all my things into my bag and quietly walked out of the office, out of the building, down the street, and into my friend's office, where I sat crying in disbelief. I turned my cell phone off, and within a week I had packed my backpack and raised my middle finger to a life crafted in response to others' perceptions, directions, and expectations. *I was going to do what I wanted to do.* I bought a EuroRail ticket for Western Europe. I bought a map. I notified my landlady, and I left town. And it was the best thing I ever did. Little did I know that I had just become a Mystical Backpacker.

This is not to say that you should quit your job and tell your boss to f*** off! The truth is, sometimes you're at the mercy of the winds of fate, and sometimes you take your destiny into your own hands. The reality is that there are two ways in which we are required to be brave in life. There's the bravery required to take advantage of opportunities that come our way, and there's the bravery required to pursue something we want when the opportunity is not presented to us. Both are equally important, for in finding our purpose in life, we must enter the flow of life and embody some flexibility in determining when we should allow the current to take us and when we should actively swim.

We follow a path, and we experience the changing scenery and the changing weather along that path. We cannot control the weather, the season, or the landscape; we can only control our response to these factors (by putting on warmer clothes or opening an umbrella or adjusting our pace and stride). Similarly, some events in our lives may seem forced by the environment itself, like my ending up in graduate school abroad. And some events are dictated by our very own choices. These are the turning points in life that provide us with the opportunities to exercise free will. Although it can be inspired and activated by both sorts, Mystical Backpacking at its core employs the latter kind of bravery.

Is Your Dream a Vision of Your Reality... Or Is It Just a Dream?

Imagine we are sitting down to play a board game. The board itself is a representation of the world. Each of us gets one plastic piece in the shape of a person to represent ourselves as a player. We have certain credits to start: a life credit, a family credit, a shelter credit, and a food credit. We also have ten dream credits, fifty imagination credits, and one hundred emotion credits. As we move along the board, we hit points at which we gain age credits, money credits, education credits . . . and so on. We also lose credits. Some may lose their family credits right away. Some may lose their shelter credits as soon as they're released from the hospital as newborns. Some may lose an enormous sum of emotion credits during a childhood trauma, and some may lose all their dream credits by the time they're twenty. In this game, all of these credits can be regained, and even those who do not begin from a place of strength or privilege can be successful. We get the picture, right? The game is our chance to act out our lives as we would want to, rather than as we feel we should or as circumstances dictate that we must.

Now imagine you can pursue any dream or imagine any kind of life for yourself. How do you spend your days? Where do you connect with your inner best? Who surrounds you? Who inspires you? Who do you inspire? In this game, you can choose any profession or lifestyle for yourself, but you can only realize that lifestyle when you have earned enough work credits and money credits to enable the fruition of the dream. However, in this game, any vision of your life is attainable. There is no profession or service that is not remunerated financially. There is no loss of love or approval from the people in your life. You are safe to make the choices you want to make.

It can be freeing to envision a life path when personal and material risks are not considerations. After all, the real world is not a board game with little consequence for victory or failure. Instead, the real world can be cruel to those who fail. But believe it or not, this game is the real world, even if it doesn't seem that way based on the view from the sandbox looking out. With hard work, sacrifice, and persistence, every dream and lifestyle is attainable, especially if you're open to variations on your original vision. If you are able to replenish your losses with gains, whether they are emotional, mental, or physical, then you can have the nerve to commit to every goal and see it through to fruition. The word *failure* only has as much weight as you choose to give it.

This can be a tough reality to embrace. Let's look at some examples of people who pursued their dreams against all odds and reached them as a result. Some of them are famous; some are known for their accomplishments. I share their stories *not* because fame, celebrity, and fortune are markers for success, but because they are people we all know; yet many of us don't realize how far they had to climb and how many roadblocks they needed to circumvent in order turn their dreams into realities.

We all know Louis Armstrong, famous jazz musician and vocalist. His popular rendition of "What a Wonderful World" is still played at every wedding you go to, can be heard in coffee shops and on movie soundtracks. Louis was born in an officially segregated America, in the Deep South of Louisiana, and was abandoned by his father and then his mother before he'd turned five. Raised by a grandmother and an uncle during this time, he was only a generation past slavery (his grandparents had been slaves), and his family was very poor. He worked as a paperboy, collected discarded food to sell, and hauled coal . . . all while still a child. Finally he was taken in by a family who bought him his first cornet. Despite such disadvantageous beginnings, when he died at age sixty-nine, he was one of the most famous jazz musicians of his time and remains as such today. He had played many of the most famous venues around the world, was in Hollywood movies, spoke out against segregation, and was the first black radio host for a sponsored national broadcast. Honorary pallbearers at his funeral included Bing Crosby, Ella Fitzgerald, Johnny Carson, and Frank Sinatra. During the last year of his life, he was quoted as saying, "I think I had a beautiful life. I didn't wish for anything that I couldn't get, and I got pretty near everything I wanted because I worked for it."[5]

Former President Bill Clinton did not start out his life with the appropriate board game credits to ensure his status later in life. His father died in a car accident before he was born, and his mother left him with grandparents to pursue a nursing degree shortly after having him. Once she returned to care for him, she married a verbally and physically abusive alcoholic. Bill confronted him, even as a young child, in order to intercept his mother's beatings. Bill's education was aided by scholarships, and he rose to become first a Yale graduate, then a governor, then a two-term president. Since leaving office, he has written bestselling books, founded a not-for-profit foundation involved in global philanthropy, and spoken worldwide for various causes, inspiring others to do good works.[6]

Superstar talk show host, actor, and philanthropist Oprah Winfrey began life in rural poverty. Shuffled about and raised at different times by her grandmother, mother, father, and stepmother, she was sexually abused as a child and at age fourteen delivered a premature son who died shortly after birth. What power of spirit and sheer determination of will would convince a child of such disadvantageous beginnings to pursue a career in television broadcasting? The first African American billionaire, she has inspired millions each day for decades. From building homes for disaster survivors to providing vehicles for children with disabilities, she has shown a generosity of spirit that has had a ripple effect on our country. Oprah's Book Club encouraged millions of Americans to spend time reading. Again, not something one would expect a television personality to promote!

Her charisma is such that advertising and marketing specialists coined the term the *Oprah Effect*. When Oprah endorses a product, it sells off the shelves.[7]

These three examples of famous individuals are representative of countless other similar stories of personal, spiritual, and material achievement that have occurred, are occurring, and will occur around the world. There have always been, and will always continue to be, people who dream a dream and then pursue it, regardless of what others tell them is or is not possible. And while the examples I highlight are of famous people, most people who achieve their dreams and live a fulfilled and fulfilling life of purpose do not become famous. As such, our perception is that this is an enigma of celebrity and not a celebrated norm. That is just not true. In all cases, we are free to create the life we envision.

Think of The Pioneer Woman. For those of you who haven't heard of her, she has a cooking show on the Food Network. But check this out: the reason she has the show is because she started a blog in 2006. Ree Drummond was a thirty-seven-year-old mother of four. She was a housewife and homeschooler. She was a "nobody" living in the middle of "nowhere" in rural Oklahoma. Celebrated by her family and friends perhaps, but not by the world at large. Her blog now has over 22 million visitors a month.[8] Why do people love her? People love her because she loves her life. She may be a homeschooling rancher's wife living in the middle of nowhere, but it's *her* destiny, and because it's hers, she loves living it.

We Aren't Defined by Our Life Experiences—We Are Defined by Our Responses to Them

What we learn from all of these examples is that the people we recognize as "special" started out as people we would recognize as "unremarkable." Their achievements are a result only of their own willingness to pursue their dreams and passion for realizing their own personal destinies. In short, their examples teach us that environment and circumstance do not define us. They may temper us and shape us, but we choose our response, and in this act we define ourselves. It is in this act, which is difficult and requires determination, that we express our spirit and write our own story. We cannot make the journey in one leap, but we must walk the path step-by-step.

When we become Mystical Backpackers, it is as though we are entering into a contractual agreement with our souls. We declare that we will put the needs of our souls first. One of the mystical dividends from this contract is that the Universe responds in kind by providing us with mentors, supporters, role models, and soul mates along our paths of discovery. In this way, we find encouragement and possibilities where our environments may not have otherwise provided such. And so in striving, we are growing beyond our circumstances with each reach.

This doesn't mean that individual attempts at success won't fail. When we reach for what is beyond our grasp, we won't always achieve the goal without obstacles along the way. Disappointments, losses, and missed marks are part and parcel of the process of trying. The euphoria we experience when a dream is realized and the pain and confusion we feel when something we attempt to realize fails to manifest are both integral elements of this journey. Consequently, we sometimes find that convincing ourselves to remain within our comfort zones (or within our ruts) becomes more and more appealing as we face these challenges. Living outside the rut can seem unpredictable and emotionally straining. How then, do we process our failures and move beyond our fear of them?

My dear friend Kari Samuels, a happiness coach, once said to me, "Our life purpose is what is hardest for us to achieve. It is an uphill journey." Her wise words remind us that we are not living our lives wrongly or poorly simply because we find ourselves on the "wrong" paths. Even the wrong path is a part of the larger journey in life. Just as Santiago in *The Alchemist* spends a year working in the crystal shop, so must we sometimes spend time by the wayside—even though we're still en route to our final destinations.[9] It is here at these rest stops that things become crystal clear. We better understand ourselves, our wants, and our needs—or better yet, what we *don't* want and *don't* need. Sometimes the pit stops refuel us; sometimes they leave us depleted. In all cases, we learn valuable information or skills for helping us navigate the road ahead. No time is ever truly wasted—when the time is spent on the journey. Waiting years to take action simply because you fear failure is not being true to your own self or to any higher purpose meant for your life.

You must move *toward what feels right*. Yet if unhappiness or stagnancy has saturated your soul, it can also muddle your thoughts about what you do want or what makes you feel positive. Mystical Backpacking provides for the gift of separating yourself—for a time—from the routine of your life and placing yourself onto a road of possibility. You begin to interact with nature, the world, the universal consciousness, God, destiny, all manner of experiences available to you at all times but perhaps more easily accessible when you are stretched beyond your comfort zone. The gift of being a part of this greater picture is that when you open yourself up to the possibilities of what your life can be, the world rises up to greet and guide you. You are not alone for long when you are open and receptive to the opportunities, messages, signs, and guidance presented to you on your journey to greater self-awareness. For in Mystical Backpacking, you will receive assurances and affirmations from the outside world as you cast the shackles from your inner world.

While the Taoists say that a journey begins with a single step, the reality is that before the step, there is a conscious thought of purpose. The journey truly begins with this moment. When I walked out of my Budapest office, blinded by tears and bitter with disappointment, I knew I could not go back. I would not go back. Doing what was "right" felt like I was casting my pearls before swine. How much of myself could I pour into a job without receiving some real manner of compensation? After my meltdown—really, my rising up—in the office that day, I remember sitting at my small kitchen table, crying into my arms and then feeling a shift occur within me. I couldn't continue on this path anymore. I was going to do what felt "right." I was going to do something uplifting! And so it was decided: I would go. And this shift, this thought, this moment is where my journey truly began.

To visualize this idea, picture your journey as a sphere that grows outward in all directions at once. At the center of the sphere is a gem. This center is the conscious thought that brought the journey to actualization. It is with this thought and in this moment that release from your current condition is realized, and the gem is ignited with a life pulse that fuels that outward growth. The decision to act brings the experience to life before a single bag is packed, before a single step is taken. This is the safest part of the venture, the one burdened with the least amount of risk and the least amount of personal fear. It is also the most precious heart of the quest, pumping life into every step. As with most "right" decisions, once made, it is as though a burden has been lifted, and anticipation for what is to come replaces the dread of another monotonous tomorrow.

While the road to self-realization is always solitary, you are never really alone. Reading these words, you are joined by others who have similar wishes to fulfill—including me. I have had these very thoughts you are now pondering. On your own odyssey, you will meet many people who will teach you, inspire you, support you, and assist you. You will also create a personal world for yourself where your thoughts and feelings become clear to you and you are able to listen to your inner voice with clarity. Your physical journey begins with a single step. Your spiritual journey begins with a decision to be purposeful. Ultimately, when you are a Mystical Backpacker, you are on a mission for yourself. You actively choose to embrace life, to wholly experience the present moment in your quest to unearth your future reality. You exercise your faith in yourself, in whatever higher power guides you, and in the world at large in a way that is rarely demanded of you. You stretch yourself to act beyond the ordinary and to embrace the extraordinary.

So, your next step in embracing the extraordinary has arrived. Here it is: your second set of Mystical Exercises! With these exercises, your foray into the sacred begins.

A little-known joy of exploring the sacred is that you can create your own sacred objects and spaces within your life. Subconsciously, you may already have done so—it's what you do when you get ready to watch a movie by setting a bowl of popcorn and chilled drinks on the table in front of you, balancing the remote in an accessible place, and getting the best snuggly blankets out from their hiding place. While the experience of watching a movie may not be what you'd consider sacred, you have, in fact, intentionally created an environment within which you can have the best possible movie-watching experience. Similarly, the following exercises are geared toward preparing your practical travel supplies for supporting your mystical journey. It's not just about acquiring them; it's about how you choose to realize them.

Mystical Exercises: Chapter 2

Create a Sacred Talisman

Acquire a gem, bead, button, or stone to represent your decision to become a Mystical Backpacker.

The Practical: It's an age-old tradition to mark events with something tangible that reminds us of our commitment, achievement, experience, or emotion. It's why we buy each other engagement rings and wedding rings. It's why we award someone with a fancy watch after a certain number of years of service. It's why we give trophies, medals, and ribbons, and it's why we frame our first dollar earned. These items are outward symbols of an inward and life-changing or life-affirming experience. The decision to become a Mystical Backpacker is just such an experience. You are affirming the value of your life. You are embarking on a life-changing journey.

To mark this occasion, acquire a physical object to remind yourself of the very beginning of your Mystical Backpacking odyssey. For this reason, let it be something akin to a gem or stone. Let it be small, so you can lace it around your neck as a pendant or tie it to your backpack. Let it be something beautiful or significant to you, so it warms your heart and uplifts your spirit whenever you look at it. Maybe it's a glass bead swirled with your favorite colors and reminding you of your favorite uncle who was a glass blower and passed away young, but you've always thought he was still with you, guiding you from the great beyond. Maybe it's a small amethyst or other semiprecious stone or crystal that marks your birth month or an energy or memory you feel aligned with. It might even be a plastic button from your grandmother's collection or a stone you find while hiking. It does not need to be valuable or conventionally attractive. It needs only to be something that you will cherish and that will evoke positive thoughts and feelings when you look at it or touch it.

The Mystical: Now that you have your small object, let's get mystical! Hold your object in your hands and close your eyes. Take a deep breath. If you're in public, be prepared to scare people into moving away from you. If you're not comfortable with that, take a moment to relocate yourself to someplace private. Good. Now, take a deep breath or two. Feel yourself relaxing. Consciously release any tensions, worries, or concerns that you're holding. Do a full-body scan and relax every part of your body, bit by bit. Shift your attention to the object you hold in your hands. Think about your decision to become a Mystical Backpacker and imagine sending the uplifting energy and positive emotions associated with that decision into this object. If you believe in a higher power, invoke the blessings of that power and ask that you be kept safe and have the courage to remain open to receiving the messages, observing the signs, and meeting the people who will serve the highest possible outcome for your soul. Allow yourself to connect with feeling safe, purposeful, and guided. All is well. When you are ready, gently squeeze your hands around your object, open your eyes, and look at it, allowing it to become a sacred talisman for you as your embark on this journey.

Remember to check out the Mystical Extras section at the back of the book, which will point you to a free guided meditation to assist you with this exercise, found on the Mystical Backpacker website.

Mission Statement

Write a mission statement for your trip that reflects the soul needs you're hoping to meet as a result of the journey.

The Practical: Most of us live our early years doing what we're told to do. We go to school because we have to. We eat our dinner because we have to. We go on vacations our parents choose and sign up for those activities they allow us to. This early training instills in us a sense of duty and responsibility that is outwardly enforced as being for our highest good. It's a strange and unnatural transition to have the helm of our ship handed over to us in adulthood and to be given the opportunities to choose what we will do. Some of us never become truly comfortable with this skill, and we continue to choose what others deem necessary or "right." It is frightening to suddenly be in charge and have the outcome of our successes reflect our worth and not the worth of our parents' parenting.

This exercise aims to clarify your own needs—your authentic needs—for yourself. A mission statement is a brief, written statement of purpose. It typically spells out the mission of a company or organization, but in this case, it's going to represent your mission as a Mystical Backpacker. This mission statement serves to guide your actions moving forward. It provides you with a sense of direction and acts as a framework for guiding you in your decision making. You may have never thought to summarize your deepest desires and innermost thoughts and feelings in a succinct write-up. Don't worry, this isn't something you're going to share with the world or put on your LinkedIn profile! This mission statement is less about career and physical gains and more about fulfilling the needs of your soul. This mission statement is something you're going to refer to every time you have a major decision to make on your trip. Will your decision take you closer to or farther from the life you wish to live?

Here's a sample mission statement to contemplate:

As a Mystical Backpacker, I become comfortable with being open to new experiences while striving to observe my authentic feelings and beliefs.

Remember to state your mission in the positive rather than in the negative. For example, the above statement would have been less successful this way: "During my trip, I won't shut down, be unfriendly, or hide in my shell. I won't spend my time in fear." You see how when you state it in the positive, it feels empowering and like you truly are on a mission? When your statement is framed in the negative, it feels more like self-criticism. It may take you five minutes to frame your statement; it may take you five days. Make sure your statement resonates for you and is filled with your personal truth and intention rather than the sentiments you think it should be filled with. There is no right or wrong statement; there is only a statement that feels right or wrong to you.

The Mystical: Once you have your mission statement written, inscribe it at the beginning of your journal on its own page. You may refer to this page anytime you feel uncertain or require a reminder of your goals. Feel free to embellish this page with drawings, paintings, collage, or in any way that resonates with your soul. You may also leave it unembellished, if that seems more suitable to you. Additionally, you may find it beneficial to say your mission statement aloud at least once a day before leaving on your trip.

Mystical Backpacking Contract

Write a Mystical Backpacking Contract with yourself. This is a variation on Denise Linn's Soul Contract in her Soul Coaching® program. Rather than creating a Soul Contract for your life, you are creating a Mystical Backpacking Contract for your trip.[10]

The Practical: As I mentioned earlier in this chapter, when you become a Mystical Backpacker it is as though you are entering into a contractual agreement with your soul. You are declaring that you will put the needs of your soul first. And in this exercise, you will write that contract. This exercise is vital. Why? Because many of us are in the habit or practice of breaking the promises we make to ourselves. God forbid we would break a promise to someone else! But when we promise ourselves to eat better, exercise more often, watch less television, read more, learn something new, finish something we started—the list goes on and on—we tend to break our promises more often than not. The most subversive aspect of this practice is that we begin to distrust ourselves. It can be deeply disturbing to begin a profound journey of self-transformation without that trust. As such, in this exercise, you will not make any promises. Instead, you will set parameters. Whenever you have doubts or hesitations or feel you may falter on your path, you will be able to refer back to your contract and act within the guidelines you set forth for yourself.

Only you know why your soul needs this journey. Only you know where your yearning for adventure, exploration, and insight are sourced. I cannot provide the language for you. However, I recommend keeping the contract simple (one page or less in length) and including language that encompasses the following points:

- A contract promises to deliver. Using the present tense, state the things you promise to deliver to yourself via the Mystical Backpacking experience (for example, *I am brave. I am open to new experiences. I finish what I start. I embrace a positive attitude.*)

- A contract specifies the parameters of the agreement. Address the time, the budget, and the criteria. For example, you might state: *I will travel for a period of up to six weeks but no less than two. My spending will not exceed X dollars, and I will be willing to stay in hostels, camp, or buy small food supplies from markets and grocery stores to economize rather than sabotage my timeline with frivolous spending.* If you don't know the numbers yet, leave a line for where they can be added later.

- A contract states the spirit of the agreement. Address not just the physical needs outlined in the previous point but also the commitments you are making to meet the needs of your soul. For example: *I commit to practicing trust in order to grow my faith in myself, in others, and ultimately, in a higher power. During this Mystical Backpacking experience, I choose to address my own soul's needs before changing my plans to accommodate others.*

The Mystical: Take your contract with you to a beautiful place that feels sacred. It can be out in nature, in a church or temple, or in your very own home with candles lit and soft music playing. Sit in a comfortable position and take several deep, cleansing breaths and close your eyes. Try to picture the vast universe, with glorious spinning galaxies, flaming stars, and the precious blue dot you live on. Try to connect with the idea that all of these realities exist simultaneously. Your own life is a thread in this fabric of existence. Imagine all the birds, fish, and land animals of the earth moving, feeding, and resting. Now shift your attention to the human race and imagine all the billions of people as they move through their days, working, playing, eating, and sleeping. Consider the preciousness of life. When you feel ready, open your eyes and read your contract. Take time to feel the full weight of each promise you have made to yourself. Allow your resolve to set and know that your contract is an act of self-love and self-care. Before leaving for your trip, transcribe your contract into the opening pages of your journal so that you can easily revisit its contents as you travel.

~~~

Even though you haven't left yet, you're already well on your way. You are already affecting changes in your life, step-by-step, and you're about to turn that spark of wanderlust into the fire that will light the way down the path of your mystical journey.

Adventure awaits!
~~~

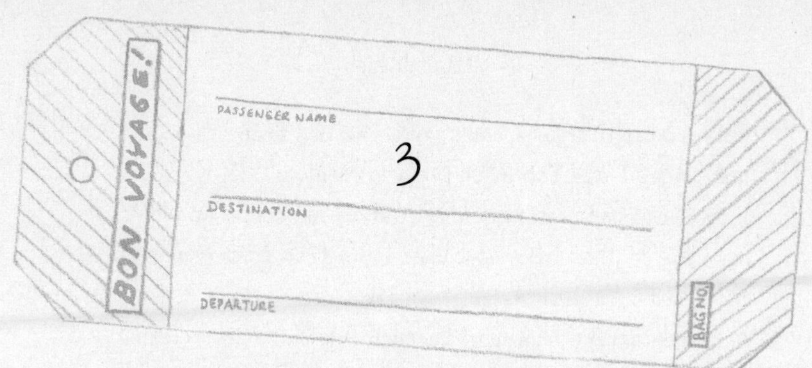

BON VOYAGE!
PASSENGER NAME
3
DESTINATION
DEPARTURE
BAG NO.

Where Do I Go? How Do I Begin?

> Twenty years from now you will be more disappointed by
> the things that you didn't do than by the ones you did do.
> So throw off the bowlines. Sail away from the safe harbor.
> Catch the trade winds in your sails. Explore. Dream. Discover.
>
> —**Widely attributed to Mark Twain**

Venice
February 5, 2000

It is 10:35 pm. It is foggy, chilly, and damp; much colder (seemingly) than Budapest. However, I am in Venice! Home to Woody Allen. Setting for the movie A Destiny of Her Own. Loved by artists, authors, and romantics. Henry James wrote "Dear old Venice has lost her complexion, her figure, her reputation, her self-respect; and yet, with it all, has so puzzlingly not lost a shred of her distinction."

I cannot wait for my own discoveries! I want to run into the streets now!

I walked here from the bus terminal and crossed my first deliciously arched bridge—over the Grand Canal—and am situated at the Universo Hotel, room #9, on Lista Di Spagna (for 50,000 lira a night). My room is ugly and littered with strange hairs, but the bed linen is white and crisp. I ate too much pizza in Mestre with Kelly and Flavio, but indigestion is the least of my concerns right now! My day has been consumed by endless conversation with Kelly and I have traveled from the Ontarioesque rolling hills of southwestern Hungary, through Austria's snow-capped mountains (literally through dark and winding tunnels) and out to the Mediterranean. Kiss me, coastline! Embrace me, little isle!

Goodbye to my lover's sweet kisses and tortured eyes. Goodbye dull job and draining existence. Hello, big world!

To bed. To finish reading A Room with a View (for the second time). Set the alarm and spend tomorrow breathing, listening, watching, and walking; LIVING!

It was exhilarating to leave behind all that had held me back. My job. My apartment. The brooding Hungarian man I'd been seeing. All evaporated behind my forward motion, dispelling like early-morning fog in the first rays of dawn. No shadows to haunt me. No regrets to raise questions in me. I felt as though I'd been freed. The days ahead were fully my own, and the prospect of filling them with joy, rest, and discovery was exciting. I felt as though I had created a situation within which more was possible for me than ever had been before. I wondered if I would meet kindred spirits or perhaps even my soul mate? Would the perfect job land in my lap? Would a new locale woo me into the future I saw myself in? For I definitely had a vision; in it, I was in a small room at the top of a building. I had a small wooden writing table pulled up to a breathtaking view. The sun was streaming in, and I was content.

Knowing I was about to leave everything behind, I felt the worries of my daily life had been swept away. I didn't have to get up and force myself to go to a job that didn't fulfill me. I could walk away from situations and people that were weighing me down and choose to be around those who lifted my spirits up. This was the first time in my life that I wasn't putting other people's wants or needs above my own. For the first time, every choice could be mine. Every direction could be the one in which I was pulled by my own needs. I was totally free!

Truth be told, such utter freedom was a bit unnerving. It didn't feel entirely safe without those checkpoints. When you live alone, it's nice to know your place of work will wonder where you are if you don't show up or your friend will start calling everyone if you aren't at the place where you were supposed to meet. I had never spent days upon days, as I was about to, without regular interaction with people I could depend upon to cause some sort of ruckus if I disappeared. Not that I was worried about disappearing: I wasn't. It was just that in doing something for the first time all by myself, I felt a bit like I was walking a tightrope without a safety net. My senses were heightened. I became aware of footsteps behind me on the sidewalk in a way I had never before. In cafés, I could feel when someone was watching me and would look up from my journal to find I was right. I had gone from moving through the motions of my days like an automaton to becoming hyperaware of the present moment. This was new and thrilling.

So, where was I going where I'd be so far from everyone else? Initially, my only desire was to experience places and things I had only imagined experiencing. I wanted to see the Pantheon—would it really amaze me? I wanted to see the Sistine Chapel—was God's finger as big as me, or more the size of my arm? Would *David* be as perfect in person as it was in my textbook's photos? Would Botticelli's Venus, Monet's water lilies, Renoir's pastel dancers pulse with a thousand colors and brushstrokes? I wanted to see the Colosseum in Rome, the Santa Croce in Florence, the Art Nouveau Metro stops in Paris. I wanted to touch Stonehenge (not realizing at the time that you can't anymore) and to sit in the reconstructed Globe Theatre and imagine myself to be in Shakespeare's time. I wanted to see Gaudi's undulating Casa Mila and the odd wet-sand-castle cathedral of Sagrada Família in Barcelona. My studies had incited my imagination, and I craved knowing the Real Thing: *the* canvas, *the* line of *the* sculpture; to feel the stone of the buildings throb in cold pulses beneath my hands, to breathe the holy air of timeless art and space. More than anything, I wanted to stop doing the endless work I felt I had to do in order to "get ahead." I wanted to actually experience the life's work of brave and inspired people who created the world they imagined.

During my first five weeks of backpacking, this is mostly what I did. I consumed with my eyes. I wore my boots out and had to buy inserts to prevent a hole from breaking right through. I moved in and out of cities and countryside and back through time to worlds removed but also juxtaposed with pop music and local teenagers applying lip gloss and sighing in boredom, sitting at the foot of human achievement, unmoved because this world was their norm. And slowly, as my senses softened and I purred through my days rather than clawed my way through them, I began to journey elsewhere too.

My thoughts mixed with my emotions in ways they hadn't before. Forgotten dreams resurfaced. I stood in the Villa Borghese in Florence and watched an artist paint a copy of a masterpiece, his paint-smeared easel set up in the cold marble room, its wild disarray in stark contrast to the carefully hung and orderly paintings, the room pungent with the smell of wet paint and turpentine, and I remembered. Oh. Yes. I had wanted to be an artist. I went outside and drew my first landscape in years. My days slumped, and I meandered and dawdled and was strangely present within each moment. Was this what it was to be Zen?

Oranges in February

When I left Budapest, I wrote on the first page of my journal:

Budapest
February 4, 2000

Budapest is rotting around me, shelling me in like a dirty cocoon. I smell her descent and observe the trying on of new jewels which attempt to rejuvenate her faded glamour. Budapest streets are lined with buildings that flirt with the eye, like debutantes at a ball. But from under the skirts of the now aged maidens, the smell of mildew and a century of cat piss repulse the pedestrian. I am oppressed by the faded glory and no longer find the darkness romantic. I, like a caterpillar prodding at its shell, need to find the way out, beyond the darkness, beyond this period of change, beyond primordial memory. I want to break through into a New World where my insides turn inside out and kaleidoscope wings spread out to carry me off to great heights. What I fear is not the journey, but the discovery. What if even the New World robs me of the will to try?

Fairly dark stuff. It's interesting that the first book I read as I made my way toward Italy was Forster's *A Room with a View*, from which I've already quoted. Even the title suggests lightness, for what is a view if not the promise of possibility, the vantage point high above the world affirming to the viewer, "*This* is your dominion." I chose the book because I wanted to have it fresh in my mind when I went to Florence. The dramatic fainting scene in the Piazza Santa Croce had instilled in me a voracious appetite for romance when, at sixteen years of age, I first saw Helena Bonham Carter collapse into Julian Sands's arms in the movie version. The young George Emerson—the character played by Julian Sands—is consumed with answering the question of the eternal why. Why are we here? What does it all mean? What is the point to our existence? And in launching into the journey of Mystical Backpacking, aren't these questions also forefront in our own minds? The answer, George discovers, is to *live*.

Similarly, there is a time for each of us when we must discover the reason for our existence and determine the way in which we wish to live. As Cecil, another character in *A Room with a View*, remarks, "It makes a difference, doesn't it, whether we fence ourselves in, or whether we are fenced in by the barriers of others?"[1] By choosing the ways in which we live our own lives, we don't resent the struggles or obstacles we face quite as much, because they are merely delays along the paths we *have chosen* to be on. Beyond these struggles and obstacles, we see the places we want to be and are fueled by these happy thoughts.

Merely ten days after my Budapest journal entry I shared above, I wrote in Rome:

February 14, 2000

It is a green February in Rome. Orange trees, burdened with ripe fruit, line the streets. Lemon trees are visible in backyards, similarly ready for harvest. Palm trees and umbrella pines sway in the cool breeze, protecting one from the brilliant blue crystal sky. In the park, couples embrace. This is the primary action that takes place here. However, many people sit alone in the sun, children and teenaged boys play with soccer balls and even now there are old men dressed in beautiful leisure clothes playing cards on top of a garbage can, pulling more and more change from their pockets with which to place bets, and they talk all the while about Lord knows what! One of their mobiles just rang and the rest of the men teased that it was probably his wife calling!

Sublime happiness in only eight days? Yes. It is possible, when you are Mystical Backpacking; you need only to be in a place that feeds your soul.

Within a week of leaving my routines and what I perceived to be my ho-hum life behind, I felt more alive than I had in years. I explored Venice as the city prepared for carnival, and a mask maker wearing a smock, beret, and wire-rim glasses held gorgeous masks to my face for me to try on.

I twirled pasta on a fork, popped delicate pastries into my mouth, and enjoyed coffee standing next to perfumed locals who were laughing and telling stories. I walked hundreds of cobblestone lanes, zigzagging between old buildings, and crossed a thousand arched bridges tucked under lines of drying laundry. I made my way to Florence, where centuries of art welcomed me in warm embrace, and admirers moved silently among them, paying reverence to the very spirit of their creation. Being in the places of my dreams made dreaming irrelevant, at least for a short while. I was whole. I was fulfilled. I was so happy!

It's no wonder to me that books such as *The Alchemist* and *Eat, Pray, Love* or films such as *Under the Tuscan Sun* resonate with us so. The story of an outward journey manifesting an inward journey is something we all hope to experience. In my experience, *leaving* was the method that most facilitated my *arriving*. After experiencing my grand adventure and endless days of happiness, I was not willing to give up the feeling by settling for less. The life I built once I became a Mystical Backpacker was one in which my dreams came true.

It may be that instead of gondolas, art, pasta, and the Pyrenees of my travels, your journey will take you to farms in Idaho, the wilds of Alaska, or the fishing villages of Newfoundland. Wherever you journey, the place must resonate with you. The story that unfolds is yours alone. The most important things for you to determine now are:

Where will you go?
What will feed your soul?
How will you journey?

Location, Location, Location . . .

If you don't know where you're going,
any road will take you there.
—George Harrison, "Any Road"

In my experience, once you've decided to journey, the most challenging part can be deciding where to go and then actually leaving. Even now, knowing what I know about Mystical Backpacking, I still have anxieties about my solo trips. I never feel the timing is right; I worry that things are really crazy at work and it's not a good time to leave, that my family needs me right now, that I really don't have the money to be taking a trip now, and so on. I also worry that I have chosen the wrong place and I'll get there and be uncomfortable and spend the trip wishing I were home. The entire planning process is overshadowed by these doubts and reservations.

Here's the reality: once I'm en route, as early as pulling out of the driveway, I am so excited I can barely stand it. Then, once I'm *really* en route . . . in the car, on the plane, a couple of hours into the trip, I am singing along with my playlist and loving life. By the third or fourth day, I cannot believe I have denied myself a trip for so long, and I know that I am in the right place and living my life fully: the magic of Mystical Backpacking begins to work on my spirit, and revelations unfold. Knowing that the planning process itself can be anxiety-ridden, expect that you will feel uncertain, unprepared, and uncomfortable. Remember that while deciding where to go is important, you can't ruin the experience by choosing the "wrong" place. Any place can teach you something about yourself.

Another thing to know about this process is that it's not necessary to go on more than one Mystical Backpacking trip. Just as you wouldn't go on a vision quest every year for the rest of your life, you won't need to journey more than once to discover your destiny. This one trip will be your big adventure, physically and metaphysically, and it will stay with you forever. For this reason, it would be a shame to shortchange yourself by making compromises and sacrifices before you've even left home. In planning your trip, feed your soul. God, Spirit, Source, whatever you wish to name it, will help you manifest the trip that serves your highest good. For *this* trip, your *ultimate* trip, start with a list of places that reflect your interests and go from there. If you've always felt an affinity for South America, don't go to Europe just because someone you know did. Instead, start your planning by looking only at the South American continent. But if you still don't have any ideas about where to go, never fear! There's a Mystical Exercise at the end of this chapter that will help you connect with your inner sense of direction.

The truth of the matter is I had *always* wanted to see Western Europe, so for me the decision was easy. From a young age, everything I was interested in (Impressionism, photography, English literature, Italian food, and the Italian language) was a product of Western Europe. I didn't look for a place I might be interested in—I ran toward a place I felt that I couldn't get enough of.

Perhaps there's a place you have always felt drawn to and you have pictures of it, have read novels that take place there, or have dreamed of it, as Shirley Valentine does in the movie that bears her name. Shirley keeps a poster of Greece on her pantry door and looks wistfully at it each day. When her friend wins a trip for two to Greece and wants to take her along, she says, "No, I can't," even though she's wanted to go all of her adult life![2] Sometimes our dreams are such a comfort to us, their realization fills us with a sense of dread. When she finally decides to live her dream and go to Greece, her life changes for the better. It is never too late to feed your soul. Perhaps, like Shirley, the opportunity to go somewhere *has* presented itself to you, and your reaction has been of the all-too-familiar "No, I can't" or "I don't want to" variety when you know deep down you should or that you *do* in fact want to. It can be important to distinguish between intuition, which often says, "No, this is dangerous," and hesitation, which says, "No, I'm afraid," and then respond to both with courage.

Maybe you've always been drawn to cowboys, bikers, gypsies, or pirates: people who wander wherever the wind takes them? Then it's time to get on your horse, into your car, onto your bike, or into your boat and go. See where the road, the trail, or the water takes you. Or if all else fails and you have *no idea* where to go, beseech the Fates to help you and throw yourself into the game at the mercy of Fortune's wheel. Go to the airport, the bus depot, the train station, or the boat terminal and buy the first ticket on the first trip you can afford. When you leap into the arms of Fate, you are assured that major events will occur, even in the most mundane place. You don't need to fly to Tibet to find your true calling—you may find it in Tennessee! But if you know Tibet is where your soul needs to be, don't try to convince yourself to settle for anywhere else. Your soul knows what it needs. This is your opportunity to meet those needs. Just as each of us has a unique life experience, so will we have a unique travel experience. The point is to be away from the familiar—away from the identity you occupy in your daily life.

I encourage you to move beyond your comfort zone by going someplace out of your element. Why go snowboarding if your favorite thing to do is snowboard and you do it every weekend already? The point is to discover yourself in relation to a world that is foreign to you; where the regularity of your comfort zone ceases to define you externally. It is much easier to define yourself in contrast to the other than it is within the established norm.

It may take you some time to determine where you're going to go, but try not to become consumed with this process. You don't need to come up with an entire itinerary and have each fare prepurchased, each accommodation prearranged. This defies the point of Mystical Backpacking. You simply need to know where you're going and to have some ideas for where you'd like to go next. Also, know the approximate cost of food and accommodations in the places you'd like to go and budget for that, plus a little extra. You will spend more than you think as emergencies come up (you missed your train, you *must* eat a steak, you *must* buy that superhot bikini, etc.). Once you start having some serious fun, it becomes easier to indulge in these extras without feeling worry or guilt.

When I first left Budapest, I knew I would start my trip with Venice, Florence, and Rome. Beyond that, I knew I would go west, likely to Nice, but on a whim I decided to skip Nice for Barcelona and ended up meeting a woman—a New Zealander named Lisa—who has since become a dear friend. Once your journey has begun, the pace and direction of the trip will be set by the adventures you have along the way. Allow for that. Remember that you are on a vision quest. Metaphorically, you are alone in the wilderness, seeking to connect with your spirit. You don't need to plan for museum entrance times and set up an itinerary that mirrors the fast-paced, overburdened schedule you left behind. Give yourself permission to meander, to sit on a park bench and think, to watch old men play cards on the lid of a trash can. Spend some time in the present moment, and see where it takes you.

But What if No One Supports My Decision?

> Courage is being afraid but going on anyhow.
>
> —Dan Rather*

Recognizing that your life needs a kickstart has all kinds of implications for you and the people in your life. It voices a statement that resonates with a thousand tones, each interpreted in a new light by the listener. Your boss, your cubicle mate, your best friend, your partner, your mom—all these people may hear you say to them, "You are part of the problem," instead of, "I have a problem." As a consequence, the very people you may turn to for support may be the least likely to provide it for you. It's very hard to have the courage to embark on your trip without feeling supported, but it's much easier if you're not relying on that support. Be honest and compassionate with your friends and family when you tell them what you are about to do. Understand that they need to be reassured that you are not blaming them or rejecting them. You are simply trying to reconnect with your authentic self. Those who love you and who love themselves want you to find happiness. They will rejoice with you when you hear your authentic voice again, when you connect with your spirit, when you find your way. But until you do, you're just going to have to bluff. Eventually, wearing this new decision will start to feel comfortable, and your capacity for braveness will have grown.

---

* I try my hardest to source the quotes I use. Well, try as I might, I couldn't figure out when the heck this quote was said. I knew Dan Rather had said it, so seeing as he's someone very much alive, I phoned his offices. In June of 2014, I spoke with Colette Carey, the director of communications at *Dan Rather Reports*, and she very kindly did some research, and still no one could figure it out. Finally, someone asked Dan himself, and even *he* couldn't remember when he first used it! He and his office know I'm using it, even if none of us (Dan included) could readily source where it was first used. I love his quote and just couldn't cut it from the manuscript.

The one thing all adventurers share is a desire to move beyond the scope of their known experience. In that regard, you are already an adventurer. Now, how do you convince others of this (especially if you aren't entirely convinced yourself)? Consider that justifying your right to be an adventurer may be a waste of time. You may not ever convince your mother or your grandparents that you're doing the right thing. Remember that you are ultimately living your life for yourself. It is your experience, no one else's. Embracing your desires is the only way to move forward. By so doing, you will grow. As we've already learned, you'll be more open, creative, and agreeable as a result. You'll certainly learn more about the world and gain a better understanding of your place in it. And you'll figure out what you really want and need out of your life to feel that you are living your purpose. When you're living your life's purpose, everyone who thought you were a screwup will end up being so proud. It's just that they likely won't feel that way in the interim.

It's the Little Things in Life: Your Travel Kit

I attended a small liberal arts college where dreadlocks, nose rings, and vegetarianism were the norm. The uniform of choice was a Mountain Co-Op jacket and backpack and L.L. Bean fleeces paired with slouchy corduroys and hiking boots. Considering my mother wore three-inch heels and a fur coat when she took me to Pioneer Village during my childhood, I was not entirely equipped for this environment. I know I owned a pair of high-heeled sneakers. I've blocked out much of the rest. Similarly, there were many things that I learned about while Mystical Backpacking that I wish I'd known before stepping out the door and which would have made me a more comfortable traveler from the start. In this following section of the book, I am going to give you the information I wish someone had given me.

First things first: it's time to put away the Gucci luggage and buy a backpack! You didn't think you'd be Mystical Backpacking without a backpack, did you? When I bought my first traveler's backpack, I was so excited I tried it on a hundred times. I stuffed it with pillows to see what it would look like full. I began to plan for patches and locks and accessories. The spirit of adventure was fully embodied in its fibers. What's so very different about traveling with a backpack is that you become the free, agile, unencumbered traveler. You won't be stuck in a crowd, dragging your hefty suitcase with the broken wheel behind you, like cattle moving from pen to pen.

Traveling light is the biggest favor you can do for yourself. When you are light in luggage, it's easy to be light in spirit too. The freedom you will feel carrying only your backpack as you leap on and off trains, trek down into subways, and run across a meadow—you can even eat your lunch propped up against your bag on the edge of the sea—will make you ever-so-grateful for your increased mobility. It's also wonderfully convenient when you change your plans at the eleventh hour and need to pack in a hurry. Aim to have everything you need on your back and keep your hands free. This way, you are ready to grab onto the handle of a departing train, steady yourself on a rocking bus, or sip your coffee as you wait for the ferry.

Buying a Backpack

The thing to know about buying a backpack is that, even though your eyes will immediately latch onto a pack with seductive colors and glamorous bits and bobs, this is probably (and sadly) *not* the pack that is best for you. The reality is that the pack has to fit you correctly along your back or else you run the risk of looking like a hobbled old peddler and developing a limp, a slump, or a dangerous tilt. For this reason, try each backpack on. You want it to have a belt around the upper buttock/lower waist that supports a whole lot of weight, offsetting the strain on your mid and upper back. It's also great to have a strap across your chest that helps to distribute the weight evenly through the upper back and shoulders. A good fit results in the length of the pack running the length of your back. Tall people need longer packs. Short people need shorter packs. Camels and horses know best what kind of comfort you're looking for, but they don't talk, so if you'd like a second opinion, remember to ask your salesperson—and find out whether they are paid by commission before you buy the pack they initially suggest! Expensive isn't always best.

The best backpack is one with three compartments. The main central compartment holds your clothes. The lowest compartment, which rests on your lower back or your backside, holds heavy things you may need to access en route (books, boots, batteries, chargers, etc.). The top compartment holds lighter things (your journal, your iPad, your lunch, wipes, a hat, sunscreen, etc.). When packed incorrectly, you will likely resemble some of the sights you're hoping to see: the leaning tower of Pisa, the chaos of the running of the bulls in Pamplona, or even the tumbledown ruins of Machu Picchu. What I learned to be the most important trick to packing a backpack correctly is this: the heavy stuff has to go in the bottom. As with most things in life: the foundation is everything.

Packing Valuables

Keep your passport, money, and tickets in a pocket separate from your bag and close to your body, under your clothes. Do not put these items in your backpack. When you're traveling alone in populated areas, remember that there are professionals who make their living robbing tourists and travelers. Their hands are deft, and you won't realize you're missing your valuables until you reach for them, which may be half an hour after they were taken. If your valuables are under your clothing, they are safer. Your back pocket is the last place you should have your valuables. Keeping stuff in your back pocket is like posting an advertisement for free stuff.

Lock it Up

You should also carry a small lock and chain. Whenever I slept on a train, I would lock my backpack to the overhead rack with a long chain and then use my backpack as a pillow, and nothing was ever stolen while I slept. Again, the less baggage you have as you travel, the easier it is to keep track of it and to keep it safe. The less valuable your luggage is to you, the less it will matter if something is lost or stolen along the way. While my warnings may invoke a bit of trepidation, know that I have never been robbed while traveling (knock on wood!). Someone I briefly traveled with was, and I was with him when it happened. Two Spaniards who playfully kicked a soccer ball back and forth with him lifted his wallet from his back pocket while I called out, "Hang on to your wallet!" He didn't. They did.

Footwear

The last thing to consider and prepare for is your most precious asset on your journey: your feet. They are the engine that moves you. I spent the first half of my trip traipsing through Europe wearing a fabulous pair of black leather boots with adorable side zippers but no arch support. I wore two large divots into the spots where my big toes were, and my feet ached deeply, past musculature and into the very bones. For the second half of my trip, I wore an ugly pair of brown-and-black orthopedic sandals. I was actually more successful at meeting handsome men during this disastrous phase in podiatric fashion—likely due to the permanent smile I wore as a result of being in such comfort. That said, with the skin of my feet exposed to the elements, I developed a hard shell of callouses that rendered my feet unrecognizable. I began to refer to them as hooves. In showers and by swimming pools, I could almost emit a *clip-clop* when trotting about barefoot. Proper shoes are your best friend and your most important purchase after a well-fitting backpack.

Following is a picture of me at the height of my backpacking odyssey. I am on the island of Santorini in Greece and have become a pro at carrying all my stuff while having my hands free. I am wearing the aforementioned heinous shoes that are very comfortable, but I have offset that aesthetic crisis by wearing a skirt, because that's just the kind of sassy gal I am.

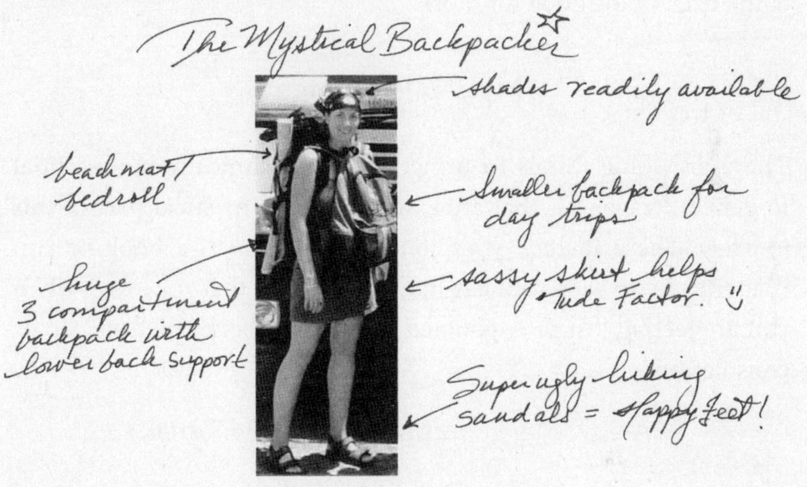

Packing Resources

For all the other things you need to pack, depending on your destination and type of travel, there are great websites to help you. Many of them provide lists of needed items. Just Google *what to pack when backpacking* for a whole slew of hits. Remember that some of these are sponsored sites, and they are geared toward selling products. You don't want this type of site—instead, look for a site that is used by travelers and has lists compiled by people who have actually been to the places you're going. You can visit the Mystical Backpacker website to see what other Mystical Backpackers packed, where they traveled, what music they listened to, and what books they read (my lists are found here too). You can also watch helpful videos, like how to best pack your backpack and read about what some of my favorite backpacking travel items are. The website is a great forum where Mystical Backpackers can chat, leave messages, find helpful tips, and leave each other helpful tips as well. Information is always useful and in this internet age is almost always easily attainable as well. Get the most up-to-date information relevant to the type and place of trip you are taking, and you'll be fine. Flip to the Mystical Extras section at the back of the book for more.

Mystical Supplies

There are some things to bring that are technically nonessential to general travel but that are essential to the mystical part of this journey. These include your journal or journals, a book or two (paperbacks, to keep your bag light), and music that you love—when you are feeling lost or frightened, there is no better pick-me-up or consolation.

A Few More Words about Your Journal

The words *journey* and *journal* begin with the same four letters because both words derive from the French language; the root word *jour* is a unit of measurement: a day. A journey is a long trip where passage or progress from one stage to another takes place over many days. It can be a physical journey across the desert or a metaphysical journey to success. In a journal, we record the events of the day: our experiences, the occurrences that took place, and our observations of both. It is only fitting that while you are on a journey that is both physical and metaphysical, you should record the experiences, occurrences, and observations you have along the way. You are doing this not just because you'll probably forget bits and pieces, or even whole cities or days (our minds are like sponges, it's true, but that also means some of the stuff in there gets wrung out) but because it is easy to see what limiting thought patterns and beliefs you ascribe to when they are written down. When you see them in print, revelations abound. It's useful to be reminded of your revelations (you'd think you wouldn't forget a revelation, but it can happen) down the road. This journal will become your most valuable possession. In it, you will find yourself. If you don't consider yourself to be a writer, this doesn't matter. You're not trying to get published here! This is your private place for reflection. It is a place to document your thoughts, your feelings, and your adventures. It's a place in your mind that you can revisit later in life because you committed it to paper.

Book It

> Coleridge said that happiness is just a dog sunning itself on a rock. We're not put on this earth to be happy. We're here to experience great things.
>
> —MELISSA BANK, ***THE GIRLS' GUIDE TO HUNTING AND FISHING***

I remember reading that quote while lying in the sun, taking a much-needed rest from my travels. I spent a few days at a backpackers' resort on a small Greek island and read this book cover to cover. A woman I met there gave it to me on my very first day. The quote affirmed the experiences I had been having, reminding me that I was on the right track. In fact, every book I read while I journeyed aligned with my adventure. It was as though each word I read affirmed my decision and honored this time as sacred. It was an uplifting, inspiring, and reassuring way to pass the time on ferries and trains, in waiting rooms, and at bus stops once the views had become monotonous or the crowds had become an annoyance rather than a fascination.

For this reason, bring a few books as well. I know you may think it's a bit crazy to pack something as heavy as a book into your bag. If you're lucky enough to have a Kindle or iPad or something that makes book bringing easy, this is a cinch (remember, countries have different outlets, so bring an adapter). If you're going old school and are bringing physical books with you, go for only a few paperbacks and smaller editions that are lighter to carry. You can make notes in the margins, read without worrying about your battery depleting, and also (the best part), sniff the pages. If you're using hostels for your accommodations, you'll meet lots of other backpackers, and there's often an informal system of trading books along the way, so you'll always have something new to read. If you've made notes in your book and want to keep it, just mail it home when you're finished reading it and lighten your load.

Choose your books as you do everything else for this trip: purposefully. (Check out this chapter's Mystical Exercises for some ideas on how to do this.) On a journey of self-discovery, it's perfectly okay to bring along self-help books and travel books, and it's equally okay to bring along fiction. As you travel, the books will resonate with you. You'll be surprised by how many events in fiction can mirror the very events in your own life! As I mentioned earlier, *A Room with a View* was the perfect start to my trip, as George Emerson asked many of the same questions I was asking. As I was freaking out at sea on the Mediterranean, I was reassured by *Feel the Fear and Do It Anyway*, and its activities kept me busy and helped me focus on my goals instead of my panic. Later on, when I met an Aussie zoologist in Greece, I was reading *The Girls' Guide to Hunting and Fishing*, which I quoted above, and boy, was it appropriate! Again, you start to trade books, and you never know what you'll end up reading that provides lessons for you in your own process for greater self-knowledge.

Sing-Along

Finally, you need some great music. Music is not just a fun way to pass the time—it's also proven to be an effective healing agent. Clinical psychologist Dr. Mike Friedman published an article for *Psychology Today* in which he discussed how the preliminary outcome of several controlled psychological studies has determined that music is "a potent treatment for mental health issues," including depression, anxiety, and chronic pain. Music has been found to have positive physical effects on the body (reducing heart rate, blood pressure, and cortisol levels) as well.[3] If music can so deeply and profoundly heal those who suffer from a variety of illnesses, it follows that music would be equally important for adventurers as we journey along the path of Mystical Backpacker.

Before each trip, I create a unique song list, and I organize it into three sets. If you want to follow my lead, put light and upbeat songs about travel, individuality, and personal expression into the first set. This set rocks and has you smiling from ear to ear, moving your leg to the beat, striding through spaces with total joy! Next compile songs with deeper meaning: songs about soul searching, symbols, society, and life questions. This is the thinking stuff, for when you spend hours looking out a train window at passing countryside, and while listening to these tracks, you revisit moments in your life that shaped your beliefs; these selections are portals for self-reflection and revelation. Finally, include a set that is calming, nurturing, and meditative. The music should be largely instrumental, to give your mind freedom to wander where it wants to as you listen. The lyrics should not guide you to the thoughts of the songwriter but should give you the freedom to think your own thoughts. Everything about this set should make you sleepy and dreamy and pleasantly relaxed.

Remember that this music is helping you along the metaphysical part of your journey. It is an emotional support to you. As such, you probably don't want to take forty hours' worth of death metal on your trip! You are looking for balance.

I have incredible memories from my original Mystical Backpacking trip that are triggered by the music I was listening to at the time. When I hear Pablo Neruda poems being recited in lush tones, I remember sitting on a train traveling the Mediterranean coast and listening to those same words. Seeing the small towns and sun-dappled sea come in and out of view as the train snaked along to the rhythm of Neruda was truly magical. I felt that this poet knew and understood the very nature of the intangible goodness I sought in life. On the island of Mallorca, I remember blasting my happy travel set with a fellow traveler, both of us singing along at the top of our lungs to Bob Marley, the Proclaimers, Joni Mitchell, Bjork, and Tracy Chapman while our little red rental car crunched along the stony roads through yellow mountains and piney woods, past cliffs, and down to fishing villages by the sea. I remember listening to ambient trance music for days on end while lying in the mirror-ball light of a swimming pool resort and browning even the space between my toes. I was so tranquil and happy, and so was the music. Even now, Café del Mar—whose fabulous CD I bought in Spain—takes me back to a night I spent on a rocking boat, laughing with friends under twinkling stars while the salt air cleansed my soul. Finally, as I was making my way home at the end of it all, I choked up in public as Joan Baez called out in her plaintive wailing tone, "Farewell, Angelina, the sky is on fire, and I must go," as the sun set on the horizon. No good-bye has ever felt so lonely or so poignant.[4]

Your journal, the books you read, and the music you listen to will be your companions on your solitary trek. Just as maps and travel guides can help you to navigate the physical spaces of the new places you're going, these items will help you navigate the inner planes. Taking the time to put these items together with care and intention will benefit you immensely down the road.

Safety First

I hate to channel my mother here, but I'm going to do it anyway: as a Mystical Backpacker, you've got to be safe and smart. God forbid something should happen to you while you're out in the world discovering things of beauty without and within. Here is where I state a lot of obvious stuff that, surprisingly, is not obvious unless stated. Since I am channeling a little bit of my mother here, you are welcome to take everything I say with a grain of salt (I admit she does crazy things like calling me at 10:00 PM when she knows I'm alone in the house to ask me if all the windows and doors are locked), but please do take it nevertheless. Don't skip this part because you know better. Read it first, and *then* decide you know better.

Use Your Instincts

When traveling, and especially when traveling alone, always follow your gut instincts and be smart. Do not hitchhike. Do not sleep in a tent by the side of a lonesome stretch of road. Do not share a motel room with a stranger. Do not tell every person you meet what you are doing and where you are going, especially if that person seems dangerous or if your gut reaction to is to draw away. Do not get into the backseat of a two-door car with strangers in the front. Do not depend on others to provide for you or to keep you safe. You must be able to do this for yourself by being wise. The moment your intuition pricks up and you feel some sort of danger, find a quick way out. Lie, if you must. "Oh, there's my friend now, on the other side of the station . . . gotta run . . . nice meeting you!" Or, "Oops! Before we go, let me just use the restroom real quick. No, no, I don't mind taking my bag. I need stuff out of it, and I'd rather not unpack it here," etc. Do not endanger yourself in order to be polite.

Choose Your Accommodations

Stay in hostels, if possible. This kind of inexpensive, safe, and secure environment will automatically put you in a place where you are most likely to meet others traveling with goals and a purpose closer to your own than those staying in a motel or hotel. But if you find yourself alone in a hostel room with the creepiest person on earth, for Pete's sake don't stay in the room! Ask for another room or move to a different hostel. Campgrounds can also be useful places, but perhaps less secure and best selected when you have friends or a group to stay with. When traveling on buses, trains, and ferries, chain and lock your backpack to a chair or shelf and do not sleep alone in travel cars. When sleeping, try resting your head or upper body on your backpack. Always keep your personal ID, credit cards, and large-sum bills in a travel pocket looped around your body, under your clothes. Keep tickets, schedules, and itineraries in a convenient outer pocket so you don't have to stop in a crowded space to riffle through your things.

Faking It

The best thing you can do to ward off any possible threats or dangers when traveling is to look like you know what you're doing and where you're going, even when you don't! Confident people are more likely to be perceived as adversaries than as victims. If you are approached by people (not with a tourist or travel agency) wishing to give you tours, arrange accommodations for you, give you a ride somewhere, help you find a place to eat, and so on, do not take their assistance and do not go anywhere with them. Just as you would not rely on this kind of randomly and often aggressively offered help at home, you shouldn't rely on it abroad. Most abductees who are taken to a second location are never seen again, and most victims who run survive. Don't save a pittance of money from your daily budget because you opted to walk alone in the dead of night through a seedy part of town to a hostel you've never been to. Please, take a cab. If you need help, go to an information booth or use your guidebook.

Be Smart

Do not leave your food or drinks unattended or with a person you may not yet be able to rely on while traveling alone (especially in a bar). Think of every scenario and be smart. Your gut instincts will get stronger as you become more familiar with being a person who is passing through and journeying to the center of self. You must rely on these gut instincts and follow them. If you have a bad feeling about something, you are probably right. Follow these visceral reactions to situations and don't allow your insecurities to cause you to second-guess your better judgment. When faced with these feelings, read this section again before making any decisions. Your life is precious, which is why you have chosen to honor it with a purpose. Do not allow others to strip you of either.

This information is not meant to terrify you. For the most part, I always felt safe while traveling and met many wonderful people along the way. In fact, the only times *actual* scary things have happened to me, I wasn't traveling at all. Once, in my twenties, a guy felt me up on the sidewalk while I was on my way to go grocery shopping. I hit him with my purse, and he ran away. Once, in my thirties, I was almost attacked on a suburban walking trail when I took a half-hour break from work. I ran away and called the police. And once, as a child, my friend and I rode our bikes to the hardware store and called my dad to pick us up when we noticed a man was following us in his car. We were ten. All of these things happened on my home front, my own stomping grounds. You are not entering a more dangerous world by traveling. I'm just reminding you to be street smart and appropriately wary.

The world is a place of light and dark. Always keep yourself in the light and you will be better than fine. You will be absolutely radiant!

The very first night of my Mystical Backpacking odyssey is the perfect example of spooky streets and imagination run amuck and glorious light at the end of it all. Friends of mine had driven me from Budapest to Venice. We spent the day in happy company speeding through Slovenia and then the Italian Alps, engrossed in robust conversation. We dined together in a little Italian restaurant, and then they dropped me off at the train station on the mainland where I was to take the short train ride out to the islands that comprise Venice. It was a cold, dark night. I wore a long black coat, elegant black leather boots, and a large backpack on my back. The warm cocoon of the happy car sped away, and I stood in the damp silence, alone. One or two people stood on the platform, but most of Italy was tucked into bed. The lights of the train were disturbingly yellow, like sickness. The blackness of the night was an inky void surrounding me. The train itself was a welcome respite. The forward motion and a fellow passenger—a woman with grocery bags—gave me a rocking sense of security. We arrived in Venice sooner than I expected. Map in hand, I made my way towards the *pensione* I was to stay in.

Venice is confusing enough in the light of day. This particular night, it was thick with fog. It was as though I had entered a gothic novel, and alone, with only my empty, echoing footsteps to accompany me, I navigated narrow streets, hairpin twists and turns and arched bridges to some distant *X* marking the spot. And there, in the film noire light of a streetlamp, I found the place. I checked in to my room, climbed the narrow staircase, looked at the wretched wallpaper, and felt horribly, uncomfortably alone. Within minutes, I was in bed with the covers pulled up to my chin, tears welling up in my eyes as I stared out the window. The fog, illuminated by the moon, was a silver shroud through which nothing was visible. The silence was palpable. Then, a loud voice pierced the air. A man, in gorgeous tenor, began to sing beneath my window. "*O sole mio . . .*" His words reached up toward me for a long time. My tears dried up. My chest inflated as my spirit surged within me. I was here! I had done it! Italy was my oyster! My soul was where it was meant to be! Here is the translation of those glorious words that made their way in Neapolitan verse to my window that night:

> When night comes and the sun has gone down,
> I almost start feeling melancholy;
> I'd stay below your window

When night comes and the sun has gone down.

But another sun that's brighter still,
It's my own sun that's upon your face!
The sun, my own sun, it's upon your face!
It's upon your face![5]

Though I didn't understand the words the man sang, through some primal intuitive force within me, their meaning filled my soul, displacing my fears of the foggy unknown. I knew I had experienced the first of many gifts this journey would provide. I was exactly where I needed to be. The singing lulled me to sleep, and the next morning, a very different Venice awaited me.

Embrace the Magic

All the world is made of faith, and trust, and pixie dust.

—J. M. Barrie, *Peter Pan*

Magical moments, like the one I just described, are happening all around us, all the time. Each time a flower blooms: magic. Each time a babe is born: magic. The new life, the new beginning, the fresh start is easily recognized as magical. But the truth is, moments far more prosaic and banal hold their own gifts of magic, if you choose to experience them. I have always loved the poem "Stopping by Woods on a Snowy Evening," by Robert Frost, because of how it epitomizes this very point.

Whose woods these are I think I know.
....
To watch his woods fill up with snow.

Being alone with your thoughts in a quiet place you are traveling through and noticing the magical or spiritual nature of that moment is deeply comforting, even though the moment and the pleasure are fleeting. As you experience more and more magical moments, you will feel their comforting effects for longer and longer periods of time. Magic helps to dispel fears. While your journey is partially about connecting with a deeper feeling of peace and faith, it's also about learning how to draw on your everyday environments to strengthen those feelings each and every day. In this way, your journey is also about connecting with those woods, with the horse, with the gift of the snow and the silent moment, as Frost's traveler does. It is these silent and subtle elements that compose the constant hum of magic that exists at all times. On this journey you embark on, you are providing yourself with the space and opportunity to connect with it. For this reason especially, it's so important to create boundaries for yourself that will ensure you have the chance to experience these magic moments. Log out of Twitter, log out of Facebook, stop Googling every little thing, stop texting. Put away your connections to the world and just be. Okay, do let your mom know you're still alive and well (especially if she's anything like my mother!), but that's it.

Don't Overplan

If you live a structured day in your life at home, and most of us do, allow yourself to make some plans for your trip but try your hardest not to schedule it to the minute. You don't need to try to see everything there is to see and not allow for diversions from the plan. Be willing to let the journey reveal itself to you rather than forcing it to succumb to your will. If you miss the bus, ferry, or train, so be it. If your reservation is lost and you end up at a different hostel, so be it. If someone keeps talking to you when you're trying to journal, put your pen down and listen. See what comes of each pregnant moment.

The journey will reveal itself to you rather than be guided by you. Don't forget that if you didn't need guidance right now, you wouldn't be on the journey in the first place. If you knew the answers, you wouldn't be looking for them now. The answers may not be where you expect them to be. While that schedule may provide a structure to your days that helps you to feel safe, recognize that it is a defense mechanism against your fear. It's all right to feel that way, but after you've felt it, put it aside. I think it's safe to say that most mystics don't spend 90 percent of their days texting and frantically checking their appointment books. Allow your inner mystic to emerge. Faith. Trust. And pixie dust.

We're going to talk location and gear (physical and metaphysical gear) in this next group of Mystical Exercises. Know that with each exercise, you are another step closer to embarking. Feel free to start rubbing your hands together with glee!

Mystical Exercises: Chapter 3

Location, Location

The Practical: Determine where you'll go. The most important thing when determining where to go is not to shortchange yourself by surveying everyone you know for their input. I did that when choosing my counter during a kitchen renovation. I wanted Kashmir White. Then I asked everyone else's opinion and ended up with something that looked like a zebra carcass. Of course, every design magazine, a bunch of hotels, and even my doctor's office have freaking Kashmir White countertops to remind me that I made the wrong decision. Moral of the story? If you know you want Kashmir White, just choose Kashmir White and be done with it. You'll be so much happier. But if you really don't have any clue at all, I hope this first exercise will help you narrow down the possibilities. Take some time to answer the questions on the next page.

1. Have you repeatedly dreamed of a place you've never been?
2. Has a specific destination repeatedly come up in your life—in conversation, in ads, or in other places you've noticed (recently or not)? What is it? Where have you seen it or heard about it?
3. Have you seen a place on television or in a movie or read about a place in a book that you feel strongly drawn to?
4. Write a list of all the places you'd like to see before you die. Which do you want to start with?
5. Is there an activity you've always wanted to participate in or learn? Rock climbing? Swimming with dolphins? Shearing a sheep? Building an igloo? The sky is the limit—brainstorm!

The Mystical: Take a moment and close your eyes. Take three deep, even breaths. Become present in the moment. Give yourself permission to connect with your authentic self. When you feel ready, open your eyes and circle the words in the following chart that best complete each statement:

I crave:	Sun	Snow	Water	Woods	Sand
	Mountains	Meadows	Rivers	Ocean	Lakes
	Sky	Heat	Humidity	Frost	Leaves rustling
	Puffy clouds	Rain	Starry skies	Nightlife	Art
	Architecture	Farms	Books	Performances	Lessons
	Dirt Roads	Country lanes	Highways	Desert	Wilderness
I want to sleep:	In a downy bed with soft and silky sheets and dreamy pillows				
	In a sleeping bag under the stars, in a tent, in a hostel, in a hammock				
	On a cot or bunk bed or bed with decent sheets and blankets				

I want to eat:	In restaurants and cafés				
	Sandwiches and snacks bought from grocery stores				
	My own cooking				
I want to:	Sunbathe	Hike	Ski	Sail	Exercise
	Rest	Ride horses	Camp	Create	Swim
	Be massaged	Ride in planes, trains, and automobiles			
	Visit museums		Shop	See historical sites	
	Meet people like me		Meet people unlike me		
I have:	An unlimited budget				
	A healthy budget				
	A modest budget				
	A limited budget				

Now, look at the words you've circled and see if you can find a trip that meets most, if not all, of those requirements. Perhaps you'll be surprised to find that a camping trip in Yellowstone National Park is what you need, even though you've always been a city person. You never know where your heart's desire will take you, but if your heart and soul are speaking to you, now is the time to listen and respond. That said, be sensible. If you've never camped a day in your life, learn how to before tackling Yellowstone!

Acquire a Backpack

It's time to buy a backpack.

The Practical: You can't be a backpacker without a backpack, so let's get you one! I prefer the three-compartment kind, but you might be taller, shorter, rounder, or leaner, and the most important thing about your backpack is that it fits you properly and stores what you need it to store. If you have a bad back, make sure you buy a backpack that offers great back support options. If you insist on taking every piece of electronic equipment with you, make sure it has compartments for keeping these things safe. It's better to have a backpack that is easy to wear and conveniently holds what you will actually bring than to buy a backpack that your friend has or the salesperson encouraged you to buy or that I love. You should love your backpack and think it's the best backpack in the world! A couple of decades of adulthood and several home renovations have taught me this important lesson about major purchases: don't buy the most expensive one and don't buy the cheapest one. The sweet spot where quality meets value is somewhere in the middle.

The Mystical: Now that you have your backpack, go ahead and take a minute to stuff it with pillows and try it out in front of the mirror. Yeah. That's right. Look at you, you're a backpacking badass. This is going to be so much fun!

But that wasn't part of your exercise, my bad. I just wanted to share in this moment with you! After your initial excitement has worn off take some time to personalize your backpack—yes, this is the assignment. If you want to add some special patches to it that bring you happiness or are especially symbolic to you, do so. Fill out the ID card. If your backpack is a dark color, add some bright ribbon or a unique luggage tag. You would benefit from either putting your backpack in a large clear plastic bag at the airport or train or bus station or taping down the straps and flappy bits. You don't want the inconvenience of having it rip on a conveyor belt or storage door because a strap has caught onto something. Just as with your journal, if you take a little time and put a little effort into personalizing your backpack, you will become more invested in your journey, spiritually, with each addition.

You attach a sacred meaning to this item, thereby having it embody the very spirit of your enterprise.

Christen It

If you're feeling supermystical, then go ahead and bless your backpack. Say a prayer over it and fill it with the positive intentions you hope to manifest on this trip (for example, "Allow this item to embody the energy of sacred connection so that I may meet the people I am meant to meet."). If you think this sounds a little too weird, think of it this way: people christen boats (even the small ones). Need I say more? You can christen your backpack without feeling like a nut job.

Reading List

It's time to choose your books and compile your personal—and spiritually attuned—reading list.

The Practical: If you're bringing a tablet, make sure you'll be able to charge it. There's no point in dragging about a useless item. For this reason, I prefer to have at least two paperbacks in my backpack. They're light enough. You can trade them or mail them home, and they never need to be charged.

The Mystical: If you can't figure out what books to bring, here are two ways to try to figure it out. Is there anything you've really wanted to read or loved reading so much that you'd want to read it again? Bring it. If you've got a whole bunch of books picked out but you can't decide how to narrow the list down to which ones you'll take, try some old-fashioned (and supermystical) bibliomancy. Spread out the books. Take a deep breath. Either aloud or in your mind, ask, "Which books should I bring with me on my Mystical Backpacking trip? Which books will serve my highest good as I travel?" and then pass your hand over the books. When you feel a *yes!* energy (you may feel excited, uplifted, or even just strongly that this is the one), you know you've found a book. Do this until you have two or three books picked out from the pile. My goodness. You just did something rather silly. Didn't it feel good?

If you don't have any books picked out at all, you can also use bibliomancy in a library or bookstore and ask to be directed to the books you should bring. Be prepared to be stared at. It'll be great.

Your Playlist

It's time to create your music playlists with intention and consideration of fueling your inner joy and spiritual sojourn.

The Practical: You will need three playlists.

Happy Music: This first playlist is dedicated to happy music that makes you want to dance and fills you joy. Include light, upbeat songs about travel, individuality, and personal expression. This set rocks and has you smiling from ear to ear, tapping your foot to the beat, and striding through places with total joy!

Contemplative Audio Tracks: The second is dedicated to contemplative music with deeper meaning and tracks of poetry, rap, spoken word, stories, and guided meditations. These tracks get you in a soul-searching mood and address the big questions about society and the meaning of life. This is the thinking stuff that might occupy your time while you stare out the window of the train at the passing countryside, determining how the events of your life have shaped you.

Instrumental Music: This set is calming, nurturing, and meditative. It can include classical, dream, trance, opera, smooth jazz,

New Age, and so on. The music should give your mind freedom to wander as it listens, which is why it's important that it's instrumental and doesn't include lyrics. This set should make you sleepy, dreamy, pleasantly relaxed.

As you build your playlists, remember that they benefit you first and foremost. You don't need to choose music that will impress others. If a twenty-four-hour Yanni playlist is what your soul needs, go for it. No one will be listening to it except you.

The Mystical: Now that you've got your three playlists, give each one of them a name that means something to you. My Mystical Backpacking odyssey happened before playlists existed. We had tapes. It was an art to master: the making of the perfect mix tape. And when you fell in love with someone, the first thing you did was make a mix tape for your beloved. But I digress. My first mix tape for Mystical Backpacking was called *Forward Motion*. I still have it. It still rocks and puts a spring in my step. And Mystical Backpacking is still one of the loves of my life. No wonder I made it a mix tape! If you want to see what my tapes included, check out the Mystical Backpacker website or flip to the Mystical Extras section at the back of the book, where I share those playlists and others I've created. If you think you'll like them, you can use them.

Attune Yourself to the Mystical

Practice observing the magic of a moment.

The Practical: Begin to notice the beauty of the world around you. Each day, take a moment to notice a moment. Discover what is happening during that particular moment and write it down. You can keep a small journal or stack of papers you call your magic moments.

The Mystical: Embracing the mystical takes practice, just like anything else worth doing. You don't become good at something without practice. As you start your mystical motor up, this exercise begins to train you to operate in a more mystical dimension. This is a great way to flex your mystical muscles before leaving on your trip, which is why it's an important exercise.

Make it Happen

Book your trip. That's right. It's time.

The Practical: Figure out your dates, your budget, your destinations, and book the darned thing. Don't overthink it. Just do it. (But if you need some support, you can always check out the Mystical Backpacking website's community forums; see the Mystical Extras in the back of this book for more information.) Tell your boss. Discuss it with your partner or your parents. Inform your roommate and cover all your costs and bills in advance. Methodically, ticking items off the list, just make it happen. It can be two weeks from now because you got a great deal, or six weeks from now when your vacation time matures to where you need it to be, or four months from now, when you graduate. Just put it on the books and make it a commitment on paper.

The Mystical: Breathe deep. Don't freak. This is going to be amazing.

As you step into the process of beginning, remember that there are two things happening at the same time: there's the very real and earthly act of preparing yourself physically for your adventure, and then there's the intangible yet no less real act of preparing your mindset for this new phase of personal growth. Occupying yourself with the physical preparations can help to divert your attention away from any trepidation. It's important to remind yourself that when you prepare to go on a quest as you are, it is normal and natural to feel some apprehension. Discomforts, obstacles, misadventures, and missteps are part of every adventure story, and with a Mystical Backpacking trip, you may encounter these both in a physical sense and also in a metaphysical sense—emotionally, mentally, spiritually.

Every hero writes his or her own story with the ink of risk, growth, and challenge. As Chaucer said, "Nothing ventured, nothing gained."[6] As you prepare to embark, remind yourself that great things are possible, and immense dividends can be gained by investing yourself in the spirit of exploration. What a glorious gift to give yourself: the time and opportunity to traverse the outer planes of the world and the inner planes of your soul as you discover your destiny.

4

Into the Labyrinth: How Do I Journey?

"There is no use in trying," said Alice. "One can't believe impossible things."
"I dare say you haven't had much practice," said the Queen. "When I was your age I always did it for half an hour a day. Why, sometimes I've believed as many as six impossible things before breakfast."
—LEWIS CARROLL, *ALICE IN WONDERLAND*

Rome
February 14, 2000:

Such magic. I love this country! I've strolled though my favorite places in Rome today. First the Trevi Fountain, where Anita Ekberg sensuously refreshed herself in La Dolce Vita (1960), then up Via Veneto (again) and am now lolling about in Villa Borghese Park. There is so much to say about Rome, one hardly knows where to begin, but since the favorite places are most inspiring . . . !

Trevi Fountain! Designed and constructed during the early 1700s, it depicts (built 1732–1762!!) Neptune standing in a huge shell, while Tritons on either side of him steer seahorses representing the two moods of the sea (stormy + docile). But the whole fountain takes up the entire wall of a building and is (like everything in Rome) massive in size. The water in the fountain is the color of the ocean and looks just like the shallows off a coastline. The sculptured fountain has huge craggy rocks, seaweed, corals and shells sculpted into it. Plus, Suzie told me that while the fountain was being built, a barber (whose shop was right beside) endlessly fought with the builders because construction was putting him out of business. He told the designer he never wanted to see the fountain again, so the designer placed a huge stone vase on the side of the fountain facing the barbershop, thereby obstructing the view from the barber's window. When another barbershop opened across the street the barber was put out of business because the customers liked looking at the fountain!

I threw a coin in (facing backwards, over the right shoulder) to ensure my return to Rome! I think Audrey Hepburn does the same thing in Roman Holiday. Hundreds of tourists flock there daily, but Italians also sit there to eat lunch and drink wine and smoke and hold their lovers and kiss them. So wonderful!

Today I went back to Trevi and sat on a bench for a while just to stare at it. The water lights up the figurines with webs of sharp light that undulate, thereby mesmerizing and relaxing one's senses. If you focus on this, the sound of the tourists becomes a murmur and life is sweet and grand.

Speaking about the sweet life . . .

La Dolce Vita means "the sweet life" (I moved to a new spot in the park. Left my shady bench and am now lying on a sunny slope.) and both times as I was walking up Via Veneto I kept thinking about the sweet life. At first, the thought persisted because of Fellini's movie. La Dolce Vita was filmed mostly here. And it is the perfect setting. Via Veneto drips with glamor, but maintains a warmth that doesn't usually go hand in hand with luxury hotels, haute couture and fine restaurants. The road slithers like a snake up towards the old city wall and Borghese gardens. Glass buildings housing restaurants and bookstores line the sidewalks, interspersed by flowerbeds bright with color even now in February. Today I saw two famous American actors strolling about (the newscaster guy from *Saturday Night Live* [who was fired] and the balding dark-haired blue-eyed guy who always plays a cop . . . but don't know his name and can't remember movie or tv show titles), and a restaurant (Harry's Bar) boasts a display case with photos of celebrity clientele beside its menu displayed outside.

However, as I was walking up Via Veneto alone today, already blissful from my sit-down at the Trevi Fountain, I kept thinking about how happy I was and how sweet my own life is. I am so blessed and fortunate to have such a travel experience and to have such inner happiness.

And so, on a meager budget befitting a self-sufficient twenty-five-year-old, I found myself on the grandest street, rubbing elbows with celebrities in the Eternal City. My life was suddenly the opposite of all I had experienced just over a week before. Budapest had been cold and gray, whereas Rome was awash in golden light. Budapest was filled with stern faces, rude clerks, and pushing commuters. Romans smiled, sang, and expressed their emotions with round gestures, arm squeezes, and jovial hugs. In Budapest, it was too cold to be outside. In Rome, thousands lazed on the greens of the park on a weekday afternoon. There was no question I was in a better place for my soul. What had been dormant and waiting like a bored dog tied up too long in a yard, all hope for release vanquished, started stirring with curiosity at a newfound and unexpected freedom. I wasn't running or gleeful just yet. I was cautiously optimistic. I was filled with a very present and tangible happiness. I did not know when it would end.

That's what it feels like to be away somewhere you want to be, with time stretching out before you. I had five weeks of my trip still ahead of me. Would it be too much to hope for it all to feel this good? I dared not consider it. I remained present under the Roman sun. I can't say I rested, for I walked more miles each day than I had at home. I can't say I was relaxed, for I was more stimulated by what was before me than I had been in a long time. I think the most appropriate summation is that I healed. It was as though the wounds my soul had incurred in my previous state of stagnation were now being rubbed with gentle salves while my lungs breathed a cleaner, more refreshing air. And as all of us do on our sickbeds, I indulged fully in my present moment and became an observer while my body and soul rested and recuperated.

At the top of the Spanish Steps, as I looked out on the vast city of Rome and saw before me tens of thousands of people and hundreds of cars and motorcycles coming and going, toing and froing, my own insignificance became startlingly obvious. Not that I was filled with a sense of meaninglessness—on the contrary, I became astutely aware of how important it is to follow your own dreams and pursue your own happiness, for the world at large will not stop and recognize this for you. That's for you to realize, both mentally and physically.

I spent a day at the Vatican marveling at the glorification of art and was profoundly disturbed by the homeless and hungry gathered at the gates while a line of brown-robed monks strode past without pause. At this place where I, having been raised a Catholic, should have felt most connected to God, I felt only a deep sadness in my soul. What did that mean? Michelangelo's *La Pietà* was caged off from the public, the bones of dead popes vied for status under more and more elaborate tombs, and miles of golden embellishments honored art, but all the while God seemed strangely silent. I realized then that the fullness I felt in my heart and the buoyancy I felt in my spirit meant God resided in me, not necessarily under the dome of St. Peter's Basilica. This is when I first *felt* the truth of the teaching "the kingdom of God is within you" (Luke 17:21).

Italy taught me so much about appreciating, embracing, and honoring the full spirit of life, and I will always carry a deep gratitude to the country for that.

The Journey Within

In the cover of one of my travel journals, I drew an elaborate labyrinth. As I was traveling, the language of the labyrinth spoke to me. A labyrinth, unlike a maze, has no tricks up its sleeve. You can trust it implicitly and relax as you move through it, knowing you will easily find your way. A labyrinth consists of a direct path to the center and direct path out from the center. There are no frightening twists and turns, no paths that end in impermeable walls, no spaces that hold the intent to confuse the person within. When I first discovered this distinction, the labyrinth became a symbol for me, representing both the physical and spiritual journey I was on. Labyrinths are meant to be spiritual tools, and there are records of their existence as far back as four thousand years. Chartres Cathedral in France has a beautiful thirteenth-century labyrinth within its walls, and many abbeys, monasteries, and churches worldwide include them in their gardens and courtyards. Retreat centers, parks, and New Age destinations have labyrinths aplenty as well. In this environment, guests are invited to walk the labyrinth in silence, and multiple people can be in the labyrinth at the same time. As you pass another labyrinth walker, you simply turn sideways so both of you can fit and pass each other, and proper labyrinth etiquette is to nod at most but not say anything at all to disrupt the process for either one of you. Walking a labyrinth alone is a real treat because you don't have to worry about etiquette and there aren't any distractions from your process. As you enter the labyrinth, you have the opportunity to reflect on your life or to meditate. Your brain, having to pay attention to the path as well as your thoughts, becomes focused. You begin to feel still and peaceful. You become centered. You may reflect on long-dormant memories or ideas that reveal something to you about the nature of who you have become, or you may enter a deeply meditative state.

The labyrinth is a mystic's symbol if ever there was one. As a Mystical Backpacker, hold the intent that your journey is a labyrinth, not a maze. You are not entering a time of frightened confusion. You are traveling a straight path to the core of your being as you walk a straight and trick-free physical path on your backpacking adventure. Knowing this is true, the moments of uncertainty or challenges you face can be perceived simply as exercises toward your own enlightenment. That doesn't mean you won't feel discomfort. I certainly did. The cover of that journal is worn by my touch, for each time I was frightened or uncomfortable I would look at the labyrinth I had drawn and remind myself that I was just where I needed to be.

Buyer's Remorse

As with any large and new commitment (buying a house, quitting a job, getting married, starting a new job, breaking up with someone, etc.), the moment you finally commit to taking action may very shortly thereafter be followed by buyer's remorse for having just committed yourself to said course of action. When I first arrived in Barcelona (the fourth city of my odyssey), discomforts piled one upon the other, and I regretted my decision immensely. My time felt wasted. My feet were killing me. My boots were nearly worn through. I couldn't find accommodation and ended up in a hostel with dirty bathrooms and facing a square rife with pickpockets. All I could do was kick myself for leaving Italy. Little did I know that Barcelona would be where the magic of my Mystical Backpacking journey would truly ignite. It was during this part of my journey that my future was rewritten. Without it, this book would not exist, for I would not have experienced the mystical encounters ahead. But at the time, steeped in distress, all I knew was remorse.

It's reassuring to know that remorse is a universal language. I remember seeing an *I Love Lucy* episode in which Lucy and Ricky buy a house in Connecticut. The first night after they've signed the papers, they take turns being completely unable to sleep because they're so freaked out by what they've just committed to. That episode was filmed over sixty years ago now, which I find comforting. It means that it's very normal to feel the panic caused by big investments of time and money, increased responsibilities, and new and uncharted paths. It means that people have been feeling this way for ages. That said, it's never fun to find yourself on a plane with a few meager possessions and the complete and total unknown spreading out before you when you have your panic-induced moment of buyer's remorse. Now that you've committed to your Mystical Backpacking journey, expect this moment may very well come. It might not happen right at the beginning of your trip. But it's likely going to happen.

How are you going to cope with it when it does? With the tools in your Mystical Backpacker's Toolbox.

The Mystical Backpacker's Toolbox

What you're doing is brave, if only because it's also scary. You are taking a leap of faith! As such, the biggest obstacle to conquer on your personal journey is fear. It may be that you fear new places or not being in control. You may even be a little afraid of what you might discover hidden within your very self as you explore yourself with an intensity or honesty you've never before employed.

There are five main Mystical Tools—both practical and spiritual—in your Mystical Toolbox for you to employ as you embark on your spiritual and physical journeys: signs, prayer, reflection, journaling, and paying it forward.[1] (See the Mystical Extras section in the back of the book for a quick-reference guide to these tools.) These Mystical Tools will assist you in coping with your fears and addressing any limiting beliefs you may be carrying as you journey. They are *Mystical* Tools, which means you can't see them or touch them, and you will need to employ faith when using them. Envision the most enlightened person you can. Now, picture you. You have the capacity and ability to be just as mystical as the best of them. As with anything, the more time you spend doing it, the better you become. Lawyers *practice* law each day. Concert pianists *practice* their performance pieces. Yogis practice their poses even if they've mastered them long ago. The more you practice being mystical, the more mystical you will be.

Before we explore each tool, I want you to imagine each soul in the universe as a grain of sand composing a beach. The beach stretches out before you for miles. Each and every grain of sand is necessary for the beach to exist at all. The grain of sand that is you is no more and no less valuable than any other. Each of our lives is a gift, and *in each and every case*, opportunities for connecting with others and with the deeper, broader meaning of life exist. These gifts are not reserved for others more special than you. It's not about deserving. It is simply a fact. Just as the world is round, these opportunities exist. If your intention is to connect with God, the earth, or some force of energy or consciousness you believe can lighten your spirit or ease your fears, it will happen. If your intention is to heal your confusion or discontent, it will happen. The tools in the Mystical Toolbox will help you reach your goals and connect with the mystic within you. Let's get to know them better, beginning with signs.

Signs

Most people will claim, even if just jokingly, that they have experienced a sign of some sort. They have seen an animal or had a dream or watched a cloud or overheard a conversation that speaks to what they've been grappling with, and they feel this is a sign. Whole books have been dedicated to interpreting the many types and meanings of signs. It's enough to convince you the human spirit either has a primal need for signs or remembers a value to signs from some other plane of existence. A sign is something in your environment that comforts you and causes you to feel better when you are worried that you aren't making the right choices. If a sign has alleviated your fear, it has worked.

If you ever become frightened on your trip, ask for a sign. Make a conscious request to be offered some affirmation. You can write your request in your journal, say it aloud, say it in your mind, or incorporate it into a prayer. There is no wrong way to ask for a sign. Then, just sit back and wait. It may take some time, or you may spot one right away. You will know when it's a sign for you. And if you're unsure, close your eyes a moment and ask yourself, "Is this a sign for me?" More often than not, an instinctual yes or no response will immediately present itself.

Yes, believing in signs like this requires you to accept divine intervention or perhaps the concepts of fate and predetermined destiny. If you're not sure that you want to align yourself with these philosophies, you may not believe this exercise can work for you. In this case, interpret the exercise as such: each day, endless activities and actions are taking place around us. We only notice some of them. The subconscious mind chooses to recognize which of these to focus on, which of these interest us, which of these we can relate to or identify with. In this case, your sign is the one that resonates with your subconscious mind. In this way, you can still appreciate a sign by recognizing it as the subconscious mind's ability to tap into latent thoughts and beliefs and determine the value of something in the exterior world that doesn't yet make sense, but will with time. So, whether you believe in God or angels or spirit guides or your dead relative or simply the brain's ability to note objects of subconscious significance, you can learn to appreciate a good sign.

When looking for a sign, don't expect *instant* results every time. This can be hard, because if you're looking for a sign—especially early on in your trip—you're likely scared or needing immediate reassurance. Having to wait for a sign when you're in this state of mind can be difficult. When we are frightened or stressed, we often immerse ourselves in chaotic fear-based thoughts and focus our attention on our responsive emotions. With the body now serving as a cocoon around us and not as a bridge for us to connect with the world outside of ourselves, we become insulated from the world. We may build upon our fears and feed our internal hysteria within this enclosed space of the mind. We create imagined scenarios that frighten us. We worry about imagined outcomes that frighten us. We tend to fall into the habit of chanting negative affirmations to ourselves: "I can't do this. I'm being selfish. I'm unworthy. I'm being ridiculous." Instead of feeling better, we begin to feel worse. It's very hard to move your focus from this inward place to an outward space. Your first attempts may result in your perceiving even more dangers and stressors and threats! In most cases, this is likely the projection of your fears on the environment around you. Once you have managed to calm yourself down and move beyond the panic, you can turn your attention outward in a more productive way and see some positive results.

Easier said than done? Here's what you need to do to achieve this. First, calm down by doing something you love to do. This will help you to ground yourself in the reality of the moment and not the fiction of your mind. Eat ice cream. Draw. Write. Take photographs.

Read a book. Watch a movie. Immerse yourself in an activity that engages and uplifts you. Pay attention to something that reassures and invigorates you. Clear the slate; wipe away your primal, physical fear.

It sounds too simple, right? As someone who used to suffer from panic attacks, I can tell you this tactic works. I try not to allow my fears to stop me from doing things and have coped with my fears (of flying, traveling alone, riding in elevators, going to the dentist, heights, swimming in the ocean, receiving poor performance reviews, debt, hospitals, tests, rejection, and so much more) by using this simple approach. We create our fears in our mind. Just as you teach an unruly child to become calm by providing him or her with an activity to focus on, so you can still your unruly mind. Tell your mind to get over its Big Bad Self and just lick an ice cream cone for a minute. Your hands may shake, and you may lick like a person unhinged, but eventually you will settle down and feel calm once again. This is when your signs will come tumbling in.

While the first step in looking for a sign is to ask for one, the second step is to turn your attention outward to the world around you. You can only see a sign if you're looking for one, and you can only look for one if you've calmed yourself down.

So, what exactly is meant by a sign? Am I talking burning bushes and stone tablets? No, but I won't rule them out! A sign can be a found object: a feather, a stone, a bead. It might also be an overheard conversation. For example, you might be wondering if you should end a relationship when you suddenly hear someone sitting next to you say to her friend, "You need to try couple's therapy." A sign might also be something you see on a billboard or in an ad that holds greater meaning for you than the ad intends—you might be wondering about leaving a toxic work environment, and in three different places in a single day you happen to see the Just Do It Nike ad. A sign could be something you see in nature—a cloud shape, a sudden rainstorm or burst of sunlight. The most convincing of signs is when many of these smaller ones combine to create a series of meaningful coincidences from which you extrapolate a subtle message. Even Carl Jung wrote on this subject and shared his own experiences of what he called synchronicity.[2] But for the purposes of the Mystical Backpacking process, know that there is no "wrong" sign if you feel that it's a sign for you.

Here are two signs I have experienced. In these examples, you'll see that I actually did receive the sign right after I asked for it (which is why they make such interesting stories), but, again, that's not always the case.

After the first leg of my backpacking trip was completed, a dear traveling companion, Lisa, and I moved to Palma de Mallorca, the capitol city of the Balearic Islands in the Mediterranean Sea, on the island of Mallorca. Although we started off living in a crew house (a communal apartment with beds rented to individuals on a weekly basis), we quickly found a three-bedroom Old Town garden apartment, sharing a large bedroom and bathroom. Our landlord and roommate, a British engineer, worked in the yachting industry, and we three quickly adopted each other as family and lived with the casual intimacy and torturous antics of siblings. We were happy. I was working on a private yacht as a steward and cook. Lisa worked as a laborer and delivery person for an array of vessels using the main harbor. We were in our twenties, done with school, not yet committed to full-time careers, and I think we were very nearly tipsy every other night for three months or so! It was the most fun I had ever had. We worked hard and played hard.

We worked on boats during the daytime, becoming deeply tanned from the reflection of the Mediterranean sun on the lapping waters and trim and fit from the manual labor and walks to and from work. In the evenings, our group of friends gathered at The Corner Bar, and we told stories and laughed, and then we'd eat roasted chicken dinners and trundle off to our apartments to rest a little. Despite repeated attempts at staying in and saving our money, we'd usually dash out to Latitudes bar to hit the two-for-one drink specials before they ended at 10:00 PM, and we'd line up four powerfully mixed Spanish cocktails and enter Wonderland. We danced on tables, laughed riotously, told stories, and listened to tales of adventures as recounted in the smoky, dimly lit haze of the predawn hours. On the weekends, we'd hit the beach, doze and brown, shock our systems with brisk topless swims in the sea. We'd snorkel, ride motorbikes, and hike in the mountains. I don't remember a rainy or cloudy day. I don't remember a day without flowers.

Even in paradise, alas, discontentment can find you. You start to reflect on your days and wonder to where they are disappearing. You start wondering about what you've accomplished, what the point to your existence might be. Friends began to leave the island, committed to work on vessels cruising the Mediterranean for the summer. Those of us who remained began to feel restless ourselves, looking for alternate plans. We felt trapped on the island and a bit depressed. We sobered up, literally and figuratively.

One night I sat with my friend Eddie on the shore of Palma's manmade lake beside La Seu Cathedral. The night was clear. The cathedral was lit up in her elegant yet menacing Gothic stance. We were railing against the state of affairs in our lives, talking candidly of our fears and frustrations. After an hour or so of gloomy yet releasing conversation, I began to cry. My voice escalated in a panicky way, and I remember saying, "I just don't know what to do with my life! Should I leave here? I just wish I had a sign!" and in that moment, a large silver fish jumped out of the lake. Its thin body flashed through the night like a sword, and it leaped majestically not once, not twice, not thrice, but four times. We were shocked. We shut up, our mouths slack-jawed. Eddie looked at me in wonderment and said, "I guess you have your answer." And so it was decided. When Lisa woke up the next morning,

I announced, "It's time to leave Mallorca." She agreed. The Universe conspired to help us do the right thing, right away. That afternoon I visited my friend Natalie in Port de Portales, a smaller and more exclusive marina down island. I told her of our plans, and it just so happened she knew of a vessel looking for crew. We met the captain, were hired, packed our bags, and left early the following morning. Just like that, our time in Mallorca was over.

The vessel that hired us was moving to Lebanon and would be renamed by its new owner. We were on her final voyage as the *Taipan*. Lebanon wasn't politically stable at the time, and it was decided we would disembark on the island of Cyprus, an hour or two before the boat reached her new home. This meant we'd be crossing the Mediterranean from Spain, in the west, to the most easterly island, very close to Lebanon and Syria and just south of Turkey. We had both phoned our parents to tell them where we were. We had provided them with the names and phone numbers of the captain and first mate, the name of the vessel, and the ports we'd be entering. That said, we would be nearly a week at sea with two men we didn't know, and I worried about the wisdom of our decision. If we were raped and murdered and thrown overboard, no one would know for weeks, if ever. I phoned my parents often to let them know I was well.

The first few days we trundled along happily, reading books between ports and meals. We wrote in our journals, dozed in the sun, saw giant sea turtles swim beside us. I wrote:

June 15, 2000
7:55 pm: Sardinia in sight.

The sky and the sea are massive; two bodies of water reflected in each other. It is only the density of the water ratio that varies. And so I sail the sea, while my mind sails the sky and my spirit hovers between the two. Another vessel and the faint outlines of Sardinia crowd my canvas, interrupt my frame of mind all too soon. Everything that is, is a shade of blue. The afternoon indigo sea has roughened and turned mercury. The dome of the sky, rich periwinkle, drains of color towards the horizon, fading to powder blue, the color of 1950s sweater sets.

The sea licks its million white tongues upward, hoping for a taste of the sky.

Around me is Africa, Europe, the Balkans and the Middle East. I am where history began. How much this aquatic theatre has witnessed. And out here, none of it remains above the surface. As Purdy says in his poem Moonspell, "Sink Down."

We were tranquil only because of our forward motion. We were anxious because we didn't know our final destination. Once on Cyprus, we would be on our own with no return trip tickets and nowhere to return to. Our thoughts and emotions heavily influenced by these oppositions, we alternated between happiness and sadness, euphoria and fear. I spent my days reading books, writing in my journal, and doing exercises to examine my past and to visualize my ideal future. This self-reflection was rewarding, enlightening, and disturbing, as self-examination often is.

One morning in Palermo, Sicily, I awoke to untie the vessel from the pier and to bring in the fenders. It was 5:30 in the morning and Palermo wore a gilt of powdered gold as the sun rose behind the shore. I stood barefoot on the boat, the chill of the sea rising from below and saturating every cell of my being. I shuddered from the cold, and a horrible feeling of panic grasped me. My mind raced with doubting thoughts once again; what was I doing with my life? Where was I going? What was the point to my existence? Was I just wasting time? Was I on the right path? My heart pounded in my chest, my clammy hands grasped the lines and trembled, my knees knocked, and my mouth went bone-dry. I felt like jumping off the ship and running on the pier. I couldn't breathe. In this moment of abject terror, I squeezed my eyes shut and prayed to God. *Please, I am so scared. Am I on the right path? Please, show me a sign—I'm terrified!* I heard a splash. There, in the deep harbor water below me, a long, thin silver fish leaped out of the water four times in rapid succession. It was the same type of fish that had jumped in Mallorca. I was stunned. I rubbed my eyes. Undulating rings of water assured me this had actually happened. I was startled out of my panic and was strangely, immediately reassured. The boat hummed away from Palermo as my drama was left behind.

So, it's possible the Mediterranean is filled with millions of this breed of thin silver fish that are forever leaping about in series of four jumps yet the only times I ever saw this fish were the two times I asked for a sign. Yes, it could be coincidence, and it's possible that any darkly tanned Mediterranean fishermen reading this are running their hands through their glossy black hair while laughing at the ridiculousness of this American woman who thinks this prosaic fish is a sign from a higher power. Or it could be that this fish-jumping event was, in both cases, actually a sign. It doesn't matter: I ended up feeling better because of it. The question, "Was this a sign?" really doesn't matter if the experience matters to you. I have decided that, in the case of signs, it is better to believe and to see where it takes you, and I encourage you to give the same a try on your travels and in your life in general. This is a mystical approach if ever there was one.

You also don't have to be in the throes of an emotional ordeal to look for signs. When there's a decision I'm trying to make, I often ask for signs. Or if I'd like confirmation that a message I believe I've received from a sign is in fact a message and not my imagination, I ask for another sign to validate it. Recently I've asked for feathers, but for over a decade now I've asked for stones in the shape of feet. I've found little foot-shaped stones all around the world, on rough hiking trails, on beaches, in city parks, and even in the woods. Whenever I want to reflect on the path I have chosen to walk in this life, I line up my stones to look like a set of footprints and am made happy by this physical representation of my past decisions. Regardless of where I am now, even if that place is a time of stress, strain, or failure, I feel a sense of confirmation that I'm walking the right path and am right where I should be. And if you don't believe in a higher power or that random things you notice can be connected or orchestrated to communicate a greater message or meaning, consider this: no matter how a sign presents itself to you, observing one can also be perceived as your subconscious reaching its arm out from the dark recesses of your mind to say, "*This* is what matters now." Pay attention to this.

Signs rely on interpretation. In my fish story, I think that we can all agree that in neither case did the fish jump out of the water and say, "Yes!" Nor did it actually say, "No!" The fish simply jumped. I interpreted the jumping as a yes. In this way, my subconscious mind made the decision based on what I needed at the time, whether I consciously knew it or not. Recognizing the message as just that—a missive from both your outer and inner worlds—and interpreting it according to what your soul most needs in that moment is all that matters. The subconscious mind is a survivalist and wants us to live well, and I suspect that, if higher powers exist, they're working under the same tenet.

As you document your signs in your journal (which I encourage you to do any and every time a sign presents itself), a big-picture message may begin to emerge. When this happens, it is truly thrilling and often enlightening.

Prayer

The second tool in the Mystical Toolbox is prayer. I'm not talking about bringing along the Talmud or reciting the Holy Rosary, although certainly if this is part of your religion, you can do that too. As a tool in your Mystical Toolbox, prayer serves several important functions: it helps you to ask for help when you're frightened, it helps you to pay attention to your blessings instead of your complaints, and it is a vehicle for feeling connected to something greater than yourself. In this third and final way especially, prayer is deeply connected to the mystical. And if you don't particularly connect with the word *prayer*, you may instead call it paying homage or meditating or being mystical or programming the subconscious mind to default to positive thinking, for prayer can be all of these things and more.

You don't even need to close your eyes or be on your knees for the type of Mystical Backpacking praying I'm talking about. You may be riding a bus, standing in line, eating your lunch, or walking on the beach and in your mind be saying your prayers. You may write your prayers in your journal or say them aloud to the sky. There is no wrong way to pray as a Mystical Backpacker! There are three main types of prayer that will be useful tools for you on your trip: Asking Prayers, Thanking Prayers, and Enlightenment Prayers.

Asking Prayers

We already touched on Asking Prayers in the previous section on signs. Asking for a sign is a type of Asking Prayer, but other types of Asking Prayers include: asking for direction, asking for assistance, asking for forgiveness, asking for answers, asking for companionship, asking for understanding, and so on. In an Asking Prayer, you are taking the time to acknowledge and understand your feelings enough to determine what course of action would help you to address those feelings. These prayers help us to feel reassured, but they also help us to better understand ourselves. For example, if every single day we ask to meet someone to fall in love with, then we learn that addressing our feelings of loneliness is a priority. If we frequently ask for financial assistance, then we learn that addressing our feelings of insecurity around our ability to support ourselves is a priority. We don't actually need lovers to feel whole. We don't actually need more money in order to feel safe. Asking Prayers set the intention to invite these very things into our lives and help us to clarify the very things we need to work on developing for ourselves internally. Asking Prayers are a very good place to start your Reflection Work, which we'll be talking about later. For this reason especially, you may wish to document the things you ask for in your prayers in your journal.

Thanking Prayers

The best thing about Thanking Prayers is that they can be random and spontaneous and surprising. Let's say you're riding a bus and looking out the window, and you see a group of children playing. All of a sudden, you feel a rush of happiness, and you're glad to have seen them because they made you feel happy. In your mind, say, *Thank you for giving me this gift today*. This is a prayer. I think if there is a God, then God's job can sometimes kind of stink. It's almost like God works at the universe's complaint department. Probably most of the prayers that come in are Please Don'ts and I Needs and Help Me Nows, and only a small amount in comparison are I Love Yous, You Rocks, This Made Me Happys, and I Am Grateful for You and Your Creations. You know, whether or not you've officially worked in customer service, that when you're subjected to a constant stream of complaints, you can become disheartened. Now, I personally believe God is without ego, so I don't think God is actually worried about all the complaining but is rather more focused on having compassion for us. But throw God a bone every once in a while, people. Perspective is a beautiful thing.

Consider that many of the people in the world don't have access to fresh drinking water and don't own a wallet, let alone have any money to put in one if they did. When you remind yourself of this, it's much easier to recognize the many blessings in your life already. While all of us have problems, and your problems are no more or less serious and real to you than mine are for me, we also need to learn to focus our attention on the simple joys and constant stream of miracles we witness each and every day and to produce praise and gratitude rather than criticism and want. Training your brain to focus on the positive rather than the negative by engaging in this type of prayer will also result in a dividend of immense personal reward. You will become a happier and more grateful person.

Sometimes Thanking Prayers simply involve taking negative experiences and focusing instead on the positives. Let's say you're eating something divine, but the service sucks. Rather than allowing yourself to get all worked up about the awful server, spend your time being grateful for the delicious food and the extra time to sit and journal. If your hostel owner is lovely, but the bathroom is never clean, spend some time being grateful that you met such a good person (and maybe throw an Asking Prayer in there that he or she gets some help with cleaning the bathroom). If you missed your train, spend some time being grateful for the opportunity to sit quietly in the sun or to catch up on your exercises. Every complaint can give way to a gift if you set your sights on gratitude. Part of being a Mystical Backpacker is seeing the spirit of all things and connecting to the bigger picture through the smaller details. Challenges are just smaller details. Your life and the world around you make up the bigger picture. Don't get hung up on the smaller details. Seize each opportunity to learn compassion and gratitude.

Here's an example of how I reinterpreted a challenging situation into one I could be grateful for. The night I arrived in Barcelona, I met a Japanese student who was taking some time to travel. He was planning on staying in a hostel that catered specifically to Asians. Since I was looking for a place to stay, I asked him if I could join him. He warned me that he didn't know if they'd let me stay there since I'm not Asian, but we decided it was worth a try. It was getting late, and he had not been able to exchange his traveler's checks, so he had no money for the subway. I paid for our fares to get us to the neighborhood where his guidebook directed us. We got off the metro at the wrong stop and had to get back on again. I paid for our fares again. We got off at the right stop and waited for over an hour at the McDonald's the guidebook said was the meeting place each night for new hostel visitors. I paid for our food. He phoned the hostel, and the annoyed person on the end of the line explained we were at the wrong McDonald's. We got back on the subway. I paid for our fares. We finally met our contact at the right McDonald's and were directed toward the hostel. We walked several blocks in the night, down dodgy side streets in a seedy neighborhood and carrying our heavy backpacks all the while. We reached the hostel, and the woman who ran it refused to let me stay because I wasn't Asian. Now I would need to make my way back to the city alone, in the dead of night, and seek alternate accommodations for myself. The young man felt terrible and apologized profusely (it wasn't his fault; he did warn me), changed his money at the hostel, and paid me back. He walked me back to the subway and we said our good-byes. I rode back downtown, walked along the main boulevard in the heart of the tourist district, and asked a young American couple where they were staying. They directed me to their hostel where I checked in, fell into bed exhausted, and slept deeply. The next morning I discovered that I was across the street from the hostel I'd been searching for and had originally planned to stay at. After breakfast, I moved—which would turn out to be the perfect time to end up sharing a bunk with a certain New Zealander who would become my lifelong friend.

Even the challenges on your journey serve a higher purpose. I was able to help the young man find his hostel because I was able to pay his way until he could exchange his money. The young couple

I approached directed me to a safe and comfortable place with availability. The next morning, my timing was such that I checked in to my new hostel at the *right time* for being given a bunk bed with a woman who was my future BFF. And I learned a great tool for my journey ahead: always know where you'll be staying the night you arrive in a new place *and know how to get there*. There was so much to be grateful for, even in this unpleasant and exhausting experience. So, find something to be thankful for, and gratitude eventually will reside within you, and you will feel like a lighter person for it.

Another way to say your Thanking Prayers is to use a section of your journal to record them. It will be fun to revisit your trip through this lens, and the exercise of writing them down will also help you train your brain to think positively.

Enlightenment Prayers

This is the advanced stuff here, people. You are not necessarily going to be tapping into enlightenment with a snap of your fingers. But, as with all things, the more you practice, the better you get.

With both Asking Prayers and Thanking Prayers, you are thinking and speaking from your own perspective. Enlightenment Prayers ask you to do the opposite. With an Enlightenment Prayer, you meditate on being a part of God (or on being part of the energy of the Universe). We begin with the premise: everything that exists is happening now. You become more aware of this while traveling than at any other time. You likely know what your friends and family are doing at home, but now you also know what the people of Milan are doing today, what the tourists in Phuket are doing, and what the monks in a Balinese temple are doing. You hear traffic or animals or the surf, and you realize that every reality is happening right now, all at once. You live your life tuned in to *your* reality, which is such a small slice of the whole. Billions of people and living things are tuned in to *their* realities at the same time. In this way, an inchworm in the Amazon is experiencing a reality that is as real and relevant to it as your reality is to you as you're living it right this second.

Since Enlightenment Prayers are more meditative and receptive rather than conscious and active, you will need to find either a peaceful place to practice or develop strategies to help you tune the world out. Try beginning here: sitting or standing in a comfortable position, take some deep and cleansing breaths. Spend some time stretching you muscles, rolling your head and shoulders, limbering up your body, and releasing any stress or upset. Tune in to the thought that everything that exists right now exists simultaneously. Picture all the different life experiences and realities happening concurrently right now. Picture this energy in whatever way works for you. You may imagine it as a white light or a feeling of love or the sound of white noise as every sound that exists hums together in unison. There is no wrong way to do this. There is only your way. If you have no idea at all how to do this, feel free to visit the Mystical Backpacker website, where a free meditation will help you get started.

I first discovered this type of meditative prayer during my time on Mallorca. I would sit on my knees or cross-legged and imagine a beautiful white light pouring down onto me from heaven. I would raise my arms up toward the white light and would feel love. Now, I need to emphasize here that I had no reason to feel particularly loved or loving during this time in my life. I was estranged from my mother, hadn't seen my father but once a year for nearly three years, and had no boyfriend. I had no family around me and was truly alone but for a few friends. So, connecting to this feeling of unifying love was really different from my daily life and very precious to me as a result. I would sit in this love for a long time, and by the time I'd reemerge, I would feel connected to all that exists. I would know that we are all part of God, one with each other. Being in this love bubble is some serious mystical stuff, I'm telling you. It's delightful and amazing and feels at once enlightening and enlightened. Once you emerge from this love bubble, it feels as though you are a much realer version of yourself. You won't feel as separate and insecure. You will feel more united with the world around you and whole in your own skin. I encourage you to find the way that works for you—there is no wrong way—and connect to all that is. When you seek enlightenment, you become lighter. Your troubles, your worries, your burdens you have carried so long—they fall to the wayside, and your spirit is buoyant, your heart fuller, and the grip of your fears dissipates. It never ceases to amaze me that in connecting with what is so much larger than myself ends up making me feel whole and connected instead of insignificant. This, more than anything, convinces me that God resides within us as well as without.

As you journey outward to know the world and inward to know yourself as a Mystical Backpacker, praying is an energetic road that assists you on both of these paths. It is an inward exercise that connects you with the biggest picture there is. Aim for Asking and Thanking Prayers to be a part of your daily practice and Enlightenment Prayers to be something you practice at least three times a week.

Reflection

The third Mystical Tool in your toolbox is reflection. I'm not talking about looking in a mirror (although mirror work can certainly be part of this process for some of us). I'm talking about reflecting on the events of your life. I love the scene in the movie *Moonstruck* when Loretta Castorini (played by Cher) goes into the confessional booth. She confesses, "Twice I took the name of God in vain, once I slept with the brother of my fiancé, and once I bounced a check at the liquor store—but that was really an accident." The priest replies, "Then it's not a sin. But what was that second thing you said, Loretta?" They discuss, briefly, and after giving her penance, he tells her in a somewhat plaintive voice and while pinching his fingers up toward heaven, "Be careful, Loretta. Reflect on your life."[3]

It's exceptional advice. In Loretta's case, we learn that when she was widowed years earlier, she came to believe she's cursed in love. Her decision to marry someone she doesn't love is her way of addressing the curse and finding a way to be married despite it. But as Nick Cage, playing the dashing brother of said fiancé, says, "Playing it safe is just about the most dangerous thing a woman like you could do." I love that line.[4]

Sometimes, the only way to move forward is by going back. In this way, reflecting on your life can be the best way to illuminate the road ahead. Why do you believe the things you believe? Why do you feel the way you do? What feelings are difficult for you to experience? What memories do you default to when you are happy or sad or upset? What have you been told by others (that does not serve your highest good) and are complicit in ascribing to? What do you regret in life? Will the things you want really be enough to undo these beliefs and memories? Are these remedies real or fiction? An honest appraisal and a digging in to the sleeping giant of your soul will truly be the work that heals you from the inside out. This is why you're traveling alone. You can't do all this reflecting when the muddle of other people's plans and wants tugs you away from it. This is soul work of the highest order.

As you journey—processing your memories and your beliefs—remember that while your memories may cause you to feel upset with some of the people in your life, you cannot control how others act or what others think. You can only control your own thoughts and actions. So, do so. Feel your feelings: good and bad. Remember your memories: happy and unhappy. Examine the beliefs you hold to be true about the world and about yourself as a result of these experiences. Do you think you are unworthy? Do you think you are misunderstood? What do you spend most of your time thinking about? What do you believe to be true? Are these beliefs real? Are these truths real? You are complicit in their existence. You accept these beliefs as true. You accept these thoughts as true. Why? Discover that. You may take only the first step of that journey on this trip. You may realize the fallacy of your belief system on this trip and return home to seek a counselor or church, a new community or teacher and continue to dig deeper and deeper into reassessing your beliefs. You may spend the rest of your life "unlearning" these beliefs. But in recognizing them, you are freeing yourself.

We are on this good, green earth whether we understand the reason for it or not. Let's make the best of it. Be healthy, know yourself, understand, and have compassion for the person you are as a result of the experiences you've had, and then let the impact of those events be loosed from your current self. This type of intense reflection will enable you to understand who you believe yourself to be and then to distinguish those beliefs from who you actually are. It is time to honor the true you. In this Reflection Work, you are removing the harness you wear in life and learning that you are free to make choices unencumbered by the dogma of your early life experiences. You are not cursed in love, despite what your life experiences have taught you. Just like Loretta, you too can choose to play it safe and sell your life short, or you can choose to take a risk and believe you deserve the life you actually want. It is always up to you.

There are a number of exercises at the end of this chapter that will help you to begin your Reflection Work. I encourage you to do them all. You may also seek out additional resources that will also serve as useful tools for you in this process. However, if you find a program that you'd like to do, please wait to do it until you return home. A program might detach you from the opportunities aligning with you on your Mystical Backpacking odyssey. This journey is about allowing the world around you to be your program, so it's important to interact with the world when you're not using your Mystical Tools. Document your Reflection Work in your journal. It will be the most valuable information you turn to in the future. You wouldn't think you could forget your breakthroughs, but some fences are tough to tear down. Turning back to this work once you return home will be something that will help you to realize new and different choices in your life.

Journaling (I Can't Believe She's Talking about This Again)

I know. I know. I've said it before. But I also know how traveling gets—at first you miss a day, and then four, and then all of a sudden you're thinking you'll write this stuff down when you get home. Don't try to fool me; I've been there! Throughout your Mystical Backpacking experience, journaling is a task you don't want to skimp on; this is the fourth Mystical Tool. Keeping a journal may seem a banal exercise, but by journaling, you are actually constructing a mystical portal. As you travel the interior landscapes of your soul and the exterior landscapes of the places you're passing through, keeping a journal builds your portal word by word. Record your thoughts and observations. Record details about the people you meet, what you read, or see or hear that resonates with you and why. If you think you see a sign, write it down. When you finish a particularly powerful prayer, record the experience. When you finish a reflection session, write down what emerges when you do.

The only reason I am able to share some of my stories with you now is because I wrote them down in my journal. For example, I had completely forgotten the story of meeting the young man from Japan and searching for a hostel. Memory is a tricky thing—the way I recounted it in my mind, I'd gone straight to my hostel and all had been immediately well. I wouldn't know the names of places I'd been or people I'd met had I not written about them in my journal. I filled my journals with words, but I also glued in photos, coasters, postcards, product labels, tickets, and all sorts of visual reminders of the places I'd been. All of my Reflection Work is recorded in my journals. While doing the work all those years ago was incredibly insightful in the moment, I continue to learn from it anew each time I reread the work now. I am able to do that only because I recorded the work in my journal. Your journal will become a doorway you step through to access your mystical experiences long after you have returned from your trip. While the dividends from your journey are something you can treasure forever, the intangible magic that occurred daily will begin to ebb from memory. As such, you will store those memories on the page and recover them morsel by delicious morsel at another time. In this way, your odyssey never fades.

Months or perhaps even years from now, you will look back through your journal and the moment when your life changed will be clear. The messages you received from people or observations you made will be recognized as signs for what was to come. You are a cartographer, recording the map of the new lands you are discovering: the new you. Do so in detail, and you will be grateful you did. You don't need to record every sneeze and every meal, but honor the broad strokes of each day in ink and you'll thank yourself for years to come.

Paying It Forward

Here it is: the final tool in your Mystical Toolbox, completing the five tools we've explored in this chapter. As you begin to experience the happiness, mysticism, and magic of Mystical Backpacking, make a conscious effort to pay it forward as well. Just as you were blessed with having the right people turn up in your life at the right time, so can you be the right person for someone else. Pay attention to the world around you and do what you can to be the best you can be. Hold the door open for others. Help a person struggling with a load of groceries. Smile at someone who looks to be on the verge of tears. As you begin to experience the mystical, you will become increasingly aware that we are all connected. Our lives coming together at once in this grand picture is the miracle of the moment. Open your heart and your spirit to it regularly and know that you make a difference each and every day. You may not see immediate returns on these acts out in the real world, but you will *feel* the return immediately. When you are being the best you can be, it feels amazing! As you move through your days being this kind and giving person, your light will touch others and help their lights to grow a little brighter too. Sensing your openness and generosity, people will spend more time talking with you, helping you, and making your life easier.

When Lisa and I were on the island of Cyprus, we experienced the glorious alchemy of this process in significant ways. We were really worried about money. We were paid a small sum of money for our work delivering the boat to Cyprus, and it was depleted by half its amount in less than a week's time on Cyprus. We still had another five weeks of travel ahead of us! What would we do? We began to economize with serious determination. We bought canned foods for lunches and walked rather than take a bus or taxi. If we rented a car, we slept in it. If we slept elsewhere, it was in a tent. Despite our worries and material troubles, as we explored the island, we walked and laughed and exclaimed and pointed, and a remarkable thing began to occur: everywhere we went, people gave us food.

I remember an old woman who flagged us down. We walked over to her gate and tried to greet her in her own language. She pressed fruit into our hands and smiled at us, chattering away and waving her hands over our heads. I think she was blessing us. One afternoon we hiked a mountain, and at the crest of it, another old woman gave us each an apple. How an old woman ended up at the top of that very tall mountain, I will never know. Yet another day we were paying for our groceries in a small supermarket, and Lisa didn't have enough money in her wallet to pay for her bill. We were putting our daily allowance into our wallets and hiding the rest of our money in our backpacks. My money had just run out with my purchase. She would have to unpack everything to get at her cash, as would I. Instead, she began to search for items to remove from her purchase. This whole exchange took mere seconds, but once the teller realized what was happening, he simply waived her on, insisting she take all her groceries and that the money she had already paid was enough.

Time and again, people greeted us with open arms and helped us feel blessed and full and safe. It was with great relief that we arrived in Greece and realized our money would go much further there. From this point on, no one gave us food. I truly believe that our ability to be cheerful and open with everyone we met and to trust that everything would work out well for us contributed to our material needs being met. It was as though our positive attitudes created a positive-energy loop between us and the world we interacted with each day. Paying it forward by projecting your happiness and gratitude out to the people around you is a marvelous way to create the right energy for the extraordinary to enter your life.

I want to take a moment to note that Mystical Backpacking isn't a religion. It's a path for discovering the secrets of your soul and feeling the connection between the divine within you and the divine without. As such, there are no rules and regulations. However, chances are you aren't used to using these Mystical Tools heavily in your everyday life. You do have to become conscious of making an effort to do new things as you respond to life in a new way. When you're on a diet, you have to remind yourself not to eat the tray of hot, fresh, sugary doughnuts. When you're doing your Mystical Backpacking, remind yourself as often as possible to use your Mystical Tools.

Now that you've tackled your tools, it's time to focus on some real-life strategies for cultivating a healthy frame of mind to accompany you and your toolbox in your travels—one that best enables those situations that serve your highest good to manifest. Your thoughts are the fuel in your engine. If you have bad fuel, progress is slow, stilted, and oftentimes arrested completely. The following strategies are all about having high-octane thoughts.

Rise Up to Meet the Journey

You might think that once you've bought a ticket, packed your bags, and actually left town, you're emotionally and psychologically invested in your journey. While you should be proud of yourself for this monumental achievement (yay, you!), don't interpret this as an indication that you are personally invested in ensuring you get all you can from it. Oftentimes, our first response to being in a new situation is to put up walls around us. It's a defense mechanism that keeps us feeling safe and makes us appear formidable or unapproachable to others. Some of us might keep ourselves forever occupied in solitary tasks (texting, emailing, reading, working on our computers, listening to our iPods), and while this does help us pass the time, it is often an obstacle to meeting new people and trying new things. Yes, read and yes, journal—but also remember that while yours is an inward journey, it's being manifested outwardly. What's especially important to keep in mind is that you need to be open enough to allow new people and experiences to come into your life while you're making new ground as a Mystical Backpacker. In this way, you rise above any discomfort you might be experiencing (internally and externally) and meet the journey head-on, receiving those people and opportunities placed on your path rather than resisting them.

One of the mystical aspects of Mystical Backpacking is to trust that you are in the right place at the right time and to follow your intuition and gut instincts when you're not. For this reason in particular you should endeavor to meet new people, have discussions, and learn from each new experience. Be open and receptive. Talk with the person you're sitting next to. Ask questions. Listen. And when talking about yourself, be honest. Be your authentic self, not the self you wish to be. You absolutely can say, "I'm a successful businessperson, and I hate my job, and I'm traveling to find my purpose in life because I don't think I'm on the right path," if that's your personal truth. You'll be amazed at the stories you will hear in return. Some of them will make all the difference. If you project a false persona, these stories won't make their way to you. When you are reaching out to the world around you in pure spirit and with an open heart, you will not be as likely to fall into the dark recesses of your mind where self-doubt and self-criticism lurk. Be open. Be honest. Receive the world around you warmly and respond to the world around you honestly.

On this trip you are learning to embrace freedom physically and metaphysically: you are discovering the world, and you are discovering and honoring your authentic self. This effort is wasted if you bring any limiting beliefs you may hold along with you and employ them in the new relationships you begin. Believe that the risks you're taking will reward you. If you're drawn to someone and think, *I'd love to be friends with that person*, then don't just sit there wishing. As Grandpa Gustafson says in *Grumpier Old Men*, "You can wish in one hand and crap in the other and see which gets filled first."[5] Wishing doesn't yield results. Take action. If you're invited to join a table of people, join them! Imagine that every possibility is like a blind date: uncomfortable, anxiety-ridden . . . but sometimes you meet someone you'll know for the rest of your life. Stick your neck out for sometimes.

You'll Never Walk Alone

Rome, the third city of my odyssey, was a turning point for me. This was where I truly began to open myself up and trust meeting new people. It was here I met Kay, a young woman who worked at the hostel where I was staying. One night, she invited me out to the local Irish pub to celebrate the Arsenals beating the Celtics in a soccer match. All the Brits in Rome were converging on this bar to celebrate, despite it being a Sunday night. I had no idea what the night held for me. The biggest celebrator at the bar was a young man named Neil who was already three sheets to the wind when we arrived and spent most of the night calling out, "Who bet, we bet, who bet, we bet, who bet, we bet, the Arsenals!" The bar was packed. Everyone was happy and joking, and we played billiards in the festive ambience. Each time I tried to excuse myself to go home and go to bed, someone would buy me another drink. By night's end, all sorts of weepy singing of Liverpool and Arsenal songs had erupted, and we closed the bar. An Italian man bought Kay and me each a rose in the wee hours of the morn—my first and only Valentine—as the next day was the fourteenth of February. As I talked with the group of people I'd been introduced to, they shared their personal stories with me.

Steve and Linda had decided to leave California the year before and had maxed out their lines of credit to open the Beehive hostel in Rome, the very hostel I was staying at. They'd been at 80 percent occupancy ever since and were so pleased with their venture and their relocated life just up the road from the Colosseum. I recently Googled them and am happy to report the Beehive still exists and has grown into a high-end, eco-friendly hostel and hotel. Nearly fifteen years later, it's been well reviewed by dozens of international travel magazines.

Adam, an artist from San Francisco, was living in Europe and working at the hostel while embarking on a spiritual and creative journey through *The Artist's Way*. He shared with me that it was proving to be a profoundly creative and spiritual experience for him.

Shane, an Irish man staying at the hostel, told me his story of personal triumph. He was working a factory job he hated and felt like he was going nowhere fast. All his friends were graduating university, and he was turning into a drunk. His family supported him for a year while he fell apart in personal despair. Then he got a job volunteering at a hospital. He was naturally good with patients, and everyone encouraged him to study nursing. His self-esteem was very low, but he gathered what little confidence he had and went to nursing school. When I met him, he was working in a burn trauma unit and was recognized as one of the best nurses on staff in the ward.

I met an American named Senjett, who had been about to start medical school and realized he wasn't absolutely sure about his choice. Born in Calcutta, he felt he was earning the degree more for his parents than himself. He told them he was taking a year off to live abroad, and he was now teaching English in Vienna. Through the people he met and the course he took there, he discovered that he *did* want to be in medicine but with a focus on international medicine. He wanted to work in war-torn regions.

Australian Suzie had stayed with friends all over the world while traveling, and her cheerfulness and friendliness inspired me to be more open myself. We spent the next couple of days together, walking arm in arm and giggling like schoolgirls through the streets of Rome.

And Kay, the desk clerk at my hostel, shared her story. She had left Liverpool without a dime to her name, feeling very much like a loser. She was now in love with her cosmopolitan life in Rome;

in taking this step and living this life, she felt like she was *someone* and was really proud of herself whenever she visited home and met an old high school friend and was able to report what she was doing now.

That night out was like a cloud of happy affirmation that drifted beneath me and lifted me up in buoyant spirit. Had I not gone, each of these beautiful souls and the inspiring stories of soul searching and risk taking in the pursuit of deep personal happiness would not have touched my soul. It was fitting the night ended with voices raised and singing the words to Liverpool's anthem, "You'll Never Walk Alone" by Gerry & the Pacemakers. If you've never heard it, Google it now and be prepared to have your heartstrings tugged. From this point on, I truly didn't walk alone.

That first night out was only the beginning of a potent time of travel when people who were aligned with my own soul searching came in and out of my life, sharing their brave stories and happy endings. That night, my trust in the process of my journey was fostered, and I began to open up my mind and heart to the people around me and speak my personal truths uncensored.

We Can't All Be Soul Mates

I was once talking with a friend of mine about the distinction between friendly-friends and soul-mate friends. Once you've entered adulthood, most of the friends you tend to make are friendly-friends. They are your neighbors, your colleagues at work, the other parents in your child's class, and so on. You may see them often, invite them to your parties, and send them holiday cards, but the conversations tend to be light and neutral or related to third-party topics (politics, news, courses at the community center, good gyms, where to shop, etc.). You don't necessarily discuss the topics close to home, close to your heart. You're not sharing the details of your childhood or the challenges of having an alcoholic parent or that your career is not what you wanted for yourself. There's more propriety, more smiling, and more chitchat. While everyone needs fun chitchat from time to time, it's not very rewarding in a deeper sense. When you have a problem, you are not calling these friends in tears to ask for their advice or reassurance. When you have a triumph, you don't necessarily call them first to share it. That's what your soul-mate friends are for.

With soul-mate friends, you don't feel the need to edit yourself. You blurt out your thoughts, however offensive some of them may be, and you are never tarnished in their eyes. You can talk candidly about your worries, your problems, your hopes, and your goals. Soul-mate friends are champions rooting for your success and try hard never to kick you when you're down. They're more likely to cry with you. Time and distance never affect your soul-mate friendships. You can go a year without talking to your friend, pick up the phone, and be in the midst of a heartfelt conversation within minutes. When you haven't seen each other in years and are reunited, you are immediately sitting across from one another, leaning in to hear better, squeezing hands, rubbing arms, or slapping backs with the body language of beloved siblings. Soul-mate friends are rare, harder to find, and precious to living a life of abundance. Without them, life can seem lonely, and you can feel misunderstood at best, alienated at worst. Soul-mate friends are your people. They make you feel as though you have a place in the world and a strong connection to the people who occupy it. During the aforementioned conversation, my friend and I were talking about how and where soul-mate friends are found. She suggested I make a list of my dearest friends and note how I came to know them. I did. It was a revelation.

Every soul-mate friend I have, I met while doing something brave. Whenever I have pushed myself to do something I didn't want to do or wanted to do but was afraid to do, I met someone who befriended my most authentic self and is still my friend today. Because I took the action to move toward my dreams, the Universe gifted me with a person to share that experience with.

It's vital to remember to rise up and meet the journey with openness and honesty. Know that as you travel this road while adhering to the rise-up-and-meet-the-journey philosophy, the right people will enter your life as a result and you will feel a sense of connectedness and belonging, despite being in new and uncharted places in both your exterior and interior worlds. You will meet new friends. You will also meet soul mates and kindred spirits. Some of them will be your friends for life.

What Might Rising Up Yield?

A major chapter in my life occurred only because I was willing to connect with strangers and trust the direction in which they took me. I was riding a train from Naples, Italy, to Barcelona, Spain. I was going to stop in Nice, France, which was roughly the halfway point between the two. My reason for stopping in Nice was simple. My grandmother always served these delicate rectangular vanilla cookies with sugar crystals on top. They were called Nice. I thought I'd honor my grandmother's memory by stopping there, but as the train pulled into Nice, it just didn't feel right to get off. The thought of Nice had me feeling empty, and the thought of Barcelona had me feeling full. So I stayed on the train and rode straight through to Barcelona.

Barcelona is a bustling city where the modern and the medieval juxtapose. I made my way to the well-reviewed hostel in the center of it all and checked in. In my exhaustion, I threw myself into the lower bunk and slept. When I awoke, a cheerful blond New Zealander named Lisa (yep, *that* Lisa) was in the bunk above me. She claimed

I had slept in her bunk. I insisted I hadn't. Turns out, after much debate, she was right. We laughed it off and decided to stay where we were. Later that day, Lisa approached me in the common area and invited me to go dancing with her that night. She was celebrating her twenty-sixth birthday and was backpacking alone. I was celebrating my twenty-sixth birthday and was backpacking alone. We were born at the same time on opposite sides of the world.

After spending several days together enjoying Barcelona, Lisa had plans to go to Ireland, and I had plans to go to Paris.

We decided to go to the train station together to buy our tickets. There was a very long line, and as we stood in the Spanish sun and enjoyed a sunny February day together, the thought of riding alone into the cold, gray north began to permeate our reality. Moments from the ticket counter, I turned to her and suggested we buy ferry tickets to Mallorca, a Spanish island in the Mediterranean, instead. She looked at me, giggled, and said, "Yes!" Less than four hours later, we were on a ferry headed toward a totally new and unplanned future. On Mallorca, I met two other soul-mate friends: one who would start as a lover and the other as a roommate but both of whom have become my lifelong friends. My life is different, and I am a different person for knowing Lisa, Martin, and Simon. When life causes me to falter, they are my touchstones and remind me of the magic inside me—the magic that *is* me.

What would have happened if I had stayed at the hostel and not gone out with Kay that night in Rome, where I learned that I was not alone? What would have happened if I had gone to Nice instead of staying on the train and riding through to Barcelona? What if I had declined Lisa's invitation to go dancing? What if I had thought she would laugh at me if I suggested Mallorca and not uttered my thought aloud? Because I was able to take the risks that felt right, I am now in a position where I don't have to worry about what-ifs—I am so deeply fulfilled by what-actuallys. In each case, because I decided to rise up to meet the journey, the journey likewise rose up to meet me. It became a symbiotic relationship, and I was truly in the flow of Mystical Backpacking.

Mystical Exercises: Chapter 4

With your outer journey now launched, you will begin to experience the mystical in your daily life, most especially if you're regularly employing the tools from your Mystical Toolbox. As such, the exercises for the next few chapters (beginning here) focus solely on your inner journey and facilitate the process of excavating the truths buried deep within you. They guide you in connecting with your driving desires, your inner compass, and the beliefs upon which your behaviors and actions are sourced. Remember that this process is symbiotic, and the magic of mystical backpacking is a result of that beautiful alchemy of traveling the outer world while concurrently traveling the inner one.

Self-awareness is a vital ingredient for self-improvement of any sort. As you tap into a lightness of being through your travel experience, it's important to use this opportunity to unburden yourself within as well. While your mind may be distracted by the glorious sights you're seeing, the constant low-grade pain caused by your sore feet, and the dilemmas your stomach faces in navigating the new menus you're sampling, your soul remembers all the truths that support you in being you, regardless of where you are.

Along the way, you'll likely find that some of those truths are actually limiting beliefs based on how you've interpreted certain events in your life. As I've said from the very beginning, Mystical Backpacking is an outward journey that facilitates an inner journey. Even though the outward journey is such a big enterprise in itself, the inner journey is the one that will free you. Completing this next exercise is a vital part of that journey. It may take you several days, and that's totally fine. You do not need to finish answering the questions in one sitting. It is important that you complete all the work below, but do it on your own time, in your own way.

Your Inner Map

Maps help us navigate the outer world. Would that we had a map of our inner world—how much easier navigating our own lives might be. Metaphorically, this next exercise helps you create a map of your inner world. The following questions and fill-in-the-blank statements make up one big, juicy exercise for this chapter. The important thing is you consider each question, and then answer it, in whatever manner you like, but I do encourage you to start and finish each question in order, not skipping around.

The Present Moment

1. This place ________________ reminds me of ______________. When I think of this memory, I feel ________________ because ________________.
2. This person I met ____________ reminds me of ______________. This reminder makes me feel _______________________ because __________________.
3. This person I met ___________________________ makes me feel ________________. When I feel this way, I am (circle):

Happy	Angry	Sad	Stressed
Worried	Enlightened	Unburdened	Safe

Inspired	Adventurous	Lonely	Connected
Uplifted	Hopeful	Other (explain):____________	

____

Rose and Thorn

Each day, record your rose and your thorn. This exercise requires you to state what part of your day was a sweet gift (like a rose) and what part was a challenge to deal with (like a thorn). Recognizing that both are part of the whole, begin to understand that your challenges bring forth your best moments as well. Recording your rose and your thorn will help you become aware of what you do or do not easily notice in life.

Happy Lessons

Make a list of your ten happiest memories in life. What has each taught you about life in general, or your life specifically? Do these lessons ring true to you? If they do, keep them. If they don't, you can identify them as false and begin to work toward letting them go.

Sad Lessons

Make a list of your ten saddest memories you've experienced in your life so far. What has each taught you about life in general or your life specifically? Do these lessons ring true to you? If they do, keep them. If they don't, list five ways in which your life or your attitude toward your life would improve by letting them go. Seeing this in writing, answer honestly: are you ready to let these beliefs go?

Meeting New People

When you meet new people at this point in your life, how do you feel? Open and excited? Do you feel defensive or lonely? Do you want to please them? Often, our behavior (which we may be unaware of) has nothing to do with the other person. Analyzing our own emotions teaches us more about ourselves than assessing other people's behavior will. Honestly analyze how it feels for you to meet new people. Once this is done, you may be a little surprised by what you've discovered.

Using this information, create a personal affirmation you can repeat to yourself internally whenever you meet new people. Affirmations are positive statements in the present tense that help to reprogram thoughts and behaviors. For example, your personal affirmation may be: *It is safe to be my authentic self, or, I employ healthy boundaries and ease into new friendships.*

Relationship Lessons

Create a table of five columns. In the far left one, list the name of each significant person you have had a relationship with in your life to-date. These can include your best friends in childhood, your best friends now, your closest siblings and relatives, and your romantic relationships as well. In the next columns, moving from left to right: include what was wonderful about each relationship, what was challenging about each relationship, and why the relationship ended, if it did. The fifth column can be a yes or no answer to the question. Were you able to envision a future with each person (a simple yes or no will suffice)? Do you see a pattern? Are there things you need to be aware of (about yourself especially) as you move forward with choosing your next relationship(s)? This exercise is great for both romantic and nonromantic relationships. (I created charts for both while on my trip.)

Favorite Things

Make at least three lists of your favorite things in different categories. For example, make a list of your favorite books, movies, quotes, poems, sports, places, foods, etc. Find your pleasures! Now, think about what common threads tie all these favorites together. What are the common themes? Adventure? Love? Triumph? Security? Home? Write these observations down under your lists. This exercise can help put you in touch with what drives you and motivates you.

The Perfect Life

If you could imagine the perfect life with no limitations, what would it look like? Write a page or two describing your ideal life in detail. Where do you live, who do you live with, what do you do each day, what foods do you eat, what do you see and experience daily—describe it all in rich detail. Remember, this is the ideal; it can't get more perfect than this. As it goes in *Field of Dreams*, "If you build it, [it] will come."[6] You can't build without a vision. So, start envisioning! This exercise will be the foundation stone for another exercise later in this book.

Top 10 Lists

Answer the following three questions about life in general:

The top ten things I dislike most are:

The top ten things that make me angry are:

The top ten things that inspire me are:

My First Memory

Describe your earliest childhood memory in detail. How has this memory impacted your thoughts and beliefs about the world, the people in it, and your experience of life? Even if the memory is a small and seemingly insignificant one, see what you can extrapolate from it.

Who Taught You to Be Happy?

Who was the person who made you happiest as a child? Why? What is the best memory you have of that person?

Favorite People

Make a list of your favorite people in your life. Describe why each of them has made the list. Do these people help you to feel loved, supported, or accepted? The qualities you identify in them are the qualities you might wish to align yourself with in your future relationships.

Least Favorite People

Make a list of the people in your life you dislike interacting with. Describe why each of them has made the list. Do these people drain and deplete you, make you feel criticized and judged? These are the qualities you may wish to avoid in your future relationships.

Top 10 Stressors

What are the top ten stressors in your life? Imagine yourself moving through your days back at home and write a list that includes your recurring stressors. Is it the phone ringing incessantly? Are parents constantly sticking their noses in your affairs? Is a hellish commute causing you to be sweaty, angry, and exhausted before you even get to work? The little things (your leaky shower that annoys you every morning, the burnt coffee at work, the dog that barks all night) can really add up to create a constant low-grade stress over the course of the day. The big stressors (the boss you can't stand, the extra twenty pounds you can't lose, an unhealthy relationship in your life) often distract us from all the little stressors—so making little changes can often make a huge difference for the better and give us the breathing room and energy with which to tackle some of the bigger stressors.

Offsetting Stressors

Using the above list, make a plan for how you might immediately address some of these little stressors once you return home. If the phone disturbs you during your most productive morning hours, maybe you'll decide you won't turn your phone on until after lunch each day. If your commute is killing you, maybe you'll decide to join a carpool. Come up with solutions you can work on implementing immediately upon your return home.

If I Could Change 3 Things . . .

If you could change three things about your life at home right away with the wave of a magic wand, what would they be? Be completely honest with yourself. Why do you want to change these three things? What fears have stopped you from making these changes? How would your life be different if you made these changes? How would you feel if you actually made these changes? Explore all your thoughts and emotions associated with these questions and write them all down. This will be extremely useful to see in print.

Grab yourself a refreshing drink and relax in a comfy spot—that was hard work! The perspective gained in answering these questions far from home and from your new vantage point will prove invaluable in the days to come. It no doubt took a lot of time, effort, honesty, and bravery to answer all those questions and to dig so deep. You have done yourself a great kindness in spending this time on yourself. You have honored your soul's experiences; you have released some uncomfortable thoughts and brought to the surface some uncomfortable feelings, and in so doing, you have allowed your soul to honestly express itself without—or perhaps, more important, despite—fear. Recognizing that this may be a new experience for you, give yourself a pat on the back. Be compassionate with yourself. Be kind to yourself. You are the beginning and the end of *you*. The most important thing is to take care of who you are at the core. You have done some incredible healing work and allowed yourself to process some pretty unforgiving truths. In bringing them to the light, you have made it possible for them to lose their hold on you. Well done!

After some time backpacking—for me it was around the three-week mark, but for you it might be sooner or later—you'll start to feel that you can't go on with the pace of sightseeing, mystical exercising, and journaling you've been keeping. Don't get me wrong; you absolutely will not want to go home! You'll just be too tired to keep going at full throttle. Your feet, your muscles, your mental and emotional stamina will all be depleted. You'll need to stop and rest somewhere for several days or close to a week. And when you do, it will feel so good you won't know how to resume regular life after all this. You'll be fully present in each moment and the need to be productive in order to pass the time will ebb. You will shift gears and reduce speed, spending more time indulging in pleasure. As the minutes turn into hours and the hours turn into days, you may begin to think or feel like you don't want to go back home again. You may even try to figure out a way in which you won't have to. The possibility of living life differently, free of responsibilities, may become a persistent thought that seduces your waking moments. You'll have entered the Land of the Lotus Eaters.

5

Idle Days: Hitting Your Stride, and Then Entering the Land of the Lotus Eaters

How to Conquer the Wild World: 1. Yell "Be Still!"
2. Stare it down without blinking even once.
Then, you will be the wildest thing of all.
—Maurice Sendak, *Where the Wild Things Are* (paraphrase)

We sailed from Palermo the morning I saw the fish jump and took it as a sign, heading through the Strait of Messina and into the churning, gunmetal-gray Ionian Sea.

Though the sun shone brightly, the winds picked up to gale force 8 and force 9 as measured by the Beaufort scale. Imagine a toy boat in a little boy's bathtub. He violently splashes the water around in glee, and the boat tosses up and down erratically. That was our experience in a very wet, choppy nutshell. The waves were up to twenty-one feet high, and our boat was small. Inside it, we were airborne half the time. We pitched about the whole day, bullying forward while the weather worsened and the faces of our crew grew increasingly grim. Seeing land nearby was immensely reassuring, and we did stay close to shore, but our progress was stunted, and by day's end, the captain conceded we had to find a port to seek refuge in until it was safe to go on.

Altogether, we spent four days in a marina in Crotone, a small town in the heel of Italy's boot. Here I entered a prolific time of self-reflection and the mental solitude needed for processing my own self-prescribed mystical assignments. I explored patterns in my relationships, both romantic and platonic. I explored familial ties and dynamics. I deconstructed my belief systems and sourced where each belief, whether limiting or expansive, had originated in my psyche. While I still lost sleep or dreamed the haunting dreams we often experience when our way ahead is unclear, I also made full use of the long expanses of blustery days in the arid sun. I remember fruit granitas cooling us in town, friendly stray dogs guarding our boat at the marina, and fuzzy green almonds fresh from the tree given to us by the store clerk at the small shop where we restocked our supplies. But most of all, I remember being on the ship for hours upon hours of quiet stillness and working through the story of my life on paper. Who was I? Why was I this person? What did I know to be true? *Was* it true? Crotone's unassuming nature fostered a time during which I found new places within myself.

I continued to experience signs and answers to prayers.

8 pm Capo Rizzuto, Crotone (south of Italy)
Another sign I'm on the right path:

Still very windy out. We're in a large port (Porto Nuovo—a commercial port) waiting to be allowed into a marina 1 km away (Porto Vecchio). We're at empty piers just holding onto them for safe harbor, but we are far from shore, far from town. We are in the middle of nowhere with water and wind surrounding us. And a dandelion seed pod blows in through the back doors and into my hand. I make a wish, let it go, and it flies back out the door again after swirling around the doorway a few (3?) times.

Setting wishes aside, I dared to envision what my ideal life might look like were it to be whole and fulfilling to my authentic self. I committed the vision to paper in letters inked to the bobbing motion of the smaller waves in port. The letters did not seem to embody struggle or want but possibility. Could it be this simple? Could I learn to understand my responses to life and surpass limitations by changing my thinking or perspective? I was becoming convinced this might be the case. Perhaps a whole and fulfilling life was both possible and plausible and not just the stuff of dreams.

June 17, 2000

My Fulfilling and Balanced Life

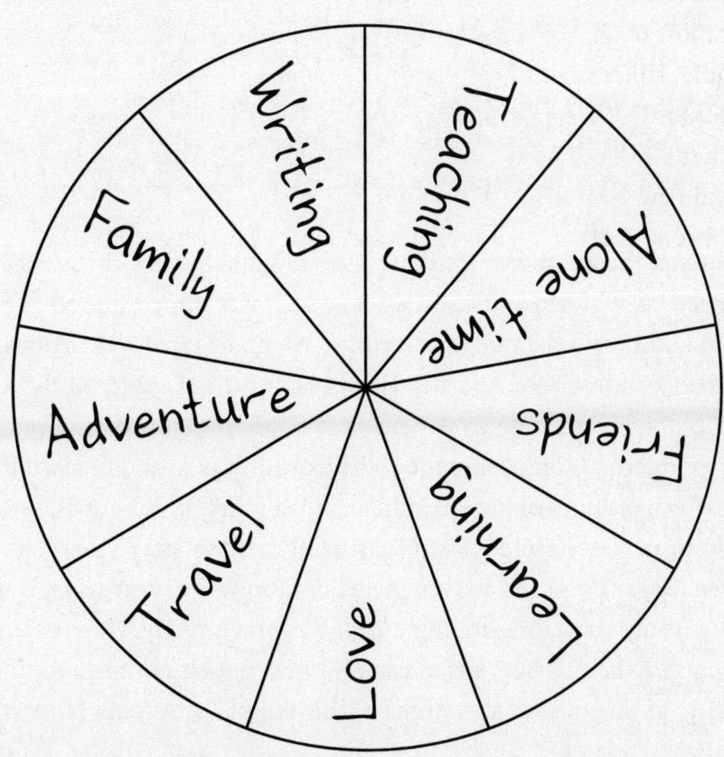

Writing

I see myself as a writer. I have my own room for writing that has a view. It doesn't have to be a big room, but it should be bright. My view is of nature: trees and water. All of my books are arranged on shelves behind my desk. My desk faces the window and is high–like a drafting table. My chair is high and very comfortable. I have my photos and quotes and mementos stuck all over the walls. I have a door to a garden with a small private sitting area just for me. Wind chimes. Incense. Dog and/or cat hanging around. Potted plants that bloom. Candles. Private space. Office with phone, fax, supplies, copier, printer, etc. is in another space. Business end of writing (publishing) does not invade creative side of writing. I start writing early in the morning while drinking my coffee. Stop for lunch and then stop work in the afternoon sometime. Have freedom to stop/start when I want. Spurred by passion, not a time clock...

Once the weather calmed, it was as though the very chaos within me had been blown away, and what was left was ironed smooth. I felt calm and repaired as we left Crotone. We made our way northward to the Corinth Canal, and I finished reading *The Catcher in the Rye* shortly before arriving in Athens. It was startling to experience the very modern accomplishment of the Corinth Canal and to learn it is actually a product of the late nineteenth century. It was equally startling to perceive Holden's story as being written sixty years before (even longer now) and to recognize how accurate a portrayal it is for many souls struggling to come into their own today. How strange a contrast then to hop into a cab and find myself at the Acropolis, staring at the ancient structures of the Temple of Athena Nike and the Parthenon.

The temple to Athena, goddess of wisdom, companion of heroes, was erected at great cost and effort in 427 BC or so, a simple building with elegant lines and intricately carved statues and friezes rivaling the skill attained by da Vinci in his *David*. The Parthenon, built over four thousand years ago, was purposefully built crooked so as to appear straight within its environment. Had it been built with actual straight lines, it would have appeared crooked. And this achievement preceded Christ by two thousand years! Is progress simply an illusion? Have only technology and faiths changed, but our humanity remains consistently, well, human? Cue a Greek chorus reciting, "Has humanity changed? Has humanity changed?" It was too big a thought to capture for long. I posed for photos at Athena and petted the stray dogs living there.

In the days that followed, we traveled to Cyprus, where we ended our delivery contract. The *Taipan* left us on the dock in Limassol, and we watched her grace and luxury slip away with quiet elegance. The captain and first mate waved from the bridge, and we waved back until they disappeared from view. With a blank slate before us, we turned toward town and trekked with heavy packs in the high noon heat. As the sweat broke on my brow, I turned to Lisa and asked, "Where's my boat?"

That first day back on the road wasn't easy. We struggled to find a place to stay and were shocked by the high prices and great cost of the Cypriot pound. Limassol didn't exactly call to us. It was piercingly hot, and the town seemed to be suffering a drought. Dilapidated commercial buildings and tacky souvenir shops huddled up next to an industrial coastline with beaches overlooking anchored freight ships. There was no sound—it was as though every person and vehicle in town was waiting out the weather, hoping for relief to settle. By the time we were finally ensconced in a clean and spacious but slightly downtrodden hostel in the center of town, all I could do was lie limp and wet under the ceiling fan and allow my body to cool. Outside the window, a water fountain with dolphin sculptures gurgled and splashed reassuringly.

Cyprus Heat
June 24, 2000

During daytime:
No words.
The heat has melted them away.
Glaring sun
and thick air
suffocate articulation,
beneath the surface.
All energy
is spent on a futile attempt
to embrace the meaning
of the word,
cool.
This evening,
the dolphin fountain in the square
waters my senses.
Cyprus is lulled.
We are lazy dogs
in night heat,
which at least delivers respite
from the rigorous sun.
Even the moon
is warm tonight.
An opalescent,
shimmering bowl,
containing the answers
to all questions,

and pouring them
drop by drop
into the simmering sea.
Music and traffic
And dolphins
that will never swim free.

As the day waned, we were filled with regret. Why didn't we stay on the boat and sail to Lebanon? Why didn't we take a ferry right away to another island? We booked tickets to depart on the very first ferry the next morning. And then the man from the front desk stopped by our room, and his kind words inspired us to change our plans. He reminded us both of the king from *The Alchemist*.

June 25 through June 26, 2000

The man working the front desk was strange in a wonderful way, and he reshaped our entire Cyprus experience. While he had our passports he looked at all our stamps and came to our room to talk with us about all of our travels. I was already spread-eagle on the bed trying to cool down and Lisa was unpacking.

He was an odd man. Very thin. Not tall, but not short either. He was wearing a long-sleeved shirt, fully buttoned, faded trouser slacks and tattered slippers with socks. His English lacked even a hint of an accent. He had thinning hair, brushed back, and his ensemble matched the interior of his hostel. It was a clean and well-maintained space that looked like a cottage from the 1940s. Whitewashed walls. Bold flower paintings. Crochet work. Vases. Checkered tablecloths. White linen. Mismatched furniture. The nameless man (for we didn't get his name) was very graceful and slow in his movements. His questions were articulate and his responses well-considered. And he rubbed his chin or his fingers as he listened to us. We have affectionately referred to him as our Alchemist King, for he is so like the King who appears to the protagonist and reshapes his future. When The King discovered we were due to leave Cyprus the next day he was unimpressed. "Well, you should have just left on the very next ship rather than stay until tomorrow. You can't do anything in a day and there's so much to see in Cyprus," he told us. He was so convincing, Lisa ran to phone the travel agency and rebook our tickets for Wednesday instead. I spent the afternoon draped on the bed, motionless and suffering the intolerable heat. Early evening, we walked 2 km to the beach, rented a car along the way (after realizing no buses or taxis went to the good Cyprus sites [and we were determined to see them!]) and I went for a swim in the cesspool-sea. But it was refreshing, even with the industry and freight ships. Then we walked through the Old Town—actually quite charming at dusk—and ate a fabulous dinner at this small restaurant. The interior of the restaurant was all stone with wood beamed ceilings, candles, torches, interesting antiques on the walls. We sat on the patio (tables on the street) and ordered the vegetarian meze. The small plates kept coming and coming! We had couscous, tzatziki, potatoes, grilled veggies, grilled cheese, fresh bread, pastas, etc. Yum! But WAY beyond our price range.

We slept incredibly well that night, even in the heat. The next day (Sunday), we picked up our car rental (guy was late, car cost more than they said, forgot to refund our deposit and we had to go back, made us pay for £18 worth of gas up front, key was broken, etc.) and headed off towards the destinations we found in a Cyprus Walks brochure and our Lonely Planet. Of course, we got lost before finding our way—but we were on the open road, in an air-conditioned car and heading for the mountains to have some respite from the heat!

What unfolded was four days on Cyprus, where we truly encountered the mystical and supernatural, in strange and subtle ways. We visited Socrates's house in Omodos (a rural life museum that is, alas, not actually Socrates's house) and bathed in Caledonia Falls. Friendly locals welcomed us.

We drove to the top of Mount Olympus and enjoyed the brisk air (oh, sweet relief from the heat!) and ate chilled fruits while looking out at the views. We visited Kykkos Monastery and were sent away by an angry priest, dressed all in black with a pillbox hat and long beard, because Lisa wore shorts. We got lost in the Troodos Mountains after dark and happened upon a firefighters' station where we shared dinner and drinks (yes, thank you) with dozens of firefighters who offered us a room for the night (no, thank you). Leaving them, in search of our campground, we drove under a black sky illuminated by so many stars, it was as though they were sand or dust scattered across the heavens. We saw piles of rocks and sticks by the side of the road (very *Blair Witch Project*) and were chased away by soldiers in the dead of night when we came too close to the Cypriot-Turkish border. Hearts pounding in fear, we raced our car away from them and parked on a side street in a small suburb, the first sign of life after hours in the mountains and woods. We spent the night in the cramped car, parked in a haunted orange grove, both of us awakened repeatedly by a strange presence that terrorized us all through the night.

On our way to the Baths of Aphrodite early one morning, a man grabbed my hand, told me his name, sat me in a chair in the shade, and put a fresh orange and knife in my hand. He was an old man with long hair and a beard. He had a small pickup truck filled with orange tree branches, the fruit still hanging off them. He set up a clothesline and began to hang the branches from the line to sell to the tourists. Later in the day, after we had been to the baths, I saw him again, dressed as a priest. I discovered he had been kicked out of the monastery for shaving his beard and selling oranges.

That night, we slept in a campground under a grove of eucalyptus. All night we breathed air that smelled so strongly of the tree it felt like inhaling Vicks VapoRub. We saw the Tomb of the Kings the next day and slept in our car the following night, parked in a beach parking lot near the ferry. The police came by and interrogated us and then parked near us, ensuring we'd be safe. In the mountains, rabbits darted. By the shores, lizards skittered.

From Cyprus, we made our way back through the Greek islands and into southern Italy by foot, ferry, and train. I consider the six weeks of backpacking through Greece and Italy the second half of my Mystical Backpacking odyssey. While Lisa and I traveled together, we journeyed apart. After Cyprus, we parted ways most days to follow our own adventures, and we'd meet for dinner to discuss them. There was little compromise, for we never restricted each other's desires with guilt or insecurity. We ambled our own individual paths, and sometimes they happened to be parallel. On the island of Santorini we spent three days' budget on renting a jeep and buying new bikinis. We explored the entire island in a day, wearing nothing but our bikinis, hiking sandals, and straw cowboy hats while driving the jeep up steep inclines and around perilous bends. The locals called us *gringas*. White stone homes perched atop volcanic rock like vanilla frosting on a chocolate cake, and each vista was more beautiful than the next, each village more picturesque than the last, so we lost track of the number of times we said, "This is beautiful." Instead, faced with such an embarrassment of riches, we'd call out, "Bored now!" and break into peals of laughter.

We visited the Valley of the Butterflies on the island of Rhodes, where hundreds of thousands of nocturnal butterflies had settled during their mating season. I went to sponge markets piled high with natural sponges of all sizes, walked among ruins, touched walls within which more than five centuries' worth of generations had taken breath, and saw octopi hanging on laundry lines, drying in the sun. Lisa and I got horrible food poisoning in Rhodes and spent an evening lightheaded and shivering as we purged our guts in tandem. The next day, spacey and exhausted, we delicately sipped Cokes and recovered our strength in the unforgiving sun. We saw an octopus and tuna and beautiful underwater life swimming alongside us while snorkeling in clear waters guarded by ancient ruins. We also spent entire days apart, exploring museums and marketplaces, winding footpaths, and wave-whipped shorelines in peaceful solitude. Everywhere the smell of the sea, the warmth of the sun, and the sharp magenta of trailing bougainvillea in contrast with the potent cornflower blue of the sky framed the narrative of our experiences. Each day, my own inner work unfolded in sync with the outer adventures I engaged in. It had turned out that being blown by the wind to wherever it wanted to take me wasn't such a disaster after all. I'd hit my stride as a Mystical Backpacker, and the Universe seemed to be letting me know at every turn.

Weeks passed. My feet grew calloused from the many miles I walked each day. My fingers grew calloused from the many pages of journal entries I filled. My soul, increasingly freed of its limitations, filled my body, light seeping out of my pores and through the ends of my fingers, toes, and hair, emanating beyond my physical borders, shining the light that is me brightly for all to see. I smiled easily at others. They smiled back. I asked questions easily, without feeling exposed or vulnerable. Information flowed to me. Always, it aligned with what I needed to hear or know or experience that day. I had no goals and ceased to feel panic, guilt, or remorse because of it. Instead,

I noticed how the whites of my toenails looked like the whites of water-washed shells in the grains of sand at the beach.

One day, we took a ferry to a tiny, seemingly deserted rock of an island baking in the hot sun. We were told which way to hike toward the campground, and a small group of us walked with our packs through undulating heat waves rising from the cracked pavement road. Then, like Prometheus' offering to Zeus, the unappetizing exterior of this barren place suddenly yielded a place of nourishment. For there, around the bend, was a haven of bright colors and tanning bodies. The coconut smell of sun lotion mixed with the bright berry smell of slightly melted popsicles and wafted over to us on a sea breeze. A mechanical crane rose above the bedlam of swimsuits and turquoise swimming pools, and the distant shrieks of bungee jumpers heralded this new land of plenty. Cold beer on tap. Hot, salted French fries by the loaded paper plate. Ambient trance beach music pulsing low like the breathing of a sleeping animal. Grass umbrellas shushing in the breeze over napping bodies. Laughter. Splashing. And rest. We had arrived at the Far Out Campground.

Ios Island, Greece
July 14, 2000

"Far Out Camping" on Ios is Club Med for backpackers. It was my first true vacation since childhood. Days occupied with lying in the sun by the swimming pool, swimming and observing people. Read several books. Drank beer in the afternoon and sucked on fruit popsicles. At night, we'd go into town and bar hop and dance. It is the ultimate place for hedonistic youths. The bars are meat markets where rampant hormones fail to subscribe to any selection criteria. People attempt snogging anyone in their near vicinity. The campground was so well equipped there was no reason to leave during daylight hours.

There was bungee jumping, billiards, a free movie played every night, there was email next door, a minimarket, postal service, phone charging stations, safety deposit boxes, free loungers and umbrellas, etc. I saw nothing of Ios itself, except for the village at night, through the haze of alcohol. The island is barren and Far Out Camping was our paradise amidst the Mediterranean moonscape. I met so many people and most everyone was friendly (and younger)!

A group of us formed a clique and hung out together everyday. We were: Lisa and I, Nikki (Vancouver Island Canadian, 21, working at a bar in London), Nathan (Aussie from Perth, 22, working in a bar in London), Chelsea (22, Aussie, working as a Personal Assistant in London), Vanessa (26, Kiwi, working as a hairdresser in London), Tracy (26, South African, working as a Personal Assistant in London), and Miranda and Nikki (Kiwi, 30, and Aussie, 24, working in London also).

The first thing to notice about those journal entries is that they're written in the past tense. That's because I didn't journal at all for days on end, and I was catching up afterward. It's also because I didn't do any reflection work or exercises at all. I simply indulged in sun, books, rest, beer, and dancing. And it was amazing.

After the exhaustive soul searching you've accomplished doing the exercises in the previous chapter and the physical exhaustion you've incurred from your sightseeing and traveling, both your mind and your body require rest. And by rest, I don't mean a good night's sleep. I mean several days' worth of lazing about, lying in the sun, napping under a shady tree, eating and drinking and doing nothing. As I did, you might add some dancing in there too. But that's it.

It's perfectly all right to do this. You deserve it! Why? Well, because it's hard to be productive every single day without taking time to rest. It's hard to be plugged in all the time without unplugging. And it's very hard to gain the benefits of all that self-reflection and to revisit the emotions and memories of your past without taking some distance from it all. It's as though you've taken all those damp and musty memories out of the attic, and now you're putting them out in the sun and fresh air to dry. It takes some time. Dealing with them once you've given yourself some R & R will be so much easier. You'll be able to look through them, one by one, and release those that no longer serve you and keep the ones that do.

When I reread my journals from the first half of my Mystical Backpacking trip (when I traveled from Budapest to Barcelona by myself), the narrative begins pinched and prompt and includes the cost of items, the times of train schedules, and the clambering details about finding places to rest, eat, use a restroom, and get a good coffee or tea in the afternoon, when Italy and Spain shut down for siesta. Interspersed are accounts of museums and records of places I'd visited and some people I encountered. I felt danger around me, and the energy of that feeling emanates from the page, roped taught between the billowy cursive lines of text. I was so used to being in control, and the discomfort caused by acclimating to some other way of being was something I dodged and resisted, like a beginner matador who uses his cape as a shield instead of an extension of himself in the magical dance with danger. Yes, there were moments of tranquil bliss in parks and coffee shops, and I was thrilled to be doing the trip, but the tone is very different from that found in the entries toward the end.

In the beginning, my feelings and deepest issues are alluded to in postscripts and hastily jotted questions like, "What is the meaning of my life?" and, "Am I depressed?" In the middle of my journal, pages and pages of my own Mystical Exercises are filled out in charts, graphs, and comprehensive detail. By the end of the journal, it's hard for a reader to picture where I am (what country, town, or city) because the prose focuses instead on how I feel, describes the people I've met and what we talked about, and how I feel in response to the conversations. I sound so happy in the writing, so safe and confident. That sense of security is conveyed also by the events I record participating in, things that only a safe-feeling person would do. I meet locals in a hostel that is fully booked, and they offer me their couch for the night, and I take it. I borrow a stranger's tent to go camping for a few days. I smoke pot and actually enjoy it instead of becoming a paranoid mess. I describe sunsets and the things I see in the ocean while snorkeling, but there's no mention of arrival and departure times or a complete record of my spending and consumption. There is a freeness of being and a sense of ease with the constant state of change I'm experiencing, and it's delightful for me to revisit on the page and in my memory.

Sleeping in a stranger's house and smoking pot may not be everyone's way of hitting their mystical stride, but for me, this was a remarkable display of trust. I am hyper-responsible, and this, coupled with my experiences as a child of an alcoholic parent (many children of alcoholics and addicts become hyper-responsible adults), means that I am often interested in being in control, feeling safe, and doing things "right." Certainly at this phase in my life, I tended not to trust things would work out all right, but did my best to ensure they would by taking action in advance. As I get older, more experienced with life, more self-aware, I address these emotional needs differently, but this type of trusting behavior at this stage in my life was remarkable *for me.* Your own healing, your own loosening up, will look different. It will be unique to you.

As you loosen up and try yourself in ways that extend your comfort zones outward, you will reach a point where you just *can't* go on. You don't want to board another train or bus, you don't want to find another bed, you don't want to reflect on your life anymore. You may feel tired and indulgent. You may just want to have some fun and stop all this working and thinking and physical discomfort. Yahoo! Do it. Party hearty. Rest. Relax. Indulge. Enjoy. Disconnecting, laughing, and experiencing pleasure are the best medicine for your heart, soul, and psyche. Give yourself permission to have some fun or to sleep for several days or to lie in the sun . . . whatever it is you need to rejuvenate. Some of your happiest memories will be a product of this time. Be kind to yourself and luxuriate in the freedom you've been gifted with. Don't bother spending a moment feeling guilty about it either.

Imagine having a child. Would you want your child to be happy with life and to have fun on a regular basis, or would you want your child to work all the time, feel guilty about pleasure, and feel unworthy of abundance? Many people believe we are created by and are children of a higher power, and as you begin to feel more mystical, you may feel this more potently than ever before. It begs the question then: does the god or other higher power you believe in want you to suffer? If a higher power named God created this beautiful world, would God want you to enjoy it, appreciate it, and embrace it? Or would God want you to ignore it while bullying through days upon days of "doing what's right"? We truly *can* give ourselves permission to slow down and to spend days on end resting and relaxing without being "wrong." In fact, it is often during these experiences we are best able to experience the spiritual, the sacred, or the mystical.

One evening back on Mallorca, Simon, Lisa, and I had relaxed with friends on a patio lounge perched over the Mediterranean Sea. The waves lapped up against the supports of the very floor our table and chairs were on. Brightly colored flags clapped loudly over the sound of the ambient music playing from inside the café, and the sky bedded down the sun in smoky lavenders and electric pinks. The mountains, a hazy blue gray, framed the backdrop. Conversation ceased, our senses fully aligned with the setting moment. The energy was sacred—a true mystical moment—and we all felt it.

Another day, a group of us drove loud jeeps through Alaro, a twelfth-century town built entirely of golden-colored stone, and up a slippery gravel road. We hiked to the very top of a mountain, where Alaro Castle looks out over the island. The restaurant there served us roast lamb, rosemary potatoes, and ruby-red wine. It was the Last Supper for me, for after that, I had truly risen. I was aware that I was no longer the person I had been when I began. I had ascended to another level, gained healing and insight, and thus, a new chapter in my life was truly born of this moment. Shortly thereafter, I remember dancing on a triple-mast schooner under a perfect blue sky and, despite fearing heights, standing with a friend on the railing and together jumping off into the fresh blue sea.

Taking the time to enjoy the pleasures of the earth and the delightful creations of humans, a love for both was stoked within me. These moments of bliss generated a peacefulness that still resonates within my soul today. Most of all, I began to feel that I could trust in the world around me. There was no battle. There was no war. There was enough to go around. All would be well. Staring out at the sea, feeling the sun warming my skin, nourished by food baked in stone ovens, my blood pumping as I danced through nature; I felt deeply connected to myself and the world around me.

Later in my journey, as I neared Greece, I remembered a dream I had had a year before. In it, I was in a beautiful seaside bedroom in a white stucco home in Greece. The wall facing the sea was open to the sea, and sunlight spilled in, the delicate rays creating shafts through white curtains billowing in the salty breeze. The room was illuminated by an expanse of white: white sheets on the bed, pristine white walls unmarred by hangings or artwork, sheer white curtains. The azure sea and sky framed by the glass doors along one wall seemed only to assure me all was well in the world. I was on the bed and looked down to see my belly huge and protracted. I was expecting and must have been full term. I looked into my husband's eyes—he seemed to be a Greek boy I had barely known in high school as an adult—and he was smiling at me. He had black hair and chocolate eyes and a rugged face. His smile was so pure. The dream, while delicious, also haunted me. It made my current reality (single, no children) seem empty in comparison. I had not known then that I would ever go to Greece. Was the dream prophetic? And if so, was the dream to be interpreted literally? These questions moved slowly beneath the surface of my consciousness. Consequently, when I first set foot on Grecian soil, a part of me began to look for this boy I had once known and feel the dream was possibly my imminent future materializing. Would I meet him again here? Or would I find my destiny in Greece in some other way, and his featuring in the dream was simply to identify the location? Was the dream itself a sign that Greece would yield a time of happiness and peace in my life? It had seemed so real.

To some extent, a part of me pursued the lingering memory of this bright and tranquil dream from island to island, waiting for that moment when destiny and fate would collide. But weeks passed without any such event, and by the time I had arrived at the Far Out Campground on Ios, I was simply tired and weathered. Mystical experiences waned as fatigue set in and my body and soul craved rest. The club on Ios seemed the perfect prescription. I spent days there soaking up the sun, talking with new friends, and reading books. I swam in the pool, dimly aware of the overhead screams as bungee jumpers in the adjacent pool dropped from the sky. Introspection had ceased entirely, and I was living entirely in the moment. A gorgeous younger man caught my eye—a blond Australian backpacker. He looked nothing like the man in my dream, and every impulse in mind said no while the rest of me said yes.

He was someone real I could interact with, unlike the man in the dream. We walked on the beach and danced in clubs at night. We held hands and talked and kissed well into the dusky pinks of dawn. My days were a steady stream of gentle pleasures. I did not want this experience to end. I did not want to go back home. I wanted to live like this forever.

Little did I know, I had entered the Land of the Lotus Eaters.

It's apropos to introduce a story from Homer's *Odyssey* here, for on your personal odyssey, how great is it to relate to Homer's famous tale and be reminded that mankind has always had the need to take risks and seek adventure in order to fulfill one's soul. This passage is from book nine, Samuel Butler's translation, and describes the Land of the Lotus Eaters.

> I was driven thence by foul winds for a space of nine days upon the sea, but on the tenth day we reached the land of the Lotus-eaters, who live on a food that comes from a kind of flower. Here we landed to take in fresh water, and our crews got their mid-day meal on the shore near the ships. When they had eaten and drunk I sent two of my company to see what manner of men the people of the place might be, and they had a third man under them. They started at once, and went about among the Lotus-eaters, who did them no hurt, but gave them to eat of the lotus, which was so delicious that those who ate of it left off caring about home, and did not even want to go back and say what had happened to them, but were for staying and munching lotus with the Lotus-eaters without thinking further of their return; nevertheless, though they wept bitterly I forced them back to the ships and made them fast under the benches. Then I told the

> rest to go on board at once, lest any of them should taste of the lotus and leave off wanting to get home, so they took their places and smote the grey sea with their oars.[1]

You'll know you've entered the Land of the Lotus Eaters when the very thought of returning to your old life seems an impossible idea to swallow. You begin to scheme, trying to figure out ways in which you might make this new reality your forever reality. *I could work remotely. I could get a job here. I could use my savings and live here for a few years, then go home and start over.* Or you may not concern yourself with the hows at all. You may simply *be* for days on end, without any worry, thought, or plan for the future. You'll know you're in the Land of the Lotus Eaters when you have stopped doing your Reflection Work and you've stopped processing the past or planning for the future. Avoidance of your reality at home is the primary objective.

While *some* time in this seemingly Zen state can be enormously freeing and gratifying, it is important for you to also be present *in your life*, not just your vacation. After all, true Zen is achieved anywhere. While you are Mystical Backpacking, you have vacated your life. This is the truest *vacation* in this sense of the word. However, scheming to extend that vacation forever is not living your life; it's avoiding it. It's not that you can't move to a new place in the world or change jobs or continue to feel happiness and contentment. If this is truly your path and circumstances align to support these types of immediate changes, so be it. However, keep in mind that the point of Mystical Backpacking is to connect with your authentic desires so you can manifest them in your day-to-day life and not just when you're on vacation. Eventually, no matter where you live or work, the challenges you face with this process will reappear. Leaving your world behind for a new one will only postpone or delay the work for a time.

Here, on the beach of the Far Out Campground on Ios, when I realized I had lost my way and needed to return to my personal journey, I was inspired to write the following:

July 11, 2000

The answers can't be found
In the stars
Or the fading lights
Of closing bars.
They won't be encoded
In disco beats
Or hid beneath
4 am sandwich meats.
Dogs are sleeping on the beach
Between couples exchanging
Sexual treats.
A western wind
Fights the rising sun
And the losing battle
Cheers me on.
If a shooting star
Is a disappointing illusion
Then literature
Can no longer be my God.
Romance
Denies reality
For awhile.
Blue eyes
And a rising sun
Blink.
Fish tremble in shallow waters.
Islanders start their cars.

I think I might have ripped off the second last line, which is basically the best line in a poem hastily scribbled in a musty tent in the middle of the night before the words were forgotten. But each time I read this poem, I am transported to that moment on Ios, on that dark dot of island facing off a million pinpricks of light in the predawn sky, where I became acutely aware that the present moment holds illusions projected by the past. Many of those stars in the night sky don't exist anymore. Only their lights exist. Many of the great authors I relate to on the page don't exist anymore. Only their light exists. The dream of Greece had been dreamed, but the reality of Greece was here to experience. And it was here, in this moment, I realized I had eaten of the lotus blossom. I was living in fiction and in dreams. It was time to resume my odyssey and leave paradise behind. Going through life blissful but unconscious of my reality was not the answer for me.

Which brings me back to Shirley. Remember Shirley Valentine, the character in the movie *Shirley Valentine*? When she's in Greece, she falls for a guy who claims that he doesn't want to have sex with her (but of course, *he does want to*). He offers to take her out on his uncle's boat and show her the island, and when she hesitates, he promises her in broken English that he doesn't want to "*make fuck with her*." She decides to take a chance and go. She has the most incredible day and ends up having glorious sex with him on the boat. It's a turning point for her. Once she makes her decision about her life (to stay in Greece and work in his restaurant), she finds he doesn't want to make fuck with lots of women. Instead of being distraught or upset or angry, she is amused and stays to work in his restaurant anyway. She is able to do so simply because she has found herself within herself. She did not find herself within the guy or in his perception of her.

When others think we're fabulous, it's easy to ride the wave of that enthusiasm for a time, and it's right to enjoy the ride. But we have not truly changed or become whom we are meant to if we do not think we are fabulous and if we haven't freed ourselves of our own constraints. We are not harnessed or determined by the dictates of others—we are either enslaved or lifted up by our own thoughts. We cannot blame others for the lives we live. We are responsible for our choices. As such, we must make them for our own best interests.

When we struggle to support ourselves with loving kindness, as many of us do, we might attempt to avoid those people and situations that ask us to confront that dislike (the very people who may help us in becoming healthier, happier people). We may find people to blame: your mother, father, teacher, or friend. You may notice in rereading your Reflection Work that you hold others accountable for your feelings but not yourself. *She* hurt me when. *He* disappointed me. I *was betrayed.* On this second half of the trip, be brave and remember to continue to afford time for yourself to be alone with you. Hold yourself accountable. This does not imply that you should deny the difficult situations you have experienced in your life, and it doesn't dismiss or invalidate the actions of others. Rather, it sets the onus for how your life develops beyond this point on you. The answers *can't* be found in the stars or the fading lights of closing bars. The answers *don't* exist in Greece or Italy or Spain or wherever you've chosen to be right now or even in the amazing people you meet while there, however important they may be to you. The answers are within you. They are *always* within you.

Every odyssey—yours, mine, Odysseus's—has a point where the traveler is tempted to stay in a safe and happy place of pleasure and inaction. But the spell of this narcotic can derail you from your quest. Indulge. Enjoy. And then move on. Don't get derailed. If you feel yourself sliding into this space, ask yourself: is your future truly in this physical place, or is it rooted in the feeling of joy you've finally reconnected with? How can that joy be manifested in your tomorrow? Does it require a specific location? When we finally tap into the feeling within, the future we create for ourselves is in alignment with our highest good. This trip is about you taking care of yourself on a spiritual level. It's about discovering your life purpose, or putting your finger on what you want or need in life. This odyssey is about finding your true thoughts and beliefs outside the parameters of your community.

Your physical travel is a catalyst. It is helping you reconnect with joy and wonder, trust and faith. Your trip is an arena within which you can determine what you like and don't like, what you want and don't want, and what would truly bring happiness and a sense of purpose into your life. The final destination, however, isn't a place in the world. It's a place within you. Continuing your Mystical Backpacking experience by using the tools in your Mystical Toolbox is essential. Leave the Land of the Lotus Eaters behind and keep traveling to the center of your being. You're almost there!

It's that time again. As you return to journeying, you now return to your Mystical Exercises as well. You're finally at a point in time where you're relaxed, inspired, and a much more stripped-down, authentic version of yourself than when you started. This is an excellent energy to tap into and a potent time for being deeply honest and intensely creative.

Since you're returning to this process after a period of rest, the number of exercises is low in this chapter, allowing you to ease back into this process without feeling overworked. These exercises focus on the practical aspects of your life, since you've been using your Mystical Tools regularly. These exercises are the beginning phase of how you will manifest your new life once you return home. As such, they are an integral part of the mystical soul work your journey honors. Take the time to invest yourself wholeheartedly in digging deep and answering these questions as honestly and authentically as possible.

Mystical Exercises: Chapter 5

We cannot be happy if we expect to live all the time
at the hightest peak of intensity. Happiness is not
a matter of intensity but of balance and order
and rhythm and harmony.

—Thomas Merton

Bucket List

Create a bucket list of everything you would like to see, experience, and do before you die. It can be as long and as creative as you'd like. Don't forget to cover several areas of your life. For example, you might have one category for your personal life, another for your professional life, and yet another for your social life. Or you can create the list haphazardly as ideas come to you. Let loose!

Source Your Joy

Living joyfully means experiencing some degree of joy each and every day. Are you living joyfully right now? Are you living joyfully at home (when you're not being a Mystical Backpacker)? Be honest. Who brings you joy? Why? What else brings you joy? Create a complete list. It can include experiences, hobbies, events, animals, people, work, sports, etc. Be as comprehensive as possible.

Express Your Joy

Setting that list aside, answer this question: How have you learned to express joy? Do you just smile while feeling joyful internally, or do you laugh and joke around? Maybe you kiss and hug and squeeze the people and pets you love when you feel joyful? Describe all the ways in which you express your feelings of joy.

Accept Your Joy

Do your expressions of joy foster even more joy, or do they cause that joy to fade? Exploring this truthfully means you can recognize where you may have inhibitors blocking joy and come up with a game plan for working around them in order to embrace joy easily on a daily basis moving forward. What could you do, moving forward, to receive and express joy more readily and easily on a daily basis?

What Do You Believe?

Describe the higher power you believe in. This may be a being, God, for example, or general energy, science, guiding principle, or faith. Do you believe God is angry or loving or a combination of both? Does Spirit believe in or advocate justice? Do you believe events are random and unrelated? Do you believe in fairness or luck? Do you believe life swings erratically from fortunate to unfortunate circumstances, or is there some guide for how to ensure you stay safe, cared for, or secure? Is your god frugal, measuring out rewards in small doses, or is your god generous, fun loving, and bringing forth abundance? Write down *all* the things you believe to be true about a greater force. *Really* think about it. Now, is there anyone in your life who has taught you to believe this way? Oftentimes, our parents or childhood experiences serve as such strong models that you may find the being you believe in resembles your parents and their style of parenting or the lessons you learned from experiences you had in childhood. Do you see such similarities? Do you think your perception is an accurate one? Considering this, is there anything you would now change in your description about God?

Are there traits you would like to add that might make the god you believe in more compassionate, loving, or accepting?[2]

Creative Balance

Many of us struggle with having a balanced life, yet know that the secret to feeling whole and fulfilled is in finding balance. We cannot hold the idea of balance in our consciousness while dogmatically pursuing the development of only one or two aspects of our life, yet that is what many of us do. In this exercise, I'd like you to create a visual representation of what your ideal balanced life would look like, much like the one I created in the journal entry I shared with you on page 127.

Below you will find a pie chart. In each slice of pie, write a word that represents a constant and regular aspect of your life that you would

My Fulfilling and Balanced Life

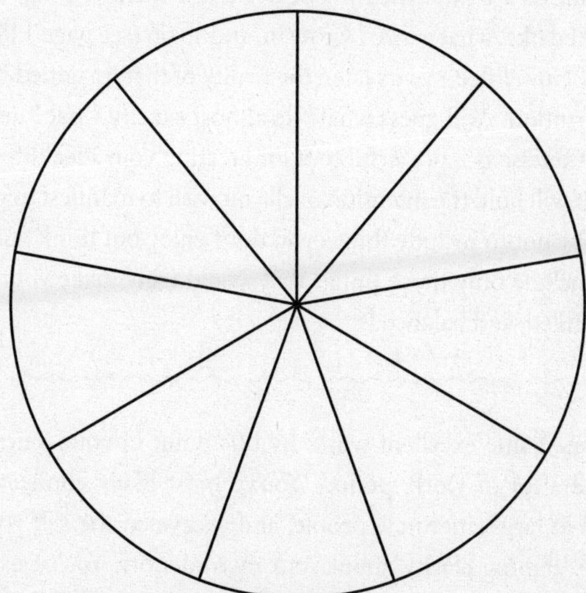

like to tend or develop. When I did this exercise, my items were: writing, travel, friends, family, romantic love, alone time, adventure, learning, and teaching. Your pie pieces can be assigned to totally different aspects of your life. They should resonate with the things you hold sacred and (want to) spend the bulk of your time on. Note that my chart didn't include exercise! I know many people for whom that would not work. Also, some people hate being alone, but without time to myself, I cannot connect with the thoughts, feelings, and inspiration that fuel my writing, so to me, solitude is an essential thing I require regularly.

Once you've filled out your sections with key words, spend some time describing your vision of each in detail. Each write-up can range from half a page to a full page in length. If you need it to be longer, that's fine too. Just don't rush through or skimp, since these descriptions are key to getting a full and observable picture of what your balanced life would look like. My first pie piece was dedicated to writing. I described my ideal life as a writer: the time of day that I spent writing, what my office looked like, what genre I wrote in, and so on (see page 128 for this write-up). Now, fifteen years later, the reality of that imagined ideal has come to fruition. And guess what? It's almost exactly what I described.

This exercise is a powerful tool for creating your ideal life moving forward. It will hold the intention of all you wish to manifest in your life. As such, try not to include things you don't enjoy but think you *should* include. Include only those things that would truly make your life feel whole, fulfilled, and balanced.

~~~

You've done some excellent work. By this point in your journey, you have done a lot of work, period. You've most likely connected with the world at large, met new people, and excavated the self you are at your core, gaining clarity about your own identity. You've used your Mystical Tools to expand your comfort zone and to connect with some-
~~~

thing larger than yourself. You've recorded your experiences in your journal, and you may have already filled one whole journal up. You've read books, listened to music, talked with new people, and taken the time to enjoy yourself and to rest. You are at the center of the labyrinth, halfway through the journey, and now its winding path shifts outward, returning you to the place where your journey began. You may actually be starting to feel like you're ready to go home and may sense your thoughts beginning to shift in that direction. While you are in this moment still a traveler on a wondrous odyssey, Dorothy's words couldn't ring more true right now: "There's no place like home."[3]

The comforts of home may be something you look forward to experiencing, but there may also be other aspects of life at home causing you to feel apprehension at best or anxiety and plain old fear at worst. After all, some of the comforts of home may be part of the reason you left for this time of exploration. Addressing those issues and revising how your home life will be realized moving forward is an important step on the way back out of your labyrinth. Creating a new reality for the home that is best suited to you and the life you wish to lead once you return to it will make your return all the more palatable, ensuring that your adventure continues once you've taken your backpack off.

Mystical Moments Photo Album

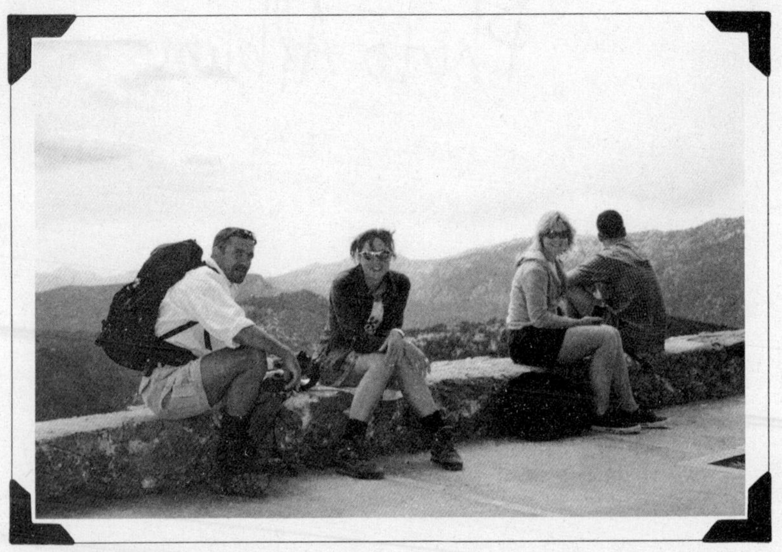

Left to right: Simon, me, Lisa, and Patrick at Alaro Castle lookout after hiking up from the restaurant Es Verger, Mallorca, Spain.

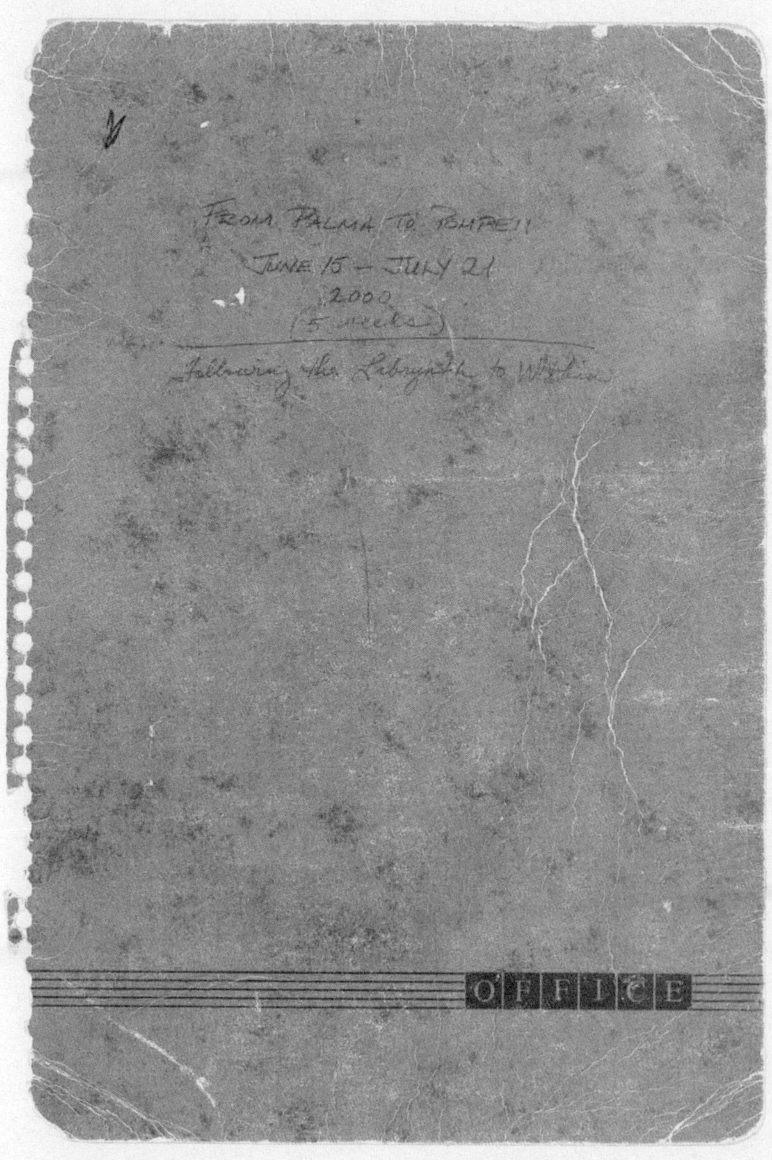

Here they are, images from the journals I kept during and after my own Mystical Backpacking adventure. This first one charts the route from Palma de Mallorca to Pompeii, Italy (via Cyprus and Greece).

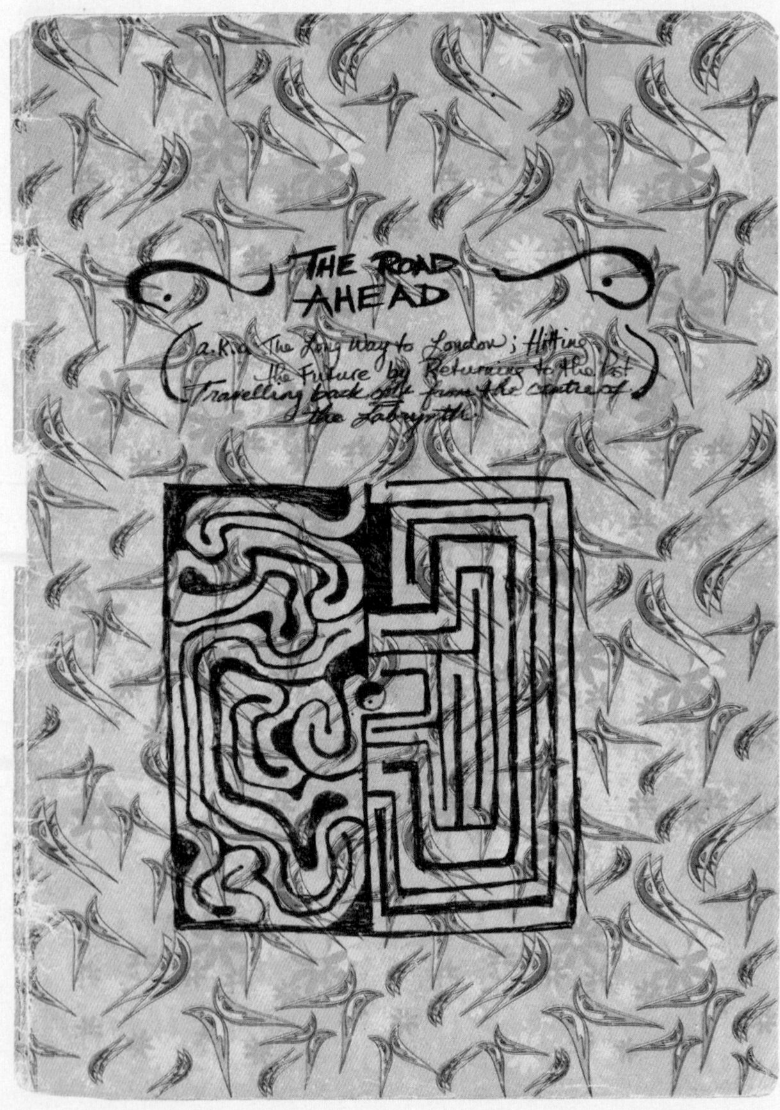

This second journal has an elaborate labyrinth drawn on its cover and charts the course of homecoming.

This third journal, with Ms. London on the cover, is the one I kept while living in London after the journey.

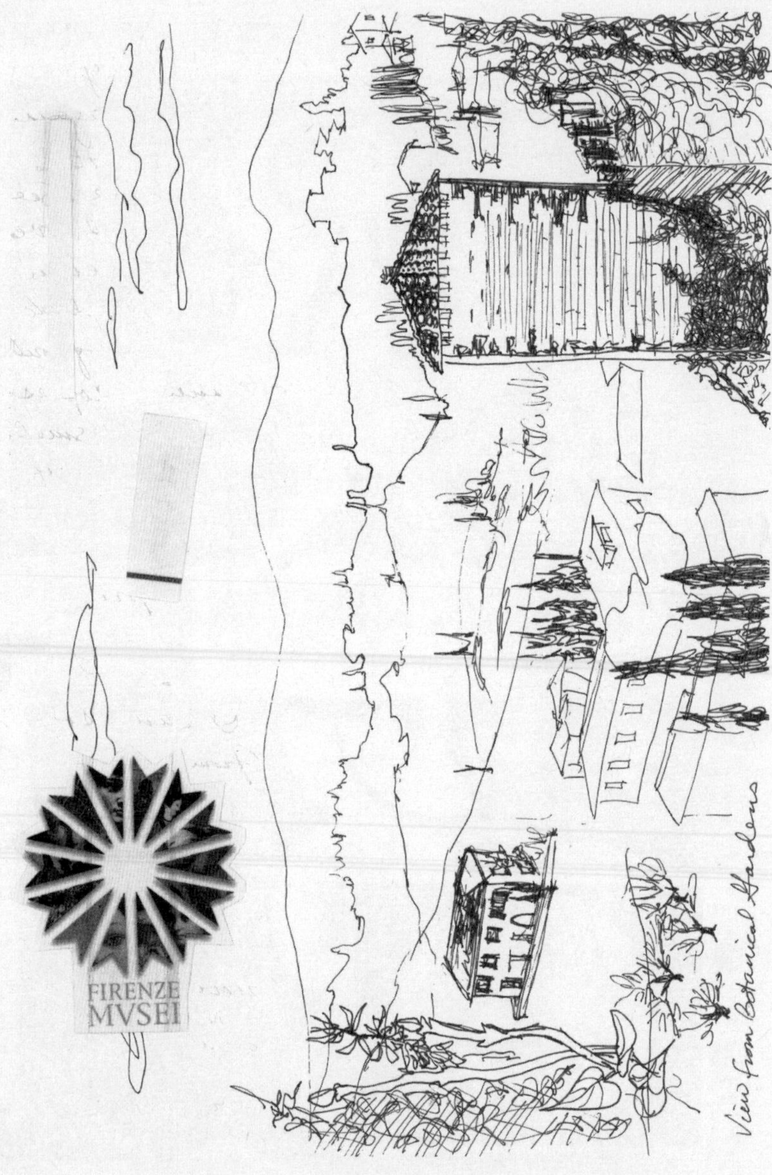

Florence: My sketch of the view from the Palazzo Pitti Museum of the Boboli Gardens and surrounding countryside.
I remember wanting to be an artist.

Trevi Fountain. Sigh.

Dear Mother, I won't be coming home as I have married a gladiator...

Arriving in Palermo, Sicily.

Me on the beach at Sa Calobra, Mallorca.

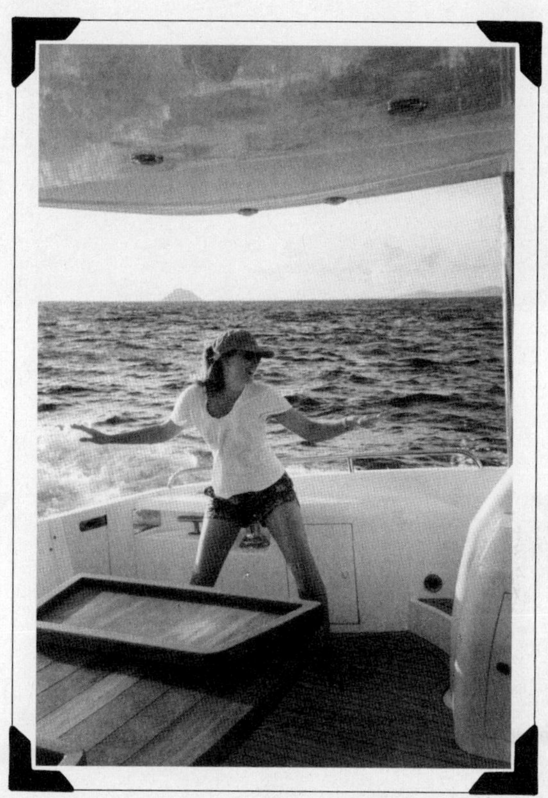

"Surfing" to pass the time.

Here we are! Very Eyes Wide Shut, methinks.

Lisa in Palma de Mallorca early in the morning: we've just arrived!

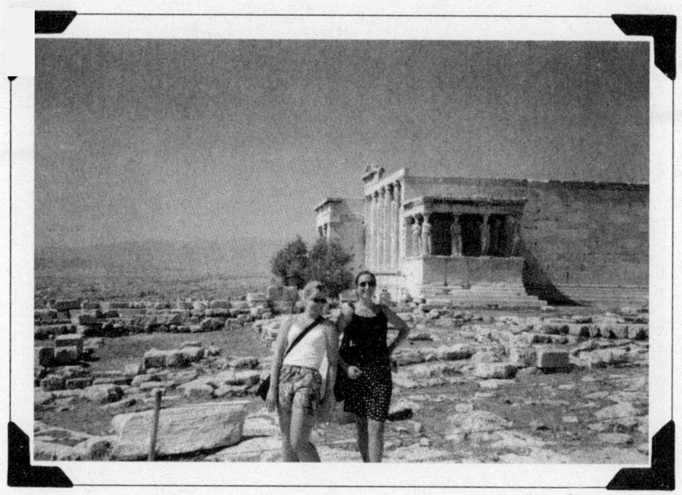

Lisa and I pose as Athena at the Acropolis in Athens, Greece.

The Corinth Canal, which joins the Gulf of Corinth to the Aegean Sea, providing a shortcut to Athens.

The Taipan leaves us on the dock in Limassol, Cyprus.
The captain and first mate wave from the fly bridge.

Troodos Mountains at sunset.
A bunch of firefighters are in our near future.

Mountaintop aria on the island of Santorini, Greece.

Calamari, anyone? Let me grab that off the line. Rhodes, Greece.

My very own Milka ad—top of the Alps!

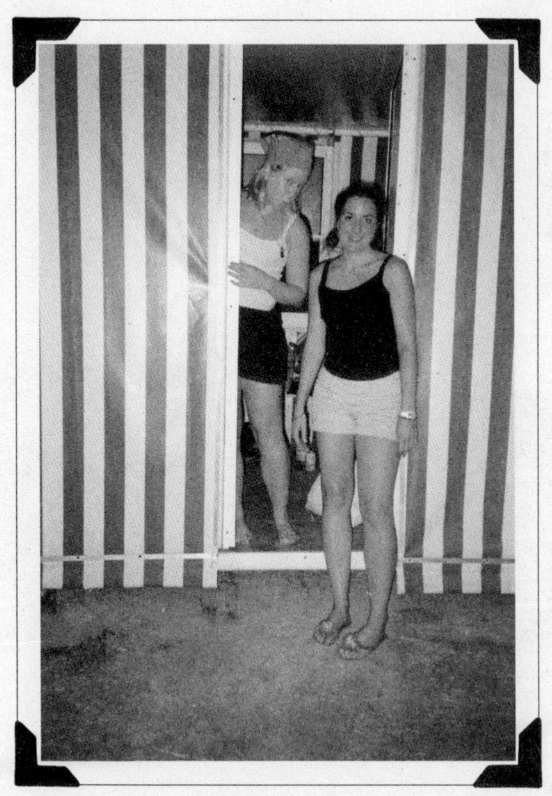

Our tent at Fortuna Campground just outside of Sorrento, Italy.

Nicolas's favorite photo (and one of mine too) is one I call Bored Now, where I fake-yawn at the stunning view from the top of a volcanic mountain in Santorini, Greece.

PART II

The Voyage Home

6

Homeward Bound

Like an ox-cart driver in monsoon season or the skipper of a grounded ship, one must sometimes go forward by going back.

—**John Barth**

After Ios, we traveled by hovercraft to one more island—Mykonos—where we stayed at Paradise Camping, a place advertised for its nude beach and "little person." There was no nudity. There was a little person. He was lovely, and the campground was, too, though it paled in comparison to Far Out. It surely was someone's paradise, but not mine. By day, I explored the quaint lanes of the wind-whipped town. Darling shops selling local art (whimsical watercolors of the famous Mykonos windmills and handmade plaster dolls and mermaids) and artsy wares (like a pale-green purse made of dyed fish bones) were wedged between brightly colored window frames and doorways overflowing with potted geraniums. It wasn't that Mykonos wasn't wonderful, because it was. I was simply growing tired of campgrounds, mosquitos, and the ordeal of seeking out every meal from public establishments. I began to long for the convenience of a kitchen, where a morning coffee could be had "for free" and without having to get dressed to acquire it. It was a relief to take that final island ferry back to Athens, where air-conditioned hotel rooms and sophisticated museums dispelled the harsh light of the islands and brought a sense of serene, sterilized order to everyday life. Daily conveniences previously taken for granted—like washing our hands in public places or finding free drinking water—were easily and readily accessible once again.

I moved serenely between displays of ancient artifacts and a visiting exhibition of Egyptian mummies in the National Archaeological Museum, disappointed to find the exhibit for the Akrotiri murals was closed (I had been looking forward to it ever since seeing the Akrotiri ruins on Santorini). While whizzing along in a taxi, a cab driver told me about how upset the farmers were about the drought. It had been a long time since I'd heard a report of what was going on in the world, and it was as though his mention of it conveyed the very murmurs of farmers speaking in hushed tones while shaking their heads in dismay. It seemed so remote a problem here in the city, where tall apartment buildings lined the streets, their lush balcony gardens spilling forth ferns and vines in long tethers. The sight seemed to contradict any news of water shortages.

From Athens, we rode a jaunty bus to Patras, and as we bounced along, I marveled to see clouds in the sky. It had been so long since I had seen clouds in the sky! I hadn't realized how all that blue could carry such weight. The respite was welcome, uplifting, and energizing. In contrast, the shoreline here was so green after the islands. Despite the drought affecting this region as well, it still felt lush to us after sunning on the island rocks for so many weeks on end.

From Patras, we took a ferry to Brindisi. Those who have seen *The Bridges of Madison County* will recognize the name of the town because that's near where Meryl Streep's character is from, and this is a conversation point between her and Clint Eastwood's character, who has been there on his travels. Other travelers we met referred to it as Sleazy Brindisi, which is perhaps an unfair nickname, since the sunny afternoon we spent there was tranquil and demure. For us, the adventure in getting there was more noteworthy and deserving of the moniker. Our funds depleting, we traveled deck class on an old and weathered ferry and spent a jarring night in the bow of the ship, soaring and falling hour after hour, wave upon wave, hearing things stored below us crashing about. We slept lightly and uncomfortably. Around 6:00 AM, Lisa's screams woke me. A Greek trucker (the ferry was full of them) had sidled up to her and run his hands up her skirt. He left quickly, but she was shaken and did not sleep anymore. In movies, these scenes carry great drama and show heroines yielding swords, guns, or high kicks and punches in swashbuckling feats of bravery, or eloquently threatening or shaming their adversary with just the right combination of words. In reality, such moments can be a small mark on a banal page of events, but deeply unnerving mentally and emotionally. The man who skulked off was no worthy opponent, and the shock of what had happened retarded all eloquence. In contrast, Brindisi itself was simply lemonade, shade, and pleasant people watching. Being there helped to dispel the darkness of those early-morning hours on the ferry.

From Brindisi, we took a train to Naples, where we arrived moments after the last train to Sorrento had pulled away. We had reservations at a campsite in Sorrento, and rather than search for accommodations in Naples, we shared a taxi with another backpacker and barreled toward our campground along the winding coastline in the pitch-black night. The taxi driver looked like the devil, complete with pointy goatee and coal-black eyes. He was young and handsome (in a sinister way) but also lurid and inappropriate and suggested we smoke hash and have group sex. We were glad to have a male backpacker with us, especially since he didn't seem to share the taxi driver's interest. We arrived at Fortuna Campground in the middle of the night and wandered around blindly for what felt like an eternity, seeking our tents. By the time we had showered and bought water at a nearby store, it was nearly three in the morning.

After such darkness faced in the tribulations of traveling, it was absolute bliss to wake up where we did. Our tent was like a little circus tent, whimsically striped in blue and white. The view from the campground was breathtaking. The void of darkness we had peered into at night gave way to such a sight of beauty by the light of day, it was nothing short of resplendent. We looked onto Sorrento and the Bay of Naples beneath. The sapphire sea was dappled with boats and sunlight, and the shoreline boasted a city perched over the sea. In the distance, Vesuvius reigned majestically. The campground was impeccably clean and organized. We caught up on our sleep peacefully, knowing we were safe and well. We cleaned our packs and did laundry. We went into town for groceries and to book our tickets for the next leg of our trip. I would be taking a train to Valencia, Spain. Lisa would fly to London, England. Until then, we had five days to enjoy and explore the Sorrentine Peninsula. If ever there was a place I could return to live, this was it.

July 19, 2000
Sorrento, Italy 10:35 am.

I love this place! Sorrento is me! Dramatic mountains, silver sea, small city with history, architectural appeal and cosmopolitan overtones. The shops carry the latest and greatest. The locals are dressed to the nines. The setting is beyond romantic. Sorrento sits on top of a cliff ledge over the sea and then sweeps up into a valley between two mountains. Terracotta rooftops embroider a carpet of green and the distant silence is misleading. Beneath the canopy the city hums with activity. I could live here. What adventures will I have today?

Sorrento's streets are narrow, flanked by Italian buildings on either side, and the walkways are impeded by vendors' stands; custom-made leather shoes, lots of leather products, ceramics (in typical Southern Italian yellow, orange, and blue colors) and kitschy tourist stuff like aprons, Pinocchio dolls, and wine corks. After eating we found a nice bench atop the cliff just above the port and sat there being silly. Lisa commented on VPLs (Visible Panty Lines) and we had a water fight that I started by tipping Lisa's water bottle when she went to have a sip. Everyone who overheard/saw us was laughing and the driver of a tiny truck even stopped to watch! It was kind of a high-stress place to sit because we were at a bend on a narrow road and every vehicle honked coming round the bend to forewarn opposing traffic. And it was a busy road.

Now we're back at the campsite that we love and we're eating chips, doing crosswords, reading, etc. Tomorrow we visit Pompeii and then Friday, we're off! I'll leave room now for my final entry documenting Pompeii—the end of this leg of the journey. Bought a new journal today in which I'll document the next leg.

When I was a child, I watched a special on television about Pompeii. Pompeii is an ancient city that was buried under a volcanic eruption. It was rediscovered in the Middle Ages and has been a tourist site for over two hundred years. At its height during the Pax Romana era, twenty thousand residents thrived there. The city grew to be an international shipping and trading port of great repute, and the residents enjoyed amenities and conveniences we would consider modern (flush toilets, spas, international banking). In 79 AD, the entire city and all its residents were buried under ash when Vesuvius erupted. That ash—dry and devoid of air—perfectly preserved a day in the life of the city. Foods have been unearthed in the restaurants, contracts and world currencies discovered in the vault beneath the bank, menus for sexual positions one could purchase at the brothel uncovered in full color and relief on the brothel wall. Plaster statues (created by pouring plaster into the voids where people and animals died by suffocation) are on display, showing the death throes of Pompeii's last residents.

As a girl, the story of Pompeii both fascinated and disturbed me. I imagined life in Pompeii over and again. I dreamed of Pompeii. I cringed when I thought of the people who hid in the caves by the sea and suffocated to death before being buried under the lava and debris of Vesuvius's eruption. I knew from that very early age that one day I would visit this place. For this reason, it was affirming to finally find myself here. As I walked through the unearthed city, the bustling marketplace and thriving industry came alive in my imagination. I felt as though I were re-experiencing a place I had known before. Life here had been cultured, sophisticated, organized, and clean. International trade had existed here, and a profusion of worldly goods and riches had been available to its citizens. People from vast corners of the globe convened here to trade, and daily exposure to new languages and currencies tempered the psyche. Pompeii residents did not need to leave home to experience the unifying aspects of the human condition, or humanity's varied and diverse marvels. People, jewels, metals, spices, and other goods from around the world came through this city, so one who lived here was more connected to the world at large than most people, save for shipmen, traders, and explorers.

As I wandered through the past, I marveled at how little the human experience has changed since this time. We still experience personal growth in the ways bestowed upon our ancient ancestors: by trial and error, successes and failures, highs and lows. One thing I knew for certain: I could no longer lie dormant within myself. It was time for action. It was time for a new beginning. After experiencing Pompeii, I wrote:

July 21, 2000

I realized how insignificant I am in my world. So why obsess about doing what is 'right' by the standards of others? I must do what is right for me.

It was odd saying goodbye to Lisa this morning. How did the end come so quick? I woke up one hour early (by accident–alarm clock still set to Greek time) and didn't realize 'til I was out of the shower. It took me 40 minutes to walk from Fortuna Campground to the Circumvesuviana train station with my pack on. But it was a gorgeous walk around 6:30 am, with the sun settling on the morning mists, the mountains so hazy they seemed dreamt, morning traffic breaking the silence, and a small dog for company.

Have I finished morphing yet? I have explored ME, myself, and being.

Now it is time for action.

That morning, Lisa and I parted ways, and I would not see her again for several months. I made my way by train to Valencia, Spain. I closed the chapter on my Mediterranean life and have not returned to those blue waters or kind islands where so much happened to change who I am. As I bid this place adieu, I wrote:

Sorrento–Naples–Rome–Ventimiglia
Friday, July 21, 2000
(on the train)

I have spent the last seven months of my life in lands abundant with oleanders and elephant grass, palm trees and pine. The Mediterranean Sea has been a constant, lapping friend. Leaving this for the interior of Europe is like watching a shooting star arc into its disappearance. Will London life signify the end of stargazing and midnight dreams, or will it start the firework show? For this seems to be the final destination for this vagabond. Reality. Responsibility. Perseverance. Dedication. Foundation and future-building. This kind of unknown debilitates me. What if I become part of an insignificant mass instead of being an insignificant writer? Already the sea has donned a tamer hue and the aquamarine sparkles of Greece have been put into seasonal retirement. Blue has turned to grey. Sparkles have turned to sheet metal. My empty pocket and rumbling stomach remind me of my aloneness.

I must become enthusiastic. I must have a positive agenda for meeting the goals of my grand plan. But first, I must eat.

I felt connected to the beauty and gifts of life. I felt better equipped to understand my responses to perceived fears and stressors. Now adept at noticing signs and coincidences, I ceased being surprised by them. Yet, though I felt more comfortable in the present moment than ever before, the future still lacked focus.

Time and again, I met teachers traveling in groups and wondered, "Should I be a teacher?" Time and again, teachers told me I should be a teacher. It seemed that everywhere I went, I met people originally from all around the world who were living and working in London. "Should I go and live and work in London?" Even though I knew I wanted to be a writer more than anything, I believed I would have to find some way to fund that endeavor. Rather than do something that wouldn't fulfill me, I sought avenues that would express and fulfill my soul in the ways I had expressed in my Fulfilling and Balanced Life Chart (page 127). Teaching and traveling were both expressions that resonated for me. As had been happening all along, signs and serendipitous meetings affirmed my path.

Portbou, Spain
July 21, 2000

Just last night I was agonizing about how I haven't really had any signs lately. As you can tell from last night's entries, I was feeling very confused and unsure. Well, this morning a teacher from Houston (Marc) simply approached me and started a conversation with me. He had overheard me mention that I was coming from Naples and was empathizing about the long journey I was making. We ended up having a long conversation about teaching and he gave me tons of information and got me really excited about teaching again. Plus, he mentioned that many of his friends who are teachers are writers as well. He told me that in the private school system teachers don't require teaching certificates. They simply need to be bright, experienced, and able to teach multiple subjects. I jotted down the names of associations and headhunters at the back of this journal.

After he left, I sat back and pondered. I thought: I'll go to London, apply for teaching jobs around Jan/Feb/Mar, stay the summer in Europe and move to the states to my new job the following fall season. Then I decided to buy another coffee and the lady working the stall (in Spain) was drinking out of a London mug! Two signs in one morning!

One thing I knew for certain: I would not live in Hungary again. My time in Budapest was over. It was time to move on, and accepting this truth soothed me. It was no longer a question that ailed me. It was a fact upon which future plans would be built.

I wasn't homeward bound yet, exactly. I spent a few weeks in Valencia, visiting my cousin and arranging visas and a work permit, so I could live and work in London if that was what I eventually decided to do. I would then travel with a friend I knew from Mallorca, who was driving from Barcelona to Budapest and had agreed to give me a ride. Once there, I would visit with friends and then travel on to stay with my aunt in Romania, where I would wait for my visa to arrive by mail. And then, I would likely live and work in London for nearly a year, saving money and gaining work experience before returning to North America. These plans had slowly manifested over the past few weeks, and while the realization of them seemed overwhelming at times, I felt the peace and excitement that a slice of certainty yields, for no matter how the future would eventually play out, I was certain it would not be in Budapest. But where would it be, exactly? How would it look, specifically? I did not know. As I settled into Valencia, my thoughts hovered not over the solid ground of cobblestone streets or within the walls of medieval buildings still functioning as public spaces today but above the city in the etheric plane where the stars and gods could point the way ahead for me. All clarity was restricted to the past, the future unclear.

Valencia is a beautiful city and served as a kind and gracious host for the transition I was experiencing internally. In the weeks I spent there, wide parks and full museums stimulated my mind, bright beaches bathed my body and soul. My cousin, too, was a great host. A student at the time, he was gone most days and I found the aloneness recuperative. During the evenings and weekends, we enjoyed an easy company, laughing, cooking, and sharing our meals and ideas with hearty appetite. Only three years younger than me, Levi shared my enthusiasm for travel and adventure, but his absolute certainty of his own future was an anchor I lacked. Being around him helped me feel grounded. We went to bustling local markets absent of tourists. We attended evening movie screenings on the green by the Palau de

La Música. We sang songs and went dancing in the wee hours of the morning, when Spain is at its social height. During quiet afternoons, we made our way through museums, where the past seemed to echo the present.

August 9, 2000

On Sunday, Levi and I had such a great day! We slept in, breakfasted, and then walked through the Old Town (and got lost!) and went to the Ceramics Museum. This museum, though I am not a big fan of ceramics museums, is fantastic. First of all, the building itself (especially on the outside, but inside as well) is a sight to behold. It stands like a nobleman from the Augustan Age: regal, grand, and primped, powdered and be-frocked in feminine garb. Inside, the courtyards, well-lit rooms, shadowy rooms, murals, chandeliers, and some excellent pieces of furniture, lighting, and drapery outfit the inner prima donna. Downstairs, two enormous (and original) coaches from the 1750s stand imperiously. One realizes that if one had been a peasant in the 1750s and this carriage had pulled up, drawn by 4-6 magnificent horses, all the gold, painted murals, silk draperies, towering magnificence, and otherworldly riches would have caused one to hurl themselves to the ground in abject fear of the god-like people within. Undoubtedly, these people themselves would inspire another bout of arrhythmia with their enormous embroidered and bejeweled silk clothes, their towering powdered wigs and their thickly made-up faces. Eeeeeek! How could peasants ever have risen up against such power?

On the same floor (the ground floor) was an exhibition of fans. Half are brand new and produced by artists. They are funny, thoughtful, clever, and freakish. For example, one has a beach scene with a shark trying to eat a surfer (very 1950s!). My favorite was black with créme lace and depicted a night sky with stars and dream constellations showing ships in space and other midnight travels. Dangling from the base of the fan was a silk tassel with a miniature blue globe. So often I have felt what this fan speaks: my mind in the starry heavens, my body lodged on earth.

The cosmically decorated fan seemed to evidence that at least one other soul had experienced and valued the astral travels of the mind and soul while being grounded to the earth plane. I did not feel so alone in this experience. The pomp and circumstance of the Rococo architecture and coaches seemed to embody the magnitude and authority of the very beliefs and conventions I, in my own life, resisted and pushed back against as I tried to chart my own story. Just as those large and wealthy people and carriages of the past must have seemed overwhelmingly powerful and impervious to the lower classes, so I realized my own thoughts and beliefs could be just as formidable a tradition to break down and rebuild. On this leg of my journey, if I were truly to experience my own Enlightenment, I would need to break with the tradition of my thoughts and beliefs and create a new reality—based on a new way of thinking—that was true and authentic for me. It was not enough to identify the limitations. I had to surpass them.

As you near the end of your odyssey, your own complex and perhaps even contradictory feelings may start to play pinball in your emotional world. Earthly desires vie for authority with the needs of your soul. On the one hand, you can't wait to soak in your clean bathtub in hot water with bubbles up to your ears. You may be looking forward to savoring the luxury of your thick, fluffy towels, your kitchen filled with spices and percolating goodness, your hand arched in a graceful pose as you point the remote at your television while you sink into the dreamy goodness of your sofa, whether in peaceful solitude or snuggling up to someone you love. Yet, you might not feel finished with your inner journey. You may not want to face the realities of work and money and responsibility again. You may feel apprehensive about seeing family and friends who may not understand what you've just experienced. Despite this reticence, you may be feeling an undercurrent of excitement about the new future you will now build for yourself, now that you better know what you need to incorporate into your daily life to bring you happiness and a sense of purpose. Then again, all that building is *hard work*, and you may not feel like getting into that particular groove again! You're ready for the comforts of home but not the discomforts. It's challenging. It's confusing. How can you run *from* something at the same time you're running *toward* it? Your new life, your future, the destiny you wish to fulfill are just ahead of you. Will you thrive in the environment you called home before you left?

Most of all, you may be wondering (as I was), *Will I be able to live my destiny and be my authentic self in this place that defines me otherwise?* This is the most jarring question of all, for it is the underbelly of the beast—your weakest spot. Returning home may feel as though your achievements may be threatened and undermined by the way life used to be, and this concern, more than any other, is a shadow upon your travels as you veer in the direction of home. What if you can't hold on to the feelings and revelations you've gained on this trip?

Consider that your spiritual journey is only halfway completed. Now, as you enter the last part of your physical journey, and thoughts of home begin to edge their way into your present moment, it's normal for a sense of confusion or uneasiness to begin to set in. You are still journeying. There are still shifts occurring. The conflicts you're experiencing are simply a response to having turned the ship and finding yourself homeward bound. You are still learning. You are still growing.

Back in chapter 4 we talked about the labyrinth as a symbol representing your journey. You're at the center now. From here on out, you are journeying outward from that center and back to the beginning—but changed. It was with some relief that I realized this myself as I found myself knocking about Valencia, Spain, feeling dislocated and confused by the flow of my life.

Valencia, Spain
July 2000

All is hazy because I am at the center!

I have traveled the path of the labyrinth to within and I have discovered my interests, my aspirations, my ideals, and I have even found my perfect partner type. So now I have to stop the center from gelling and move back out the labyrinth path into the Real World. It is a two-part journey and I must have the patience to see it through and the courage to be true to myself.

Follow the labyrinth from within to without!

The New You

No matter how shaky the path back out of the labyrinth may feel at times, you *can* hold on to the new you. You will not forget what you've learned. You have become more agile, more confident, a stronger person. You have outfitted yourself with an arsenal of tools and a new understanding of your place in the world. While you may not be able to live in vacation mode in perpetuity, you will be able to reinhabit your old stomping grounds with a new sense of purpose and vitality. You will be able to create a life that rises up to meet your dreams, and the seam between the two will, with effort, become less and less perceptible, not because you lose your grasp on your dreams, but because you realize them. Continue to look outward and you will see that the universe is helping you, just as the little old women bearing food and blessings helped Lisa and me in our time of need back on Cyprus. The mystical journey is still about you, despite the world at large coming into sharper focus as you return to your own reality.

Just as they have been throughout your journey, people will continue to come into your life to help you through this time. My friend Abe, a boat salesman I knew from Mallorca, was driving from Barcelona to Vienna, and I hitched a ride with him on my way to Budapest. While I no longer had my apartment there, my friends, some family, and all my possessions were there. We stopped in Kitzbühel, Austria, to stay with his friends, Nicolas and Kristina. Nicolas was a well-known photographer and Kristina a fashion designer, although she was taking time off to be with their baby and toddler. It was here at their mountain home in the Alps that I finally caught up on journaling. I record the journey from Barcelona to Austria in staccato:

Kitzbühel, Austria
August 15, 2000

Breakfast and the Buquebus to meet Abe. Then stress and underground garage and good-bye and coffee and 100 km of lost driving. Then 3 am and sleeping lakeside in a Mercedes outside of Lyon. Then breakfast (superb!) at 7 am in the north of Provence while talking religion, philosophy, and extra-terrestrial life. So wonderful, with brioche, café au lait, and croissants with ham and cheese. Then on to Switzerland and topics of love, mesmerism, ghosts and the rest, the much-needed rest, taken on the passenger side. Then a Best Western in Switzerland with free cakes, coffee, and a spa! Mineral water massages by cornfields in Swiss mountains with blue sky. Then Lisa in crisis and laughter before the phone credit ran out. Then dinner, dessert, bed, and the next day occupied with upset stomach and driving. Arrival in Austria. Drinks lakeside. Dinner in the Alps and a journey to Peru—Kristina's Peru—with wild dogs, blood, witches, shamans, energy-sucking babies, socks that never dry, castrated horses in a desert oasis, a microclimate to swim in out on the coast, the jungle to trek through—such heat, such heat! Then blow out the candles and lie under feathers while breathing mountain air. Then breakfast and stories of love—unrequited, after she was so certain! And meeting Nicolas (he was not for her) and never being without him since! 3 years and 2 children! Then down to town to walk and take photos, drink coffee, eat lunch. And this. This now. By the lake at the top of the world. Black water, water-colored mountains, every millimeter of earth producing green. And I write until I feel green and blue and black and tranquil and water-colored. How good it is! Even my page is sun-dappled now!

You wouldn't necessarily think a salesman driving his Mercedes across Europe would be so interesting. You wouldn't think a housewife with two small children and living in a small town in Austria would have such stories of adventure to share. When the Universe is helping you realize your destiny, you will constantly be surprised by the people who enter your life and reveal their personal odysseys to you. Continue to listen to their stories. See what you can learn from their experiences. What can they teach you? Kristina taught me, by way of her own experience, that one can be adventurous and still meet someone, fall in love, marry, and have children. One does not exclude the other. Abe taught me one can be materially successful and be spiritual. Again, one does not exclude the other. These were two questions I was grappling with at the time, as I headed back to a world where responsibilities and material success measured one's accomplishments with a value beyond which adventure and mysticism could outwardly provide.

As I swam in and out of melancholic thoughts now that I was homeward bound, I wrote a poem about the particular brand of sadness that accompanies the end of a long journey (*tristesse* is the French word for melancholy).

August 15, 2000

Bonjour tristesse!
Did you know I missed you?
I have depended on you so!
You are my valley
from which I always rise
up out of,
so I need you.
For there cannot be
great heights without you.
And though I am always
the first
to bid good-bye
that doesn't mean
I don't cherish you.
On the contrary,
when you surprise me
with your hello,
I cherish you all the more,

for I know I will reach
a summit
after we have lingered
in each other's tears.
Bonjour tristesse!

In my experience, lows tend to precede highs. When you pursue your destiny by following your dreams, life is not necessarily easier. Personal growth, just like material growth, is hard earned and requires tenacity, work ethic, and grit. This is a path that includes tears: tears of sadness, tears of fear, tears of frustration. What is easier about your life when you choose the path that is right for you is that the path has meaning. The only tears I have ever been truly tortured by were the ones I cried because I felt the effort of my current endeavors wasn't worthwhile and that the sacrifices I was making were meaningless to me. When you endeavor to realize that which has meaning for you, even the tears you encounter along the way are your friends. And just as I suspected, after a day steeped in the remorse of anticipating the end of my odyssey, a day of brilliant heights (literally) succeeded us, for the next day we climbed a mountain and adventured at its summit.

Kitzbühel, Austria (Tyrol)
August 16, 2000

A most brilliant day!

We went into town today and took the funicular up Mount Hahnenkamm. I was so nervous climbing that steep height inside a suspended and swaying box. But I survived! At the top we hiked up and around the mountain, past chewing cows and wildflowers. The vista, the air, the sun, the breeze, the sound of bells! Cow bells! Such happiness!

We took so many photos and posed in so many places. Abe filled my straw hat with wildflowers and we laughed. Then we played badminton at the top by the restaurant and we ate around back where the children play. We had a divine lunch! I ate dumplings stuffed with cheese (turo) and salad with sour cream dressing, and coffee with apple strudel bathed in vanilla sauce, and aranygaluska. After feasting we laid in the sun and just existed. Then we went to a friend's house for schnapps and I drank a nut-flavored one. The cabin was, at one time, owned by the Austrian painter Alfons Walde. He used to paint there . . .

It was sunshine and stories and a feeling of being surrounded by kindred spirits. They were all self-employed artists, and I did not know then that this was what I would become just a few years down the road. At the time, I simply basked in the camaraderie, breathed the high mountain air deep into my lungs, and enjoyed the conversations.

People Who Test Your Patience

How poor are they that have not patience!
What wound did ever heal but by degrees?

—Shakespeare

The other thing that may begin to happen as you are homeward bound is that you will encounter people who will test your resolve, your patience, or both. It's as though the Universe is providing you with a taste of what is to come, easing you back into the waters of your future reality, one bit at a time. By the last leg of our trip across Europe, Abe was not just driving me to Vienna, he was also driving me nuts! I wrote quite a lengthy diatribe about his many flaws and my judgments were harsh, to say the least:

Budapest, Hungary
August 22, 2000

What has brought all this doubt about? Well, traveling with Abe didn't help.

But traveling with him has taught me something. Abe is a decent, well-meaning, and truly good person, but he is not happy in so many ways and he is not LIVING his life, but surviving it. To explain: Abe is hyper-organized. All things that occur in his life are pre-planned, calculated, expected, and as safe as possible. He has well-stocked first-aid kits, insurance for everything, maps, phone numbers, connections, etc. He insures passengers in his car. He calculates that if he drives between 100-110 km/hour he will save $300.00 in gas over the course of the trip. If he speeds, he does so in 5–or–10 minute bursts, then pulls into the slow lane, slowing to 100 while remarking, "Well, that was enough of that for a while." He stops for a 10-minute break every hour. He then cleans all his mirrors and front windshield, plus checks his tires. His stereo saw volume 17 for all of 30 seconds before being discretely (every time I turned my head) lowered to 8. All things occurring unexpectedly and not planned for or prepared for cause Abe to turn bright red, tense up, in short—fly into a blind rage, which he attempts to suppress.

Walking with Abe is a marathon. He must always be half a step ahead and he pushes you in the direction he wants to go. He ensures you follow a step or two behind by speeding up anytime you try to keep pace with him, until you're both aimlessly racing through town, at which point he'll say, "We've really got to slow down, you're just walking too fast and I can't enjoy the city."

Abe only ever talks about himself or his interests; his successes (he was an Olympic winner in archery [he says with a barely concealed gloating smile, then repeats statement when there is no response] he cave dives, he has sold 8 boats in his first year as a junior salesperson, he speaks 6 languages, he horseback rides, he plays the clarinet and pan flute, he is a chef) and he'll only discuss pan-flute craftsmanship, sales strategy, gas mileage, car quality, license plate numbers (identifying where each car is from by said numbers), and his plans for the future.

In short, Abe is a control freak and someone obsessed with competing and winning. He will learn languages that help him in sales (but not because he's interested in them), he's completely uninterested in people's lives and experiences, to the point where he is so in control of what he is learning that he doesn't take the opportunity to learn from other people through conversation.

Abe is always falling in love with women and then finding flaws in them or being rejected himself. Orphaned as a child, raised by the state, denied his opportunity to study music (which is what he wanted), he is a product of the Modern World and (although he is quite religious) lacks any connection with his spirit and the things in the world that are magical and beautiful. For all his comments about passing cars, he never once remarked, "What beautiful mountains, what gorgeous countryside, etc." I really began to feel drained, depleted, unsure, unsuccessful, and disheartened by his company. Even though he is a wonderful, kind, and good-hearted person in many ways.

Of course, Abe's behavior upset me not because he was so annoying but because it reflected back to me the very behaviors that resided within me and that I was trying so hard to distance myself from. I could see my own disappointments in life feeding my own fears: of failure, of not measuring up, of not being the best I could be. I could see that my nature would lend itself to responding to fears as Abe's had: by competing, measuring my worth in accomplishments, losing my sense of self and the pursuit of my dreams in the process. I knew my own romantic relationships were subject to my own fickle nature; I, too, would fall in love fast and furious, only to throw men away or be thrown away myself. I couldn't wait to get away from Abe, if only so that I could turn away from these very traits within me. These traits were connected to the old me. Would they return once I was home?

The people who test you by getting under your skin have also entered your life for a reason. The traits they exhibit that cause you to clench your jaw or grit your teeth are likely reflecting back to you the very aspects of yourself that you are struggling with. Examine each annoying person from this perspective. Can you see yourself mirrored in each set of behaviors? Can you connect with a feeling of compassion for that other person by determining what would cause him or her to behave in such a way? In the case of Abe, I could understand that as an orphaned child, he must have felt very much abandoned and that there was very little that he was in control of in his life. After he was denied the pursuit of his dream to be a musician, the state wanted him to have employment that would allow him to be financially independent. Without any safety nets (parents, relatives, etc.), Abe had to ensure, always, that he was his own safety net; hence his need to anticipate and prepare for any emergency. With his worth measured by his ability to perform within the orphanage system, he had no other way to express his worthiness than in accomplishments.

As a child of strict Eastern European parents, I also wanted to have some control over my life. Raised with the mindset of "children should be seen, not heard," I didn't always feel that I could contribute to the decisions made about my life. I sought financial freedom from a very young age, earning money through part-time jobs as early as possible. While I didn't like how Abe's behaviors manifested outwardly, I could understand and have compassion for where they came from. Still, I was looking forward to having some breathing room once I got on the train that would go from Vienna to Budapest. Who knew I could experience such a sense of solitude on a train filled with people? I did. And it was delicious.

Just Keep Swimming

As my forward motion brought me closer to home, I transitioned from the dreamy world of travel to the solid ground of a reality I now had to be answerable to. But the signs did not stop appearing. When I didn't see them during my days, I experienced them in my dreams. One night I dreamed I was on a boat, looking over the starboard bow when I spotted two silver fish swimming in the water beneath me. I heard someone call out, "Look! Tuna!" and the fish heard it too, so they inverted themselves in the water, heads down and tails up, and pretended to be buoys! Then they sensed my presence, and feeling safe, they slowly surfaced, and as they did, they changed shape and color. They swam sideways on the surface of the sea, and iridescent colors of electric blue, green, and yellow undulated in their skin. They rose out of the water and swam in the sky above my head, turning every color of the rainbow. As they turned their final color, pink, they swam away from me in a wide, elegant, sweeping left-right movement, just out of reach of my hands. I awoke feeling magical and affirmed. That was the last I would see of them, and I have never again experienced fish as signs.

The truth is, trying to hold on to that Mystical Backpacking feeling for forever is just like trying to catch the tail of a fish swimming away from you. It slips from your grasp, and you stare out after it into an empty sea or sky. Being back in the "real world" may feel more like being a fish out of water. There you are, flapping and flailing about on dry land, waiting for someone to save you. So, here's the most valuable knowledge I can impart to you at this point in your journey: No one is coming. No one will save you. Just as you've been asked to do from the start, you must save yourself. And when you do, you connect with your inner hero in ways that build your confidence and comfort zones simultaneously. You may be back at home, but the journey isn't over yet.

The only way to truly be in the flow of all that magic you've tapped into on your travels is to do what Dory teaches us in *Finding Nemo*: "Just keep swimming. Just keep swimming."[1] Now, forward motion doesn't mean you should suppress the gloom and dismiss the sadness you may be feeling. It's never easy to come back from vacation, and it's even harder to come back from Mystical Backpacking. Feel your feelings. Process them. Write down your thoughts and feelings in your journal. This, too, is part of your journey, even though it may feel like a road block. Once you've finished with feeling and processing, get back to work on journeying! You may have *discovered* your destiny while being a Mystical Backpacker, but you haven't even begun to *realize* it. The future may be bright, but it's certainly not yet in focus.

Let's start turning knobs and fiddling with buttons to try and get things looking a little clearer. The clearer your vision of the future is, the easier it will be to manifest. The next set of Mystical Exercises aims to equip you with two vital tools for moving forward purposefully into your future. The first is a set of plans to help guide you in building the life you imagine. The second is to create a visual representation of the empowered feelings you've gained from your Mystical Backpacking odyssey. This will be something you can reflect on, meditate on, or be inspired by as you return to a life that is perhaps less overtly adventurous. Staying in touch with the feelings you've experienced as an adventurer will help you chart the course forward and seize the opportunities that come your way with courage and enthusiasm. The plans will help you make the right choices for realizing a life that has a much higher likelihood of satisfying your physical needs as well as the needs of your soul.

Mystical Exercises: Chapter 6

Bran thought about it. "Can a man still be brave if he's afraid?" "That is the only time a man can be brave," his father told him.

—George R. R. Martin, *A Game of Thrones*

Looking Ahead

Create a three-year, five-year, and ten-year vision for your life. Begin by imagining what your ideal life would look like in three years' time, five years' time, and ten years' time. Document this ideal in either a bulleted list or as a detailed description. Just as you did with the Fulfilled and Balanced Life Chart, be as detailed as possible. Don't omit things that are important to you because you don't believe they are attainable or because you feel undeserving. Stay focused on what would truly bring you happiness and a sense of well-being achieved by living a life of purpose. The things on your list have to have meaning to you, not necessarily to the world at large.

It's also important that your plans are reasonable and the accomplishments are attainable. Let's face it: you probably won't be a world-famous musician in three years if you don't even know how to play an instrument right now. I'm not saying it's impossible, but attainable goals tend to be much more satisfying in the short run. In three years you can learn to play an instrument. In five years, you can be playing in a band. In ten years, you can be playing professionally and have your own music for sale. Build your three-, five-, and ten-year plans with targets you're likely to reach and you will feel like a huge success when you do.

Taking Emotional Inventory: The Voldemort Exercise

As we travel through life, we accumulate the weight of our experiences. Sometimes, what we choose to carry is a feeling we can return to that reminds us how wonderful life can be (like the memory of an afternoon spent with a lover, or a particular event that was fun from start to finish). Sometimes, we choose to carry feelings and memories upon which we move forward in life with a bit more cynicism (like our anger towards an ex-friend or resentment of our perceived mistreatment by another), and sometimes, we carry shame and guilt (over our perceived failures or the wrongs we've done unto others). Oftentimes, we aren't aware of how all types of memories and feelings can limit us moving forward. When we spend a whole first date comparing the very real person before us to an idealized partner, whether from the past or from an imagined future, we limit how our future relationships might play out. This is just as undermining as our anger and resentment toward others can be, simply served up as a more palatable dish.

Take some time to write out three lists. The first names all the things you're angry and resentful about, the second lists all the things you feel guilty or ashamed of, and the third shares your happiest memories. Now, explore how each item on your list limits you in the present moment and write these points out beside each item. For example:

Anger	How This Affects My Present
I feel angry toward my cousin for her display of jealousy and my perception that she would like to deny me advantages in life.	I distrust my cousin. I distrust many relatives. I believe their love and kindness is insincere.

Resentment	How This Affects My Present
I resent being paid less than my male counterpart at work.	It makes me feel angry toward men in general, and I am rude to the men at work.

Be as thorough and comprehensive with all three lists as you possibly can. In the next chapter, we'll be working with these lists some more (in a much more mystical way). Remember: it's okay to be honest, and no one but you need see your lists. This is a private exercise aimed at clearing your own emotional baggage. Even though you may feel the tone is accusing of others, you are using this exercise to tune in to your own belief system and to ultimately free yourself of those beliefs that hold you back or limit you. Give yourself permission to be authentic and to put down on paper even that which you don't permit yourself to speak. You can call this your Voldemort exercise!

What Fulfills My Soul

Based on all the work you've done in your journals and exercises and the experiences you've had during your travels, what truths have you unearthed about yourself? What activities would fulfill your soul? What career or occupation would fulfill your soul? What relationships would fulfill your soul? What practices would fulfill your soul? List them in your journal or exercise space under the heading What Fulfills My Soul and describe them in as much detail as possible.

Once I left Abe in Vienna and boarded the train, it was as though I were at the bottom of a funnel. All the whirling and spinning excitement of unplanned, organic travel I had experienced was suddenly compressed into an orderly deposit on home turf. I felt the comfort and embrace of my options narrowing and my tomorrows becoming more predictable but also felt the suffocation and constriction of returning to the pigeonhole. Four rocking hours on the train passed. Fields and sky flashed by. And then, just like that, I was back. Back where I had begun, not so long ago. But I was no longer the person who had departed. Just as my backpack had become my comfortable friend and companion, its colors faded and its straps somewhat tattered, so had I become comfortable with my truths and fully present in the dream of what my future might hold.

7

A New World—Home Is

> Success means having the courage, the determination, and the will to become the person you believe you were meant to be.
>
> —**George Sheehan**

Once the train pulled into Budapest, I was excited and thrilled to be with friends and family again. It was nice to be home and to know my way around without looking at maps, to know where to get what I needed without reading a guidebook, and to sleep in a familiar bed with old friends nearby. I met with friends in cafés and living rooms, bars, and restaurants. I wanted so much to share all that I had learned and experienced and felt that if I could just talk about my experiences, I would keep that mystical feeling alive. After all, my entire being was different, my worldview altered. Conversation may be the very bellows needed to fan the fires ignited in my soul.

Yet, based on my friends' reactions to me, this metaphysical change didn't seem to be outwardly perceptible. I must've looked and seemed the same to them! They wanted to laugh and gossip and share their stories and find out what I'd be doing next, and I didn't really get asked about what I had experienced while I was gone. Consequently, I felt a little lonely and strangely absent from the present. The mystical began to evaporate, and I was left wondering . . . did I really experience all that I felt I had experienced? Was I delusional, believing in signs and jumping fishes and old women bearing blessings?

In lieu of adventure stories, we talked of future plans (the one thing I was absolutely, without a doubt, totally unsure of). I surveyed my friends for input, and of course, everyone had an opinion and most of them conflicted. I recorded their thoughts in my journal:

Budapest, Hungary
August 22, 2000

Here I am on this journey, right? And I keep expecting it to be over, to end, or to have already ended unbeknownst to me. I am back where I started so many (6) months ago and I feel like I have come full circle. But I must stress that I haven't. This part of my past is simply a place to revisit to prove to myself that I indeed need to follow my dreams and not what others deem as "successful." Maybe Kelly is right. A group of us had drinks on Saturday night at Café Kör and he insisted I had so many opportunities in Budapest what with being a Westerner who speaks Hungarian. And I do have usable skills here. But, that is not what I want! Keeping too many doors open and embracing too many possibilities confuses me and results in me losing my focus. It's a test or a reminder and I must have the courage to see and move beyond. Budapest is NOT the place for me. I don't want to be a business executive. I want to be a writer. London is the place I should be going to.

Then two of the guests at our dinner party piped up and said they didn't think London was a good idea financially. They recommended New York instead. Kelly insisted I stay in Budapest. In short, by Saturday night I was a lost and doubting stressed-out mess. So I ditched the whole party and met up with Michael who convinced me to stay on my path and do what I want to do and not what other people think I should do. I felt so much better! Plus, yesterday I met up with the dinner party crew and they had changed their minds and thought I should pursue only my dreams and not viable career options just because they are viable. So, even in Budapest I am learning, growing, and finding answers.

Somehow, a part of me knew that this, too, was a part of the journey. The questions and suggestions were a challenge to my resolve. The Universe may have conspired to bring me to this point, but how committed was I to fulfilling the needs of my soul? Would I do what it takes? Did I have unflappable resolve? It was as though Budapest itself—and all my friends present here—were going to find out. It was a bit destabilizing. After all, I had just spent months tracking my future like it was an elusive tiger padding through the jungle. Suddenly and unexpectedly, I was confronted by it in a clearing.

As anxieties mounted, Vacation Hangover set in; physical exhaustion combined with deep feelings of remorse as sunny carefree days faded and reality stepped in. The party was definitely over, I was suffering, and the week ahead looked grim. All things mystical ebbed from the flow of daily life. In resistance, I charted the lengths of the Danube and the crowded expanses of Pest's trendier neighborhoods, oblivious to the beauty of twinkling shorelines and romantic boulevards, focused instead on maintaining the momentum, confidence, and clarity that Mystical Backpacking had yielded. As I passed the golden Buda Hills at sunset, my thoughts strained toward Greek islands and the sound of taut ropes moaning and creaking as boats rocked in Palma de Mallorca's marina. I thought of the well of peace and love I had accessed through meditation, the confidence I had felt in response to signs and strange synchronicities, the gratitude I had felt for all I had been experiencing and witness to. I also thought of afternoon kisses, steamy nights, early-morning stars, and midnight dancing. The echoes of Ibiza trance music pulsed faintly in my heart, out of sync with Budapest's *schlager* music cackling on sidewalks and spilling forth from open windows and doorways.

Both the mystical and the pleasurable had yielded such a profoundly spiritual awakening within me. Would these feelings be tucked back into bed, where slumber would reclaim me? The quiet shushing of palm trees bristling in the breeze was replaced by cars honking in traffic and clouds of exhaust fumes rising from hot pavement. Austria's cool mountains and downy pillows were gone, lumpy sofas and the stiff mattresses reserved for spare rooms took their place. Holding on to my happiness was physically challenging. Holding on to the mystical seemed impossible.

Despite the fog I was in, some inner light illuminated new gains. I had many things now that I hadn't had before. I had acquired a host of experiences and insights that were empowering, positive, and uplifting. So many what-if questions had been answered, their power over me no longer an obstacle to forward motion. Most of all, I felt connected with a sense of purpose and the driving forces within that would see it realized in new ways. I now had a short list of what I wanted out of life. First and foremost, I knew I wanted to be a writer. That was the heart of the matter for me. I also better understood that I needed to be surrounded by beauty and creative people, environments being fundamental for inspiration. To earn money in the interim, I knew that I would like to own my own business or teach. I knew I wanted to marry someone, and he would also need to be a dream chaser. I knew I wanted to have children and balance the ever-changing aspects of a creative life with a reliable and steady home life. Before my Mystical Backpacking odyssey, I was not able to articulate any of these aspirations with any clarity or surety and certainly not unapologetically. But now it was clear to me. I was sure. I wasn't embarrassed or sorry for wanting what I wanted.

I just didn't know how I would get there yet.

What I missed most immediately about traveling was feeling like a hero. While I had been backpacking, I had truly felt that I was the hero of my own life. I was out in the world adventuring! I had no idea how things would end up, but I knew what I was searching for. I had faith in a greater power without and I accessed a greater power within, a power I hadn't previously known I had. What was I supposed to do now that the journey was over?

No one ever tells you what happens to heroes after they find what they're looking for. No books or movies or songs told me what to do from this point on. What example was I to follow? And what kind of a flawed hero was I anyway? As questions fostered doubt and doubt caused confusion, I felt more like Icarus with his melting wings. I was falling out of the sky.

I didn't want to respond to my fears as I had been doing thus far in my life: by pretending to be someone I wasn't. I remembered the fish from my dream: feeling unsafe, they had inverted themselves in the water and pretended to be buoys. It was only when they felt safe that they flew through the air and were able to show all their beauty and magic. So, what was I going to be, a beautiful, iridescent creation soaring to great heights and showing all my true colors or a drab and frightened version of myself, head buried, hoping not to be noticed?

The past is easily summarized and other people's issues much easier to identify than our own. When we have beliefs that retard our ability to express ourselves authentically (and all of us do, to some degree), then addressing those beliefs is vital. If I were going to believe it wasn't safe for me to be my authentic self, then I wouldn't be able to be my authentic self. It was that simple. Of course, I didn't see that then. I'm still working on seeing it now! Figuring out what we want and need out of life doesn't mean we get handed a road map for getting there. That's the joy and lesson of living a life. You pursue your vision step-by-step, adventure along the way, and occasionally realize dreams. Living a full life means that we keep dreaming and we keep pursuing those dreams. When we do that, we actively participate in creating our life. And when we create, we are one with God, one with a higher power, in sync with the awesome current and force of that which is much greater than us. Things get mystical. We are airborne, rainbow colored, in our full glory.

This book promised to make you the hero of your own life and to connect you with your destiny. Well, what kind of hero are you going to be? If you're trying to be a flawless hero, you will likely miss the mark. If you can accept a flawed hero as an ideal, then you can be your own hero, because we're all flawed and that's part of what makes us humans so wonderful. As you chart your course forward, remember to keep being a hero for yourself. It doesn't mean you have all the answers or that you know where you'll end up. It just means that you keep your eye on the ball: your destiny.

So, where and what is your destiny, anyway?

Your destiny resides in the pages of your journal and in the many depths of self that you've excavated by way of the exercises along the way. In being out in the world and experiencing extraordinary things, you've plugged in to the source of your truth. If you've come up with a list that says you want to be a painter, then that's it. If you've time and again returned to your longing for children, there you have it. If all you've focused on each time you connect with joy is your need to throw a basketball through a hoop, then that's it. If every place you've traveled you've taken photos and written journal entries about ironwork, then you have found your passion! When you take up the thing that brings you the greatest joy, you are fulfilling your destiny. It is as simple as that. Because when we are happy and joyful and inspired, we don't spend our time worrying about destiny or all the things we should be doing. We're fulfilled by what we've got, even if what we've got hasn't reached its full potential. And if we perceive ourselves as spiritual beings having a human experience, it's likely the creator or the higher power from which we came wants this for us too: to do that which fills us full of spirit and contentment and even joy. When we do just that, we feel our contribution is worthy.

Do yourself a favor: don't survey everyone you know for what they think you should do next, as I did. Don't expect everyone to want to hear about your journey: not the physical one, nor the mystical one. A few people may surprise you, but it's best not to hold out hope for these few, either. Yes, it's true that when you've been to heaven and all anyone wants to hear about is whether your luggage arrived safe and sound, it can be the most alienating feeling in the world! Consider that your friends and family have been dealing with the daily grind for all this time. Some of them may already be on their path, working toward their dreams. Some of them may feel confident and comfortable with their lives and know exactly where they're going. There are people who have never felt lost or without direction. There are people for whom words like *destiny* and *dreams* hold no court, for they are content and fulfilled by the lives they lead.

Consequently, it's perhaps unreasonable to expect your friends and family to receive your stories with the enthusiasm they reserve for celebrities. Remember: they are not seeking their dreams in you. You have been seeking your dreams in the world. These are two very different and mutually exclusive things. So, it's best to expect nothing. Not because I'm suggesting you be a cynic, but because I'm reminding you: the answers can't be found *out there*. The answers are within you. You're not alone, even if you feel that way. There are others just like you out there. Continue to seek the mystical. After all, you are a Mystical Backpacker for life, not just while you've got a backpack strapped to your back.

I have to admit that I lost sight of this when I returned to Budapest. I was back in this beautiful city I started in, but with no job to return to and no future plans set, I was like Pavlov's dog. Being home triggered my awareness of what I perceived to be my failures and disappointments: how I had grown to dislike the life I had there, how I could have been more financially successful than I had been, how I had quit my job and run away. I focused on thoughts that undermined my confidence and disempowered me. I revisited limiting beliefs and (unintentionally) absorbed them into my psyche, allowing them to pollute my thoughts as I strategized my next move. In contrast, it was amazing how much the odyssey part of my travel adventure had supplied the opposite, for each day of backpacking I had felt increasing confidence and empowerment. Having experienced these feelings, I now knew (perhaps for the first time ever), what feelings I was aiming to sustain.

The challenge to being back in the place you started is not to get sucked back in to the same old story. Rather than slip into old routines, recognize where your environment triggers emotions and behaviors you thought you had overcome and left behind; notice where your certainty begins to wobble. Focus on finding ways to ensure those triggers are recognized and find ways to disempower them. They can consume a lot of your time and energy if allowed to run amuck in your brand new future.

At this phase in my journey, I began to prospect. I cast out lines in different directions to see where I might have a catch. I sent out applications for teaching jobs while waiting on visas. I emailed contacts and networked. I focused on manifesting one or two aspects of the fulfilling and balanced life I wished to live. For now that the outward journey was complete, it was time to begin to create the life I'd been imagining.

I did end up working in London for nearly eight months. During this time, I saved money and traveled more. After exploring every nook and cranny of London, I soaked up the south of England, exploring Stonehenge and the Cissbury Ring, skipping rocks on stony beaches and ambling through seaside towns. I stayed in haunted thatched-roof cottages centuries old and navigated the New Forest with Lisa and Simon from Mallorca, enjoying a plowman's lunch sitting in a meadow next to a man holding a Guinness in one hand and the reins to his horse in the other. I crossed the channel and dipped my toes in Paris, where I argued with my lover on the Pont des Arts bridge and bought myself French perfume and red snakeskin Mary Janes as a salve, so I would always be able to evoke some positive memories whenever I'd return to the City of Light in my thoughts and dreams. I still have the shoes, though the lover is long gone. And of course, I will always remember the croissants. I flew to Ireland and drove a rented car in a wide circle around the north, visiting Galway and the Giant's Causeway, passing haunted-looking abbeys and stone mansions and brightly painted villages smelling of salty sea breezes and beef pies. These adventures were fun but not soul shifting. That had already happened for me.

In the fourteen years since my Mystical Backpacking odyssey, I've traveled more, yes. To different countries and to different states of being: I married. I had children. I built up my own business. I saw this future for myself in Greece—in my mind's eye and in my dreams. And you know what? I'm here in the future for which I laid the groundwork on my journey as a Mystical Backpacker. I don't think I would have made it here without the Mystical Backpacking experience, if only because articulating what I wanted to come home to was solely achieved by going out into the world and discovering it. And I love it. I love my messy, unpredictable, joy-filled life.

Of course, it didn't take me fourteen years to realize a dream. It took me fourteen years to realize all of the dreams, to some degree. Leaving Mystical Backpacking was like traveling a telescope from the wide range, in. The clarity of the big-picture vision for my future was often obscured by the out-of-focus present. But having that vision of my future meant that my compass was always pointed in the right direction as I charted the course ahead. And step-by-step, I found my way.

Within a year of finishing my Mystical Backpacking odyssey, I was employed as a full-time technical writer. Within three years, I had started my own business. Within five years, I was married, and within six years, I had a child, and we had bought our first house. Shortly thereafter, I had my second child, and within ten years, I had a blog with readership and began teaching seminars and workshops. Within fourteen years, I'd written my first book. Piece by piece, my pie is being realized. Having something to work towards, aspire to, or excite and uplift you, is a grand way to live, especially when you are fulfilled by the pursuit of your dreams because they are in alignment with your soul's purpose.

Discovering my destiny was something Mystical Backpacking afforded relatively quickly and with a lot of fun. Manifesting my destiny thereafter has been a lengthy process—in fact, it's supposed to take a lifetime! After all, wouldn't it be boring if we got everything we wanted all at once? Of my time spent as a Mystical Backpacker, I think Hemingway summed it up eloquently when he said of his time living in Paris during his twenties, "If you are lucky enough to have lived in Paris as a young man, then wherever you go for the rest of your life, it stays with you, for Paris is a moveable feast."[1] Mystical Backpacking was a personal odyssey that tempered and forged the person I am today. It is an experience written on the very fabric of my soul. I hope I continue to adventure through life and to write about my adventures until I'm old and gray, but my happiness is no longer housed in some future moment that has yet to be realized. It's in my present. It's always in my present. That's the gift of living your soul's purpose, whatever that may be for you. Mystical Backpacking afforded the clarity I needed to discover what that is for me, and that delectable feast is with me always.

Mystical Exercises: Chapter 7

If you have built castles in the air, your work
need not be lost; that is where they should be.
Now put the foundations under them.

—Henry David Thoreau

You've come home enlightened in every sense of the word. The dissatisfaction you felt before has been replaced with a kicked-back sense of accomplishment and true sense of self. Nobody wants to give up this feeling, nor should anyone have to! So, the question is: how do you incorporate all the gifts you've acquired on your voyage into the life you left behind, thereby creating the life you want to live?

The uplifted, inspired feelings you gained from being a Mystical Backpacker needn't wither on the vine simply because you've returned home. Just tend the fruit. As you settle in to the familiar scenery of your old life, the most important thing to remember is not to settle for less in regards to you and your needs. You can choose to settle back into what is no longer right for you, or you can choose to renovate your old world. Yes, it may seem harder to break from routine and expand comfort zones in this environment because there's nothing external forcing you to do so, as there was when you were backpacking. When the external motivating pressures slip and slide away as you readjust to your life at home, the solution is to create external pressures of your own to help keep your momentum going. The Mystical Exercises you complete now will take you, uncomfortable step by uncomfortable step, in the direction you want to go.

It is time to renovate. Out with the old, dated things that no longer work efficiently or support your positive mindset. In with the fresh, new, shiny things that provide you with a sense of well-being and offer an environment within which your daily tasks are a pleasure to perform. That said, just as you wouldn't start a renovation project without some plans, you don't want to start overhauling your life by tearing out walls with a sledgehammer before you've even talked budget or what will replace said walls. That type of discomfort is the worst kind of all. Your home is supposed to be your refuge. Your life can also be a refuge, a place where you feel loved, loving, satisfied, comfortable, and as though all is well in the world. Let's each create a life with a sense of purpose and a well-laid-out plan, rather than attacking it with a vengeance and becoming overwhelmed by the destruction.

On your Mystical Backpacking trip, you figured out where you want your house built and what you want it to look like. Remember your exercises from previous chapters? They are your first draft of blueprints. You breathed life into this vision, and you set the most important foundational stone: your intention. Without intention, no project ever begins. However, you don't build a house by starting with the roof, so you're not going to start building your dream life with finishing touches either. You'll start from the ground up, building walls and floors board by board. The exercises in this final exercise section will help you do just that.

A Letter of Congratulations

Write away, right now. Write a letter of congratulations to yourself, recognizing all the inner and outer growth you have been brave enough to engage in. Be kind. Tell yourself what you would tell your own child or a person you're responsible for loving, supporting, and fostering the best in. You have come a very long way from where you started. Acknowledge your journey and gift yourself with kind praise. If you'd like, place this letter somewhere readily accessible and read it when you need a reminder of how wonderfully brave, adventurous, and true to your spirit you are.

Mystical Backpacker Vision Board

Create a vision board that illustrates the feelings you have experienced and the lessons you have learned on your Mystical Backpacking odyssey. Using magazines, old books, photos, and advertisements, select images that express a feeling, concept, or representation of your experiences. You may also include your own journal entries and personal photos, the bead or talisman you chose to represent the trip and which traveled with you, or found objects and signs you accumulated along the way. Cut out the images and arrange them on a blank poster board. When the images seem to be in the right place and the look feels good to you, glue them to the board. Place this board somewhere in your home (perhaps by the mirror or on your bedroom wall) as a visual reminder of your trip. This board will remind you to realize the lessons you learned on your travels in your daily life at home and to have these soul-truth lessons inform your decisions as you make choices about your life in the next year.

Immediate Changes: The Renovation Begins

Destress your nest. In your Mystical Exercise assignments from chapter 4, you made a list of your top stressors in your life at home, and you created immediate solutions to implement on your return. It's time to dig that list out and start making those changes! That list is your starting point. If you didn't do this exercise, or if you can add to it now, please do so. Address your stressors with as many solutions as you can. Let's face it, these stressors are distractions you don't need right now. As you work on this exercise, remember that you are tweaking your physical environment in subtle ways to improve your day-to-day quality of life now. It can be simple. No paper towel holder in the kitchen and the paper towels keep falling into the sink? Install a paper towel holder. Not enough light at your desk? Buy a lamp. Your gym has disgusting showers that gross you out? Change your gym to one you like. Focus on the solution that makes the most sense and that you can accomplish quickly. The easier your current environments are to navigate and the more functional and satisfying they become, the less aggravated you will feel as you move through your days. Ease and functionality are the keys here; without all these little stressors draining you, you will have lots of extra energy for tackling the bigger changes in your life!

Big changes (like finding a new job or ending a relationship) are not a part of this exercise. Let's say you're dissatisfied with your job and are planning to find a new one. That's great! However, finding a job might be a long-term goal, not a short-term stressor. It might take you anywhere from a month to six months or even a year. It's probably not a good idea to take a sledgehammer to your job until you have a replacement or a nest egg to get you through a time of unemployment. But if you do, then swing away! You know what is right for you. Know that some changes are going to take time, dedication, and even some backbreaking work to effect, so don't start swinging that sledgehammer recklessly—swing it with intention.

Let's take the job example a step further. If finding a new job is a long-term goal but you're experiencing short-term stressors in your current workplace, what can you do to immediately address the issues? Well, let's say that one of the reasons your job's wearing you thin is that you have a cubicle mate you can't stand. Ask to be moved. If you can't be moved, set some boundaries. Maybe this means that you ask that person to keep his or her possessions out of your side of the cubicle. Maybe this means you say you can't help with personal problems while you're at work. It's never rude to set boundaries that allow you to thrive. If you are polite, compassionate, and kind in setting your boundaries, then some of the discomfort you feel in doing so will be alleviated. This doesn't mean your mouth won't go dry and your hands won't shake. They might! Confrontation is an unpleasant thing for most people, but pushing through your fear and discomfort will result in things improving for you. Remember zip-lining in Peru or jumping off that high-up rock into the azure waters of the Mediterranean or trying a new food for the first time? Mystical Backpackers are brave, and you've already exercised the very skills you need to draw on now.

Perhaps another reason your job is giving you pains is that you have to sit in an uncomfortable chair, and you are stiff and sore by the end of the day. Ask for a new office chair. If the company says no, then buy your own and bring it into the office over the weekend. Hopefully, no one's going to fire you for wanting to sit in a comfortable chair, especially if you do your job well! You might also schedule a fifteen-minute walk during you midmorning break, a fifteen-minute walk during your lunch break, and another fifteen-minute walk during your afternoon break. This will get your body moving, limber up your muscles, and help your body to feel better. Again, sitting in your uncomfortable chair and complaining about it may be a hard habit to break, but it's time to break it. It's your body, so the onus is on you, not Big Brother, to take care of it. You're not going to be at this job forever, so you may as well be comfortable for as long as you're here. And if you love your job but hate your chair, you've still solved a big problem, haven't you?

In both of the above cases, you effected an immediate change. You changed the energy of your emotional environment when you created a boundary by addressing your cubicle mate's behavior, and you changed your physical environment by improving your physical comfort with a new chair. Your days at work just got better, and in turn, your daily life quality improved.

Go through each area of your life and make immediate changes, step-by-step, to improve the quality of your life this very moment. Do as much as you can now, but this practice will also be a useful tool to use again and again in the future. Check in with yourself every six months or so to see if your little stressors need a spring cleaning—it can make a world of difference.

Set Short-Term Goals

Plan your short-term goals for the year ahead. Now that you've addressed the things you can immediately tackle, take out your list from the first Mystical Exercise in chapter 6, where you created a three-year, five-year, and ten-year vision of your life. In order to realize these visions, you're going to want to start charting a step-by-step course for making your way toward them. Using those lists, create a list of short-term goals you can achieve in one year's time that will move you in the direction of realizing your three-year vision. Consider this list the starting point for your plan for the next year. Some of these goals will be realized within a month; some may take the full year. Be thorough and be honest. Would you benefit from finding a new place to live or work? Would you like to join a program or start therapy or find support for working on some personal issues or challenges? Would you like to make new friends or restructure some of your current relationships so they're healthier? Would you like to join a spiritual group or church, or change your existing one? Would you like to get certified or complete a diploma?

Now that you've planned for changes, take your plans one step further. Register, sign up, pay your deposits, submit your applications; get things on the calendar now while your forward momentum is still in full swing. While you do want to ensure you don't overburden yourself, make sure to challenge yourself a little.

Remember: the most successful one-year plan is realistic. It's probably too much to expect to start a business, write a book, fall in love, and finish your degree all in one year! But these goals can definitely be accomplished in your three-year or five-year visions. The more realistic your plan, the more attainable it is, and attaining our goals is the fuel that feeds the fire of our forward motion. After all, there are few feelings more satisfying than the exhilaration of reaching a goal. It boosts your self-confidence, inspires you to keep up your momentum, and motivates you to realize the next goal you've set. Accomplishment is a great partner to purpose. When we have a sense of purpose, we're inspired to accomplish. And when we accomplish, our sense of purpose is validated. For this reason especially, try not to create a one-year plan that is too demanding and doesn't reward you with accomplishments along the way. It is very easy to become demotivated and discouraged when months go by without any sense of accomplishment or triumph. As the hero of your life, you need triumphs in order to feel heroic! Ensure you have them by planning out small, reachable goals along the way in your one-year plan.

Another essential element to this process is *fun*! You can't just work like a dog without replenishing your energy. Be kind to yourself and allow yourself to enjoy your successes along the way. Try to schedule breaks, special treats, and time for magic as well. There's nothing as motivating as a fun trip to look forward to in the dead of winter or attending a concert with your friends from work. These events inject fresh energy into your daily dynamic. Schedule a weekend with your best friends and do something special; go fishing and drink craft beers or cheap wine while telling dirty jokes, go to the spa and get pedicures and massages while updating each other on your love lives. Anticipate needing some rest as well, and schedule that throughout your year too. If you need eight to ten hours of sleep a night, make sure you get it. If you know you want to spend some Sundays lying like broccoli, get veggie with it! Try to schedule minibreaks and vacations too: a weekend relaxing on the beach or an afternoon hiking through a gorgeous stretch of wilderness or whatever leisure activities you enjoy. Plan for ways to recharge your batteries.

A realistic yet challenging one-year plan should include at least three big achievements and three small achievements. An example of three big achievements might be: move to a new apartment, complete that six-week certification course, and find and pursue a new job that fulfills you. The reality is it may take you a month or two to find the perfect apartment, and it may take a month or two to save up the money you'd spend on deposits and moving and buying the new stuff to outfit it. It may take a couple of months to save up the money for the certification course, and you might need to wait another month or two before it's offered. It might take you a month to create the perfect resumé and work on your cover letters. And it may take up to six months after that to land your dream job. It all adds up, and in one year, you can realistically expect to fulfill these three major changes in your life.

Concurrently, you may begin the process of change in other areas of your life as well. We could call these your three small achievements. You might join a community garden and start growing your own vegetables, train to run a half marathon, and start seeing a counselor or coach. These small changes are really about creating new routines in your life that are aligned with your soul's purpose and fulfilling your dreams along the way. When you put yourself out there to participate in these new routines, you will encounter both people who will become your friends en route as well as opportunities for new doors to open before you. New friends and opportunities will lead you to fulfill your dreams in unexpected ways. Just as you did while Mystical Backpacking, when you rise up to meet the journey of your life on the home front, your adventure continues.

Once you finish this exercise, it will give you a sense of calm and well-being to know that you have measurable goals and attainable successes coming down the pipeline. This alone will ensure you feel that you are continuing to move forward in the flow of life and not just sitting on the sidelines holding an empty soda cup and droopy flag.

Create Alternative Solutions

Address setbacks and obstacles by redefining and working around your can'ts. Create a list of all your can'ts and create solutions for each. As you begin to work on realizing your one-year goals, you will inevitably encounter minor setbacks or outright obstacles to the timeline you've charted. When you do, keep in mind that there are no immoveable obstacles—even mountains can be scaled, and the words I can't can always be circumvented. Can't get that perfect resumé together? Hire a professional resumé writer to do it for you. Can't declutter your apartment because you have become an early-onset hoarder? Hire a professional organizer, give that person the keys to your apartment, and leave town for the weekend! Can't afford to hire professionals? See if you can barter with friends and other professionals. I've bartered for things many times, and it's amazing how many self-employed professionals are willing to go this route. If your proposal is fair and offers them something they need or want in return, many people will at the very least be willing to discuss the possibilities. If you don't ask, you'll never know. If the person says no, you're right where you started anyway. You literally have nothing to lose.

If the obstacle you encounter is one you can't address (let's say you missed the application deadline for a program you want to take, and after you called the program and asked to be considered anyway, they said no), think back to how you dealt with similar obstacles while on your odyssey. You missed a train? There was another one coming. In the meantime, you were blessed with the opportunity to sit in the sun and journal, or to have a coffee with an interesting person who was also waiting, or to wander around a charming town you otherwise would have missed. Remember the lessons you learned while Mystical Backpacking and incorporate those into your life on the home front. Be honest about your can'ts (the limiting beliefs you ascribe to) and be creative in disabling obstacles and creating flow.

Releasing Blocks to Create Emotional Flow

In this exercise, we re-introduce work that has both practical and mystical components. As mystical experiences perhaps begin to wane on the home front (not that they necessarily will), this approach helps us stay connected with the mystical experiences we've come to enjoy and embrace so well while traveling.

The Practical: Refer back to the lists you created in chapter 6, Taking Emotional Inventory: The Voldemort Exercise. You created three lists, what makes you angry or resentful, what makes you feel guilty or ashamed, and what you're happiest about. If you didn't do that exercise, please go back and do it now. These lists are hands-on and meant to be used. They help to clarify some of the emotional weight you've accumulated in your life. This next part of the exercise is where we get mystical again.

The Mystical: Go for a walk and collect stones for each item on the anger and resentment lists and green or dry leaves for each item on the guilt and shame lists (remember: leaves of three, leave them be!). As you gather each and every individual stone and leaf, I want you to consciously state (out loud or in your mind) the specific anger or resentment from your list that this one object represents. As you collect each object, you are intentionally accumulating a visual representation of all that emotional weight and taking the time to properly address and articulate each item of hurt list by list.

Once you've gathered all your stones and leaves, take them home. If your leaves are green, put them in a sunny window or a place where they can dry out over the next week. Place your stones in a dish or basket or on a window ledge where you can see them each and every day. Live with these items visible and present in your most-used spaces for a whole week. In the meantime, you may continue to work on other Mystical Exercises.

After a week has passed, write a word on each stone to represent each and every item of anger and resentment from your lists. Write a word on each leaf to represent each and every item of shame and guilt on your list. If and when you feel ready to do so, the next part of this exercise will begin your process of releasing these emotions and freeing yourself of the burden of carrying them into your future.

Now, plan two special dates with yourself. The first is an evening bonfire. The second is a morning visit to a body of water (it can be a stream, river, pond, lake, whatever you wish and is convenient).

For your evening bonfire: Create a sacred, safe space for yourself where you can have an outdoor bonfire at night. You may wish to bring out some of the things you collected while traveling (stones, feathers, signs, or souvenirs) as representations of how you have become empowered or light candles or play music to set the tone—whatever feels sacred and special to you. When you're ready, say a prayer or set your intention to release your guilt and shame. If you're having challenges with this part of the exercise, there is a free meditation download that can help you with it on the Mystical Backpacker website—just flip to Mystical Extras at the back of this book when you're ready.

Now, become fully present and aware of each event as marked on each leaf. Concentrate on the feelings you have about each particular issue, and as you throw the leaf into the fire, allow yourself to fully release the energy of this event into the fire, where it is transmuted into a new energy and goes out into the Universe, no longer in and of you, freeing you to move into your future unencumbered. Consciously release each and every leaf and corresponding emotion with intention, one by one. Close your ceremony with a prayer or statement or deep breathing and know that you have effected deep and meaningful change at the soul level.

For your morning water walk: Bring your stones to a place by water where you can be alone with your thoughts and, just as you did above, create a sacred space for yourself. Concentrating on each stone and its corresponding word, allow yourself to fully feel the events and emotions represented by each. As you pick the stone up, concentrate on the event and once you feel it profoundly, state your intention to release this anger or resentment so that you may move forward into your future unencumbered. Allow the energy associated with this emotion to leave you as you place the stone into the water (or throw it, whatever you wish) and see it going out into the Universe, transmuted into something new and separate from you. Consciously feel the release. Go through each item on your list as you throw away your stones, one by one. Close your ceremony with a prayer or statement or deep breathing and know that you have effected deep healing at the heart and soul levels.

Well done! This was an intense exercise that required a lot of time and energy, but you have honored your soul deeply by taking the time to do this work. From here on out, you will feel a lot lighter.

Create Sacred Space

Create an everyday sacred space. While you were traveling, the world you passed through became a sacred space as you connected with your mystical side and exercised your Mystical Tools. When you return to the home front, those mystical feelings ebb, and it can feel like mystical occurrences happen with less frequency. To offset that, this exercise asks you to create a sacred space in your life where you can reconnect with your mystical side. It may be a place where you meditate, pray, or write . . . or it may be a place where you adventure and conquer. It might be a shelf where you place special things or a whole room dedicated to what you hold sacred and pure. Your space may include candles, photos, flowers, and icons, or it may be empty, with just a cushion to sit on. It should resonate for you. In creating this space, the mystical will become a part of your daily life.

Become Your Own Hero

List your heroes. They can be superheroes from comic books or television; they can be film characters or people who actually exist and inspire you. For each, answer the following questions: Why are they your heroes? What traits do you attribute to their heroism? What challenges or obstacles do they possess (not just externally or physically, but internally as well)?

On another piece of paper or a new journal page, list the strengths of your heroes at the top of the page. Do you already possess any of these strengths? What skills would you need to develop or foster to see yourself as the hero of your own life?

On a new page, list the challenges or character flaws your heroes face. Do you identify with any of their challenges or flaws? What strategies can you apply to these challenges or flaws that would serve you in creating positive beliefs and expressions moving forward?

This exercise is geared towards reframing yourself as the hero of your life on the home front. While you were Mystical Backpacking, you acted as the hero of your own life. The trick now is to keep this vision/feeling alive. By becoming a Mystical Backpacker, you have connected with these feelings and know them to be true and possible. Maintaining them back on solid ground is about being able to draw on these feelings and connect with them again in everyday life.

But what kind of hero are you going to be? Are you going to be nearly perfect, like Superman? He is strong, humble, and noble, and he can do everything . . . except when there's kryptonite around. Then he's totally disabled. In the 1978 movie, he says things like, "Don't thank me—we're all on the same team," and, "You really shouldn't smoke." He apologizes when he uses his X-ray vision to see what color Lois Lane's underwear is (and he only looks because she asks him to).[2] How hard would it be for you to be perfect all the time and then debilitated by your one weakness? Or are you going to be a flawed hero, like Starbuck from the reimagined 2004 *Battlestar Galactica* series? Starbuck has flaws aplenty (she drinks too much, has a volatile temper, is promiscuous) but is capable of great things and brave in the face of danger, no matter the cost. Starbuck says things like, "I don't give a damn what you believe," and, "I'm hung up on a dead guy, okay? And it's pissing me off."[3] While both heroes have a destiny and fulfill it, one does so while being perfect, neat, and tidy and living a secret life, thereby never being truly known for his true self. The other does so while falling apart and pulling herself back together amid chaos and engaging in a lot of unnecessary confrontation to address her feelings of alienation. Both these examples are at extreme ends of the spectrum.

To live a healthy and balanced life, we need heroes who are fallible and who choose life over death and connection over self-sacrifice. The reality is, life is messy. You can't actually make it neat and tidy or will your future into submission with orderly behavior because there are external forces at work that are perpetually destabilizing: the economy, politics, weather, and other humans. All you can do is tap into what drives you and keeps you feeling motivated and then find a way to chase that amid the ever-changing landscape of the world at large. That's all. If you can find uplifting and empowering attributes to connect with, while concurrently accepting your flaws and working through challenges, you are more likely to be able to sustain the feeling of being the hero of your own life.

Congratulations. You've done so much work exploring your inner world while exploring the outer world. You have turned your ship into the direction of your dreams and it's time for us to head off in different directions. As you chart your course ahead, I leave you with this parting thought. Sometimes, you will fail (I know, this is a bummer; I'm sorry). It will hurt or feel bad or be humiliating. But every failure experienced on the road to your dreams will inevitably yield a lesson or gift down the line. I have experienced this to be true time and again.

On Failure

The best gift that time and experience has afforded me is the understanding that there is truly no such thing as failure. I don't deny having wept bitterly while announcing, "I am a failure," at low points in my life. I have. And when you're experiencing these throes of low self-esteem, having someone tell you there's no such thing as failure is just about the most infuriating thing ever. When you do encounter what you perceive to be a failure, it's time to bring out those Mystical Backpacking tools again. They will show you the way through the darkness and bring you back to the light of understanding. Take time to rest. Take time to enjoy life. Take time to heal. Take time to connect with the mystical. At these times, I ask you to remember that there are forward strides in life, but there are also diversions that serve the purpose of teaching us lessons and skills we need for realizing our dreams at a later time. Sometimes, just like *The Alchemist's* shepherd boy in the crystal shop shows us, setbacks are the most valuable gifts we receive. At the end of *The Alchemist*, Santiago reaches his goal of finding his treasure by way of the pyramids, even though it happens only after many unplanned yet productive waylays en route.

Confusion occurs when, despite accepting setbacks with grace and mounting obstacles with gusto, despite putting yourself out there time and again and taking risks that grow your circle of comfort, the thing you wanted most of all will still not come to pass. You might save up your money, take that course, and fail the final exam. You might break your leg the week before your trip to climb Mount Kilimanjaro. You might breeze through interview after interview and still not get the job. Our egos tend to have no other way to label these sorts of setbacks than with the word *failure*. The worst part about these types of failures is that the void created when a dream fails to manifest can result in a crisis of faith. While it's confusing and disturbing to experience failures anytime, once you've become a Mystical Backpacker, it may seem especially so. After all, you've experienced so much enlightenment, so much spiritual connection, and so much deep self-awareness. How is it possible that the Universe would then punish you this way?

Way back in the introduction, I mentioned that during this process you'd likely raise your arms while crying out to the sky, "Why, why, why?" Well, this is what I was talking about. Becoming a Mystical Backpacker doesn't make you impermeable to failure or disappointment.

When I wanted to go to Belize and be an artist on an archaeological dig but ended up interviewing old women in Transylvania instead, that felt like failure. When I wanted to marry my boyfriend and ended up earning a master's degree on the other side of the world, alone in a new place: failure. Both forced compromises felt at the time like I was assigned to second best. In neither case did I reach my treasure. But ultimately, I would not have become a Mystical Backpacker, nor would I have realized my dream of being a writer and writing this particular book had these dreams come true. And this is where the mystical caresses our shoulders and touches our lives with its benevolence once again. Sometimes, unseen forces steer the course of events, taking the very wheel from our hands when we are dangerously close to going off course. At these times, it can feel as though we've fallen flat on our face and had to face embarrassments of epic and humiliating proportions (according to us). As I said before: Trying isn't pretty, which is why, I think, so many people don't. But certainly, the answer cannot be that we don't try.

Fearing failure and the emotional mess that often surrounds it is deeply connected to our worry about what other people may think about us. Remember this: the only people sitting around relishing other people's disappointments are those who do so in order to justify their own lack of trying. Those are not your people. The Wright brothers attempted flight more than a thousand times before they actually invented a machine that could fly. They fell out of the sky more than a thousand times! Think about that. How much less effort is required to realize your dreams? It doesn't mean that your dreams are any less important. It just means that you probably won't have to fall out of the sky a thousand times in order to realize them. The next time you're considering chickening out where the pursuit of your dreams is concerned, ask yourself, "What would the Wright brothers do?" Believe you can fly, and you will.

Remember, too, that no single risk or act will result in you realizing your dream. Dreams come true because of a cumulative series of risks and a sequence of events where you exercised your brave muscle. Some of them will yield successes, and others will yield failures or alternate routes you hadn't previously considered. Holding yourself back from taking one risk—any risk—because you fear it will result in failure is to ultimately forfeit your dreams, even those you don't yet know you have (like becoming a Mystical Backpacker instead of a married artist who documents archaeological digs in inky sketches).

Keep in mind, too, that not all uniquely presented options yield a good fit. Follow your instincts. Just as you didn't accept help from that weird guy hanging out at the bus depot when you arrived in a new town, you don't need to move forward with situations that feel wrong at home simply to force yourself into taking a risk. When you follow your gut, you always come out on top. Learn to distinguish between your ego's worry about looking like an ass and your gut's survival instincts kicking in. When you're having a moment of doubt, ask yourself why you're having it. Is it your ego? Is it your survival instinct? Are you telling yourself you can't or are you warning yourself that you shouldn't?

The first time I ever left town to explore dreams in uncharted territory with the taste of adventure ripe in my mouth I was a teenager riding in a white Corvette with the T-roof open and Led Zeppelin's "Ramble On" playing on the stereo. I was heading to a far-off beach where I would fall in lust with a pro volleyball player and paint watercolor pictures in a wooden cabin drenched in the honey-warm colors of old stained-glass lamps. The nights were hot and the midnight windows blue with starlight and moonbeams. My muscles loose, my thoughts rich with possibilities and poetry, my soul was activated by this awayness. I left behind my problems of the day, and I was free. Like the seagulls riding the wind above the crashing surf, I was light and soaring. The magic of that song and the wind and the colors of love and peace, sunshine and surf were painted in watercolor on my very soul. What a pleasure trip it has been to time and again have those mystical seeds prosper in the rich soil of the adventures that followed.

Zeppelin said it then, and it still rings true for me as my adventure anthem now:

The time has come to be gone.

Afterword

The Spirit of Mystical Backpacking

If my ship sails from sight, it doesn't mean my journey ends, it simply means the river bends.

—JOHN ENOCH POWELL

Mysticism is an old rite. In many ways, it has not been appreciated in recent history perhaps because it's the path of contemplation and surrender. It is the hard way but the rewarding way. I would be remiss in writing a book about employing a mystical approach to finding your path in life without taking a moment to clarify my own stance on God. I use that word with trepidation throughout my text because the word itself closes so many doors. Many of the modern expressions of religion and spirituality I've personally experienced are ones demanding acceptance and compliance, the very antithesis to the path of the mystic. For me, dogma is for sleds and arctic huskies, not the place of prayer. For me, penance is embodied by the consequences of our actions rather than the steeping in shame because of them. I do not need gurus and prophets to tell me God is ever present. I have found God in nature. I have found God within, having experienced God firsthand. Listening to someone else's experience of God is an interesting anecdote or a familiar chord resounding but not a direction for me to take. I believe that God puts us in the flow of God, and whether we see it around us or not is up to us. For all of these reasons, I am a proponent of finding the truth of God out for ourselves.

My favorite line from the *Tao Te Ching*, one which I believe summarizes the experience of God best is, "Tao called Tao is not Tao."[1] If Tao is "the way" or "the path," then we cannot name it or define it, for in our doing so, it ceases to exist as such. Similarly, Kierkegaard's statement, "Once you label me you negate me"[2] best describes for me the most awesome and indefinable concept of God. The more we try to pin God down, to speak for God as a representative of rules, truisms, and guidelines, the further from God both the speakers and the followers risk getting. If it is true that God is everywhere at once and we are a part of God and one with God, then we need look no further than within to find the God that is real and true for us. It is this God sense within that is our best compass as we chart our ways through life.

I am not a religious person. I am a spiritual person, and I have chosen a mystical path. The God I have chosen to embrace is one I briefly feel the presence of during meditation, a practice I have taken up in lieu of church-based worship. While the vehicle of Mystical Backpacking led to some experiences of God for me personally, I cannot promise it will do as much for others. Tao called Tao is not Tao. Regardless of our interpretations and individual faiths, we are all one with God anyway, regardless of what labels we give ourselves—or God, for that matter. Ants and sand, stones and feathers, the sun and the moon are the same to all of us, regardless of our words for them. In the human hand, it is just as much an ant, a stone, or a feather to a child from a small village in Zimbabwe as it is to the socialite on Manhattan's Upper East Side. So it is with God. While I hope that a byproduct of Mystical Backpacking is that you find a personal experience of God in whatever form speaks to your soul, my goal in writing about Mystical Backpacking is that you connect with your authentic self in such a profound way that the way ahead—for you personally—becomes undeniably clear.

When you follow your own path and allow your most authentic self to guide you, then, regardless of your personal beliefs, you live your life as an act of faith. Jung wrote, "An initial mood of faith and optimism makes for good results,"[3] and I believe this can be said of life in general. If you find nothing more than faith and optimism on your own Mystical Backpacking odysseys, then I have best served God in sharing my own story of seeking and finding with the world.

From where I stood in a high mountain meadow surrounded by lowing cattle chewing cud, the snow-topped, jaggy Austrian Alps in the distance, I could have spread my arms and twirled like Maria in *The Sound of Music*. I can still feel the sharp, fresh air that filled my lungs and see the enchanting, ever-so-quiet Hansel-and-Gretel towns that spread out beneath me like a child's play set just out of arm's reach. In town, as people gathered for a festival, horses clip-clopped on cobblestone, and women wearing traditional costumes of red, black, and white with bright-yellow straw hats perched like birds atop their heads smiled easily in the streets.

The view from the meadow was strikingly different from the one I had experienced in Mallorca, when I'd sat on the stone wall and looked out at the Mediterranean Sea and quiet white boats. There, the air had been a warm embrace and carried nestled into its breezes the smell of adventure in rare and mysterious scents I couldn't place. There was, however, a unifying factor between the meadow and the Mallorcan lookout—an intense feeling of lightness and innocence, a purity of the life experience condensed into quiet simplicity.

Mountaintops bookended my journey, and in between these disparate yet familiar peaks, I scaled my inner mountains. Examining personal demons in the very place where Plato wrote about the cave, I brought my beliefs into the light and assessed which ones I should keep that would serve me moving forward in life and which had to be released and allowed to disintegrate in the hot, arid sun. I left behind the burden of responsibility I had felt in Budapest and entered into an adventure that introduced a concept I had never before considered: the responsibility I had to my own soul. My journey, which grew organically from one place to the next, connected me deeply to this truth, each step en route unearthing a personal treasure buried deep, striking a chord to a song long unsung but deeply familiar and reinforcing the foundations of my spirit. I return to the tattered pages of my own story from time to time to remind myself of this when the way ahead seems unclear. There is a breath of life that emits from within the spiral bindings of my journals, and I remember not just an exhibit or an afternoon but revelations big and small that forged the hero of my own life I turned out to be.

Life is a journey, and we are all adventurers. How we choose to express and appreciate the spirit of that adventure is up to us, but to scale any mountain, inner or outer, is heroic, if even for a moment—and to be the hero of your own life is the best place to be, if even for a moment. I am not the first Mystical Backpacker nor the last. I simply stopped to write it down and then waved a flag and called out, "Hey there, you, fellow traveler! Yeah, you! Look what I've found. Come see for yourself." And for those of you who want to, who will, and who have, I share this message, which was sent to me from a friend when I started my own journey:

"Jolly boating weather/And a hay harvest breeze/Blade on the feather/Shade off the trees/Bon voyage, my darlings."[4]

Bon voyage, my darlings.

Acknowledgments

I thank my husband, Eli, who met a Mystical Backpacker, married her, and never stood in the way of her fulfilling her dreams. Thank you for putting up with the foibles of the writing process and creating time and space for me to dance with the keyboard and steep in my own thoughts. Thank you to Viola and Nora, who bring adventure to the home front every day and give this traveler a reason to grow roots. Thank you to Levi and Cristi, the first two soul mates I met when I crossed the pond and who taught me that joy, laughter, and acceptance can override sorrow, fear, and resistance. Thank you to Lisa, who joined me at the midpoint and, like jasmine in the night, bloomed her own magic alongside my own unfolding. What an honor to share that sacred space with you. Thank you to Alda Caprara, the teacher who made a difference. Thank you to Sharon Maxwell, who told me long ago to write this book and who has shown me that friendship is its own adventure. Thank you to Dana Johnson, who has hunted ghosts and prepared for cougar attacks with me and has always been game for acting on bad ideas. Thank you to my agent, Regina Brooks, who listened to my pitch and scored a home run with it. Thank you to Anna Noak and Sylvia Spratt, editors who understood and whose suggestions and contributions made the book better. Thank you to Kari Samuels, who not only saw the book as a reality long before it was and introduced me to my agent, but also helped me to grow as a person during the early years of our friendship. Thank you to Christina Sullivan and Nanette Davidson, who share the laughter and the tears of day-to-day life with me. Thank you to Kathy Miles, whose kind encouragement offered in a mid-winter parking lot made a difference. Thank you to my mom, Eva Kapitan, who championed the book from the very first draft. Thank you to my dad, Martin Papp, who kept quiet when he couldn't champion (very hard for an atheist to change his spots, you know). And thank you to Spirit for the grandest adventure of all: life itself.

Mystical Extras

For mystical content referenced throughout the book, please visit themysticalbackpacker.com to begin exploring. Here are some starting points.

Guided Meditations

A free guided meditation to get you started can be found at themysticalbackpacker.com in the "freebies" section under the heading "Meditations." There are four free Mystic Meditations to assist you with exercises from chapters 1, 2, 4, and 7.

Communities/Message Boards

One topic you can explore here is where to set your Mystical Backpacking experience. But don't forget to trust *yourself*! The Mystical

Exercises in chapter 3 offer some questions to help you shape where you'll go.

Packing Lists

You can watch a video about how to best pack your backpack on the mysticalbackpacker.com in the "freebies" section under the "videos" heading, or on Hannah Papp's The Mystical Backpacker channel on Vimeo.com: vimeo.com/channels/830518. You'll also find information about packing in chapter 3.

Music Playlists and Reading Lists

Find Hannah's playlists and reading lists at mysticalbackpacker.com and on Hannah's Pinterest page: pinterest.com/HannahPappPins.

Mystical Supplies

Journals: Bring a notebook or two to start your journey—and be prepared to buy more along your way! (You can always mail your completed journals home, so you're not carrying too many.)

Books: A paperback or two will give you comfort, help you pass downtime, and provide you inspiration and guidance.

Music: A playlist divided into three sets—light and upbeat, meaningful, and calming and nurturing—will improve your mood or enhance the mystical aspect of your journey.

Mystical Toolbox

This is a summary of what we discussed in chapter 4.

Signs: Feeling freaked out? Ask for a sign. Record your signs and your interpretations of them in your journal.

Prayer: Prayer is an energetic road that leads to the mystical. There are three types of prayer to employ:

> *Asking Prayers*: Ask for signs, help, guidance, direction, etc. Articulate your wants in words. Make them a spoken reality rather than a latent or dormant secret wish.
>
> *Thanking Prayers*: Notice the world around you and express your gratitude for all the precious experiences you are able to witness or participate in each day. Shift your perception from want to abundance. Record the things you're grateful for each day in your journal (or start a gratitude section at the back of your journal).
>
> *Enlightenment Prayers*: Sitting in a comfortable position and taking deep breaths, imagine yourself bathed in white light and experiencing the feeling of love. Imagine this love connecting all living things in an energy of unity. Connect (or attempt to connect) with this feeling for twenty minutes at least three times a week.

Reflection: Using the exercises throughout this book, take an honest appraisal of your inner and outer life and reflect on your deepest, most sacred truths. Do not worry about others seeing or judging your honest appraisals. Concentrate your energy on finding the courage to be honest with yourself.

Journaling: Record the experiences of your inner and outer journeys in detail. In doing so, you create a sacred text that charts the transformation you are experiencing. Also, journaling enables you to revisit moments, revelations, and turning points (which may not be obvious as such at the time).

Paying It Forward: Find ways each and every day to express kindness and consideration toward others. Be someone else's Earth Angel.

Connect With Hannah Online

Facebook: facebook.com/pages/The-Mystical-Backpacker/1537821663130902
Twitter: @mysticbackpack
Vimeo: vimeo.com/channels/830518
Pinterest: pinterest.com/HannahPappPins

Notes

Front Matter

1. Merriam-Webster Online, s.v. "mystical," accessed October 11, 2012, www.merriam-webster.com

1: What Exactly *Is* a Mystical Backpacker, and Do I Need to Become One?

1. Wolf Moondance, *Vision Quest: Native American Magical Healing* (New York: Sterling Publishing, 2004).
2. Tom Shachtman, *Rumspringa: To Be or Not to Be Amish* (New York: North Point Press, 2007), 4.
3. James W. Fernandez, *Bwiti: An Ethnography of the Religious Imagination of Africa* (Princeton: Princeton University Press, 1982).

4. Ralph Metzner, *The Ayahuasca Experience: A Sourcebook on the Sacred Vine of Spirits* (South Paris, ME: Park Street Press, 2014).

5. Julia Zimmermann and Franz J. Neyer, "Do We Become a Different Person When Hitting the Road? Personality Development of Sojourners," *Journal of Personality and Social Psychology* 105 (2013), 515-530 doi 10.1037/a0033019.

6. William W. Maddux, Hajo Adam, and Adam D. Galinsky, "When in Rome . . . Learn Why the Romans Do What They Do: How Multicultural Learning Experiences Facilitate Creativity," *Personality and Social Psychology Bulletin* 36 (2010): 731, 515-530 doi 10.1177/0146167210367786.

7. Ava Gardner, *Ava: My Story* (New York: Bantam Books, 1990), 30–33.

8. David Meuel, *Women in the Films of John Ford* (Jefferson, NC: McFarland, 2014), 110.

9. "Michael Jordan 'Failure' Nike Commercial," YouTube video, 00:30, posted by JayMJ23's channel, August 25, 2006, https://www.youtube.com/watch?v=45mMioJ5szc.

10. Fred R. Shapiro, ed., *The Yale Book of Quotations* (New Haven, CT: Yale University Press: 2006), s.v. "John A. Shedd."

11. Orison Marden, *How to Get What You Want* (New York: Thomas Y. Crowell Compay, 1917), 45–46. Orison Marden was an American self-made man who lived from 1850 to 1924. He published fifteen books, held a degree in medicine, and owned a hotel, despite being orphaned when he was seven.

2: I Never Win Anything: Life Before Travel

1. E. M. Forster, *A Room with a View* (New York: Dover Publications, 1995), 24.

2. Ibid., 24.

3. Garth Henrichs, Quotes.net, STANDS4 LLC, 2015. "Garth Henrichs Quotes." Accessed February 23, 2015. http://www.quotes.net/quote/14117.

4. *The Sound of Music*, directed by Robert Wise (1965; Los Angeles: 20th Century Fox), DVD.

5. Laurence Bergreen, *Louis Armstrong: An Extravagant Life* (New York: Broadway Books, 1997), 491.

6. Bill Clinton, *My Life* (New York: Knopf, 2004).

7. Jennifer Harris and Elwood Watson, *The Oprah Phenomenon* (Lexington: The University Press of Kentucky, 2009).

8. Amanda Fortini, "O Pioneer Woman!" *The New Yorker*, May 9, 2011, http://www.newyorker.com/magazine/2011/05/09/o-pioneer-woman.

9. Paulo Coelho, *The Alchemist* (New York: HarperOne, 2006). Paulo Coelho's *The Alchemist* is a book about a Spanish boy whose dream is to see the pyramids of Egypt. Upon reaching the North African shore at great personal expense, he is robbed. Of necessity, he begins work at a crystal shop and is in turn disappointed, then resolute, and finally, wildly successful, increasing sales dramatically. He enjoys this but eventually remembers his dream of the pyramids and makes a new attempt to realize his dream.

10. Denise Linn, *Soul Coaching: 28 Days to Discover Your Authentic Self* (New York: Hay House Publishing, 2003), 16.

3: Where Do I Go? How Do I Begin?

1. E. M. Forster, *A Room with a View* (Toronto: Bantam Books, 1988), 96.

2. *Shirley Valentine*, directed by Gilbert Lewis (1989; Hollywood: Paramount Pictures), DVD.

3. Michael Friedman, "Does Music Have Healing Powers?" *Psychology Today*, February 4, 2014, http://www.psychologytoday.com/blog/brick-brick/201402/does-music-have-healing-powers.

4. Joan Baez, vocal performance of "Farewell, Angelina," by Bob Dylan, released 1965, Vanguard, LP.

5. Charles W. Harrison, vocal performance of "My Sunshine," by Eduardo di Capua, recorded 1915, Edison Blue Amberol, 78 rpm. Charles Harrison was the first to record "O Sole Mio" in English under the title "My Sunshine."

6. Geoffrey Chaucer, "The Reeve's Tale," *The Canterbury Tales*, line 349, 1374.

4: Into the Labyrinth: How Do I Journey?

1. Susan Jeffers, *Feel the Fear and Do It Anyway* (New York, Ballantine Books: 1998). This is my personal reimagining of Susan Jeffers's Whole Life Grid, which can be found in this excellent book.

2. Roderick Main, ed., *Jung on Synchronicity and the Paranormal* (Princeton: Princeton University Press, 1997), 93–102.

3. "Snap Out of It," *Moonstruck*, directed by Norman Jewison (1987; Beverly Hills: MGM, 1998), DVD.

4. "You Run to the Wolf," *Moonstruck*, directed by Norman Jewison (1987; Beverly Hills: MGM, 1998), DVD.

5. "Inspect the Cannelloni," *Grumpier Old Men*, directed by Donald Petrie (1993; Burbank, CA: Warner Brothers, 2009), DVD.

6. "If You Build it, He Will Come," *Field of Dreams*, directed by Phil Alden Robinson (1989; Universal City, CA: Universal Pictures, 1998), DVD.

5: Idle Days: Hitting Your Stride, and Then Entering the Land of the Lotus Eaters

1. Homer, *The Odyssey*, trans. Samuel Butler (Seattle, WA: Steed Publishing, 2011), 78–79.

2. Scott Peck, *The Road Less Travelled: A New Psychology of Love, Traditional Values and Spiritual Growth* (New York: Simon & Schuster, 1978).

3. "There's No Place Like Home," *The Wizard of Oz*, directed by Norman Taurog, King Vidor, Victor Fleming, Mervyn LeRoy, and George Cukor (1939; Beverly Hills: Metro-Goldwyn-Mayer), DVD.

6: Homeward Bound

1. "Just Keep Swimming," *Finding Nemo*, directed by Andrew Stanton (2003; Emeryville, CA: Pixar Animation Studios, 2003), DVD.

7: A New World—Home Is

1. A. E. Hotchner, *Papa Hemingway: A Personal Memoir* (Boston: De Capo Press, 2005), 57. As recalled by his friend A. E. Hotchner, to whom he said this in conversation; it is after this that *A Moveable Feast* is posthumously titled.

2. *Superman*, directed by Richard Donner (1978; Burbank, CA: Warner Brothers, 2002), DVD.

3. "Scar," *Battlestar Galactica*, developed by Ronald D. Moore (Season 2, episode 15; New York City: NBC Universal Television, February 3, 2006), DVD.

Afterword

1. Lao Tzu, *Tao Te Ching*, trans. Stephen Addiss and Stanley Lombardo (Cambridge, MA: Hackett Publishing Company, 1993), 1.

2. Soren Kierkegaard, quoted in John Vriend and Wayne W. Dyer, "Creatively Labeling Behavior in Individual and Group Counseling," *Journal of Marital and Family Therapy* 2, no. 1 (1976): 33.

3. Roderick Main, ed., *Jung on Synchronicity and the Paranormal* (Princeton: Princeton University Press, 1997), 96.

4. William Johnson Cory, "Eton Boating Song," Eton College, first performed 1863.

Me at the top of Mount Alaro, Mallorca, Spain.